Get the eBook FREE!

(PDF, ePub, Kindle, and liveBook all included)

We believe that once you buy a book from us, you should be able to read it in any format we have available. To get electronic versions of this book at no additional cost to you, purchase and then register this book at the Manning website.

Go to https://www.manning.com/freebook and follow the instructions to complete your pBook registration.

That's it!
Thanks from Manning!

A Simple Guide to Retrieval Augmented Generation

ABHINAV KIMOTHI

MANNING
SHELTER ISLAND

Manning Publications Co.
20 Baldwin Road
PO Box 761
Shelter Island, NY 11964

Development editor:	Ian Hough
Technical editor:	Arturo Geigel
Review editor:	Dunja Nikitović
Production editor:	Andy Marinkovich
Copy editor:	Lana Todorovic-Arndt
Proofreader:	Keri Hales
Typesetter:	Tamara Švelić Sabljić
Cover designer:	Marija Tudor

ISBN 9781633435858

To Pallavi and Zara—my greatest sources of love, strength, and inspiration

brief contents

contents

v

preface

How machines understand human intent has always been a subject of deep interest for me. Although I embarked on my journey into AI and machine learning in 2007, it was in early 2016 that I became fascinated by natural language processing (NLP), while building a virtual data analyst. When Google released BERT in 2018, I became convinced that NLP was on the brink of a revolution.

In 2022, following the release of text-davinci-002, a model in OpenAI's GPT-3 series, I decided to join Yarnit, a generative-AI-based content marketing platform, to build the AI backbone of the application. The mission was to create a platform where enterprise content marketing teams could generate marketing assets—social media posts, blogs, emails, and more—at high speed, large scale, and lower cost, with greater accuracy. It quickly became apparent that no generative model could achieve this effectively without incorporating brand-specific knowledge and access to proprietary data. This realization led me to explore retrieval-augmented generation (RAG).

Large language models (LLMs) often fail to meet user expectations. While they are incredibly effective at storing and generating knowledge, they are also prone to hallucinations—confident yet incorrect outputs. This is where RAG provides a breakthrough, allowing LLMs to retrieve relevant, real-time, and factual information before generating responses. The beauty of RAG lies in its simplicity of concept combined with the nuance of implementation. The transformative potential of RAG in overcoming LLMs' core limitations is what has kept both researchers and practitioners deeply engaged.

When I began researching RAG, it was still a relatively unexplored area. Formal learning resources were scarce, and most knowledge was scattered across blogs, social media posts, research papers, and discussion forums. I shared many of my own findings on social platforms and in blog posts. Eventually, the idea of consolidating all these learnings into a comprehensive book took shape.

With the goal of creating a simple, practical resource for technology professionals building LLM-based applications, I started working on this book in mid-2024. Over time, it has evolved into a foundational guide to RAG, covering both breadth and depth, while ensuring practical implementation through clear explanations and simple Python code.

I firmly believe that RAG is an essential skill for anyone working with AI applications and that mastering it requires a solid conceptual foundation. This book is designed to provide just that. Writing it has been an incredibly enriching experience, and I have learned a great deal along the way. I hope you find it both enlightening and enjoyable.

acknowledgments

Authoring a book requires countless hours of research and dedicated writing, especially on a rapidly evolving topic such as RAG, where new research emerges almost every week. This book would not have been possible without the unwavering love and support of my wife, Pallavi. Her encouragement and patience sustained me throughout this journey, and for that, I am eternally grateful.

I am deeply thankful to my co-founders, Jyotirmoy and Akash, and the entire team at Yarnit, who have significantly contributed to my understanding of RAG. The hands-on experiences of building real-world AI applications have undoubtedly enriched this book, making it a more valuable resource for readers.

I would also like to express my heartfelt gratitude to colleagues and mentors—Ashish Rishi, Satyakam Mohanty, Pradeepta Mishra, Megha John, Sandeep Acharya, Akshit Sharma, Vishal Sinha, and many others—for their insightful discussions and guidance over the years. Their perspectives have shaped my philosophy and approach to data science and AI.

A special thanks go to the exceptional team at Manning Publications, beginning with Andy Waldron, for providing me with this incredible opportunity. I am deeply grateful to Ian Hough for his invaluable feedback and guidance throughout the writing process. I am truly indebted to my technical editor, Arturo Geigel, for his thorough review and pertinent feedback that has made the book better. A huge thank you to Azra Dedic, for significantly improving the graphics in the book. I also extend my deepest appreciation to Robin Campbell and Aira Ducic for their outstanding work in promoting and marketing this book. Thanks also to the production team for all their hard work in preparing this book for publication.

My deep gratitude goes to the AI research community as well, whose relentless pursuit of knowledge and innovation continues to push the boundaries of what's possible. In many ways, this book is a reflection of the collective knowledge shared by researchers, open source contributors, and practitioners who have generously published their insights in papers, blogs, and forums.

To all the reviewers—Abhishek Gupta, Alejandro Cuevas Rivero, Alex McLintock, Alireza Aghamohammadi, Amit Dixit, Anindita Nath, Anindyadeep Sannigrahi, Aryan Jadon, Ashish Sarkar, Aushim Nagarkatti, Avinash Tiwari, Babloo Kumar, Balaji Dhamodharan, Balakrishnan Balasubramanian, Bert Gollnick, Bhargob Deka, Brian Daley, Charan Akiri, Christopher G. Fry, Harcharan S. Kabbay, Harshwardhan S. Fartale, Igor Svilenkov Božić, Iván Moreno, Lalit Chourey, Louis Luangkesorn, Louis-François Bouchard, Manas Talukdar, Márcio F. Nogueira, Marine Serré, Naga Santhosh Reddy Vootukuri, Neelesh Pateriya, Peter Cotroneo, Peter Morgan, Richa Taldar, Riddhiben Sunitkumar Shah, Robert Vince, Sameet Sonawane, Sashank Dara, Stephen Wolff, Subhash Kumar Periasamy, Vinesh Gudla, and Yanqi Luo—I am indebted to you for your valuable insights and suggestions, which have elevated the quality of this book.

Finally, I sincerely thank everyone who has been a part of this journey. Your support, wisdom, and generosity have made this book—and my dream of becoming an author—a reality.

about this book

Retrieval-augmented generation (RAG) is transforming the landscape of applied generative AI. First introduced by Lewis and colleagues in their seminal paper "Retrieval-Augmented Generation for Knowledge-Intensive NLP Tasks" (https://arxiv.org/abs/2005.11401), RAG has quickly become a cornerstone of modern AI, enhancing the reliability and trustworthiness of large language models (LLMs).

A Simple Guide to Retrieval Augmented Generation is a foundational guide for individuals looking to explore RAG. It offers a gentle, yet comprehensive introduction to the concept, along with practical insights helpful in using RAG to their advantage.

Who should read this book?

This book is for technology professionals who want to be introduced to the concept of RAG and build LLM-based apps. It is a handy book for both beginners and experienced professionals alike. If you're a data scientist, data engineer, ML engineer, software developer, technology leader, or student interested in generative-AI-powered application development, you will find this book valuable. Upon completing this book, you can expect to

- Understand the fundamentals of RAG, including its components and practical applications.
- Learn how non-parametric knowledge bases work and how they are created.
- Build a RAG system, with a deep dive into the indexing and generation pipelines.
- Gain deep insights into the evaluation of RAG systems and modularized evaluation strategies.
- Familiarize yourself with advanced RAG strategies and the evolving landscape.

- Acquire knowledge of available tools, technologies, and frameworks for building and deploying production-grade RAG systems.
- Learn about state-of-the-art RAG variants, such as multimodal and agentic RAG.
- Get an understanding of the current limitations of RAG and learn more about popular emerging techniques for further exploration.

While prior exposure to the world of ML, generative AI, and LLMs is always helpful, this book is a foundational guide and does not assume that you have a deep understanding of the concepts. You'll develop a deeper understanding of LLMs as you go through the first chapter.

This book is also interspersed with code snippets in Python, using the LangChain framework. It is important to note that the code snippets act only as supplementary illustrations to the concepts and are aimed at readers who want to get a hands-on experience. Only a beginner-level understanding of Python and APIs is expected from those who want to try the codes.

Generative AI is still an emerging technology domain. You can upskill yourself using this book and explore a whole new set of opportunities in your current and future endeavors.

How this book is organized: A road map

This book has nine chapters divided into four parts. Part 1 of the book provides a fundamental understanding of RAG:

- Chapter 1 starts by defining RAG and its need and significance in the LLM-powered AI domain, discussing a few real-world applications of RAG-enabled systems.
- Chapter 2 discusses the main components of a RAG system. It introduces the two main pipelines: the indexing and the generation pipeline. In addition, it also introduces the concepts of RAG evaluation, among other topics.

Part 2 shows how to build a basic RAG system with the core pipelines and their evaluation:

- Chapter 3 discusses and demonstrates an end-to-end indexing pipeline to create a knowledge base for a RAG system. You will learn about the concepts of data loading, chunking, embeddings, and vector storage through examples.
- Chapter 4 sheds light on the generation pipeline, which enables the real-time access to the knowledge base and LLM to generate contextual and accurate responses. We talk about the retrievers, retrieval strategies, and prompt engineering for RAG, with an overview of the available LLMs.
- Chapter 5 examines different RAG evaluation techniques in depth and considers them from the perspective of the question, response, and context. We also discuss the significance and the development of a ground truth dataset. This

chapter will also contain details about popular frameworks and benchmarks used in RAG evaluation.

Part 3 will guide you in improving your RAG pipeline and lay out a blueprint for the layers required to build a production-ready RAG system:

- Chapter 6 looks into the advanced concepts in RAG from the perspective of naïve, advanced, and modular RAG implementation. We discuss important components and pre-/post-retrieval strategies. This chapter also provides optimization techniques to improve RAG system performance.
- Chapter 7 reviews different tools and technologies that enable the RAGOps stack. You will learn about the critical layers without which any RAG system will fail, the essential layers that improve system performance, and the enhancement layers that focus on system usability, scalability, and efficiency.

In Part 4, you will learn about the popular state-of-the-art variants of RAG and a RAG development framework:

- Chapter 8 discusses the state-of-the-art RAG variants, including multimodal RAG, knowledge graphs, and agentic RAG.
- Chapter 9 concludes the book with a RAG development framework that will assist you in planning the development of a RAG system.

The book is meant to be read sequentially, with the final chapter providing an overview of all the concepts introduced in the book.

About the code

All code examples in this book are written in Python. You can get executable snippets of code from the liveBook (online) version of this book at https://livebook.manning .com/book/a-simple-guide-to-retrieval-augmented-generation. The complete code for the examples in the book is available for download from the Manning website at www.manning.com, as well as in Jupyter Notebook format on GitHub at https://mng .bz/a9DJ.

This book provides many examples of source code in chapters 3–6. Source code is formatted in a `fixed-width font like this` to separate it from ordinary text. Sometimes code is also in **bold** to highlight code that has changed from previous steps in the chapter, such as when a new feature adds to an existing line of code.

In many cases, the original source code has been reformatted; we've added line breaks and reworked indentation to accommodate the available page space in the book. Additionally, comments in the source code have often been removed when the code is described in the text. Code annotations accompany many of the listings, highlighting important concepts.

liveBook discussion forum

Purchase of *A Simple Guide to Retrieval Augmented Generation* includes free access to liveBook, Manning's online reading platform. Using liveBook's exclusive discussion features, you can attach comments to the book globally or to specific sections or paragraphs. It's a snap to make notes for yourself, ask and answer technical questions, and receive help from the author and other users. To access the forum, go to https://livebook.manning.com/book/a-simple-guide-to-retrieval-augmented-generation/discussion.

Manning's commitment to our readers is to provide a venue where a meaningful dialogue between individual readers and between readers and the author can take place. It is not a commitment to any specific amount of participation on the part of the author, whose contribution to the forum remains voluntary (and unpaid). We suggest you try asking the author some challenging questions lest their interest stray! The forum and the archives of previous discussions will be accessible from the publisher's website for as long as the book is in print.

about the author

ABHINAV KIMOTHI is a seasoned AI practitioner with over 15 years of experience developing cutting-edge AI and machine learning solutions. Throughout his career, Abhinav has led AI projects across analytics, predictive ML, NLP, and generative AI—some were successful, while others provided valuable lessons. Driven by curiosity and a passion for innovation, he continues to push the boundaries of AI to create effective solutions. You can learn more about Abhinav at https://www.abhinavkimothi.com/.

about the cover illustration

The figure on the cover of *A Simple Guide to Retrieval Augmented Generation*, titled "Le Marchand D'Habits," or "The Clothes Merchant," is taken from a book by Louis Curmer published in 1841. Each illustration is finely drawn and colored by hand.

In those days, it was easy to identify where people lived and what their trade or station in life was just by their dress. Manning celebrates the inventiveness and initiative of the computer business with book covers based on the rich diversity of regional culture centuries ago, brought back to life by pictures from collections such as this one.

Part 1

Foundations

This first part of the book introduces the core idea behind retrieval-augmented generation (RAG) and the high-level design of a RAG system.

Chapter 1 deals with various challenges that AI systems based on large language models (LLMs) face. Furthermore, it illustrates the ways RAG addresses these challenges to improve the reliability of such systems. The chapter also provides a brief overview of the workings of LLMs and some popular RAG use cases.

Chapter 2 discusses the steps involved in building a RAG system. This chapter details the basics of two core RAG pipelines and other essential components of a RAG system.

By the end of the first part of the book, you should have a foundational understanding of a RAG system and be ready to dive deep into the intricacies of RAG.

LLMs and the
need for RAG

1

This chapter covers

- The limits of LLMs and the need for RAG
- The RAG basics
- Popular use cases of RAG

In a short time, large language models (LLMs) have found widespread application in modern language processing tasks and autonomous AI agents. OpenAI's GPT, Anthropic's Claude, Google's Gemini, and Meta's Llama series are notable LLMs integrated into various platforms and techniques. Retrieval-augmented generation, or RAG, plays a pivotal role in the LLM application by enhancing the accuracy and relevance of responses. According to Grand View Research (https://mng.bz/BzKg), in 2023, the global RAG market was estimated at some $1 billion USD, and it has been projected to grow by 44.7% annually, which makes it one of the fastest-growing AI methodologies.

This book aims to demystify the idea of RAG and its application. Chapter by chapter, the book will present the RAG definition, design, implementation, evaluation, and evolution. To kick things off, this chapter begins by highlighting the limitations of LLMs and the need for an approach such as RAG. It then introduces the concept of RAG and builds toward a definition. The chapter ends by listing the popular use cases enabled by RAG.

By the end of this chapter, you will gain foundational knowledge to be ready for a deeper exploration of the RAG system components. In addition, you should

- Have a strong hold on the RAG definition.
- Understand the limitations of LLMs and the need for RAG.
- Be ready to dive into the components of a RAG system.

November 30, 2022, will be remembered as a watershed moment in the field of artificial intelligence. This was the day OpenAI released ChatGPT, and the world became mesmerized by it. ChatGPT turned out to be the fastest app ever to reach a million users. Interest in previously obscure terms such as generative AI and LLMs skyrocketed over the following 12 months (see figure 1.1).

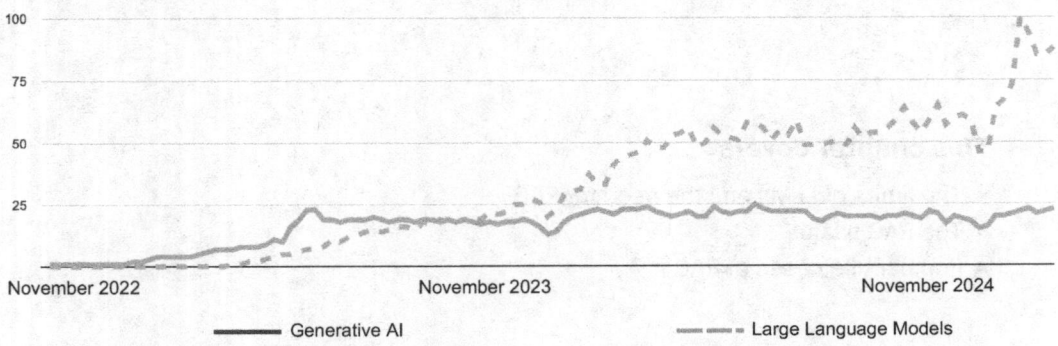

Figure 1.1   Google trends of "Generative AI" and "Large Language Models" from November 2022 to November 2024. Source: Created by the author using data from trends.google.com.

As the use of platforms such as ChatGPT exploded, the weaknesses of LLMs were exposed.

1.1   *Curse of the LLMs and the idea of RAG*

LLMs such as those powering ChatGPT, Ask Gemini, and similar have been shown to store knowledge. You can ask them questions, and they tend to respond with answers that seem correct. However, despite their unprecedented ability to generate text, their responses are not always accurate. Upon more careful observation, you may notice that LLM responses are plagued with suboptimal information and inherent memory limitations.

To understand the limitations, we will use a simple example. Those familiar with the wonderful sport of cricket will recall that the Men's ODI Cricket World Cup tournament was held in 2023. The Australian cricket team emerged as the winner. Now, imagine you are interacting with ChatGPT, and you ask, "Who won the 2023 Cricket World Cup?" You are, in truth, interacting with GPT-4o, or o1, LLMs developed and maintained by OpenAI that power ChatGPT. In the first few sections of this chapter, we will use the terms ChatGPT and LLMs interchangeably for simplicity. So, you ask the question and, most likely, you will get a response as the one in figure 1.2.

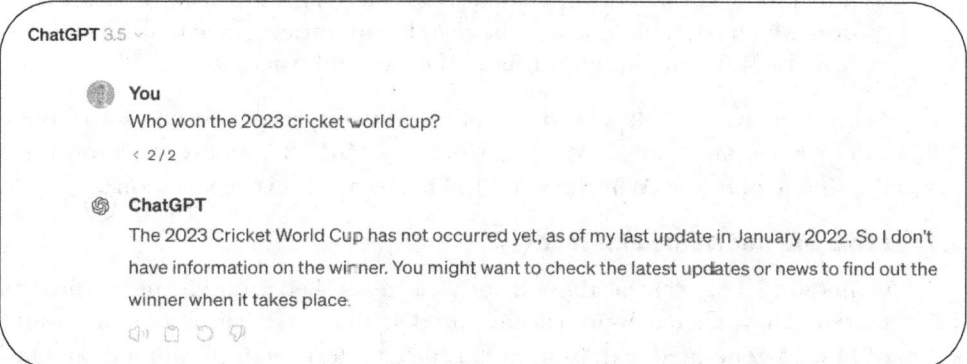

Figure 1.2   ChatGPT (GPT 3.5) response to the question, "Who won the 2023 Cricket World Cup?"
Source: Screenshot of the author's account on https://chat.openai.com.

ChatGPT does not have any memory of the 2023 Cricket World Cup, and it tells you to check the information from other sources. This is not ideal, but at least ChatGPT is honest in its response. The same question asked again might also provide a factually inaccurate result. Look at the response in figure 1.3. ChatGPT falsely responds that India was the winner of the tournament.

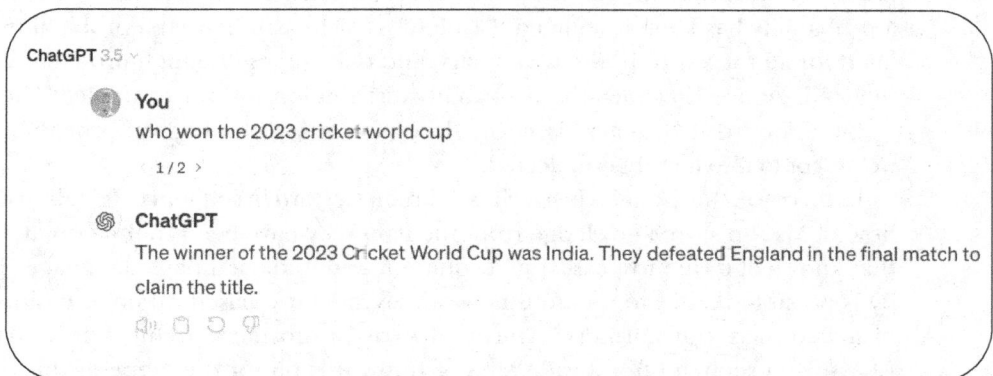

Figure 1.3   An example of hallucination. ChatGPT's (GPT 3.5) inaccurate response to the question,
"Who won the 2023 cricket World Cup?" Source: Screenshot of the author's account on https://chat
.openai.com.

This is problematic. Despite not having any memory of the 2023 Cricket World Cup, ChatGPT still generates the answer in a seemingly confident tone, but it does so inaccurately. This is what is called a "hallucination," and it has become a major point of criticism for LLMs.

> **NOTE** In September 2023, ChatGPT's "Browse with Bing" feature was introduced, which allows ChatGPT Plus users to fetch live information from the web for more accurate and up-to-date responses. This is a feature of the application, which is enabled via agentic search and retrieval mechanisms. The underlying LLM doesn't inherently have the latest information.

Many users treat LLMs as a source of information as an alternative to Google Search. In our example, we also expected ChatGPT (GPT 3.5 model) to know the answer to the simple question. Why does an LLM fail to meet this expectation?

1.1.1 LLMs are not trained for facts

Generally, LLMs can be thought of as a next-token (loosely, next word) prediction model. They are machine learning models that have learned from massive datasets of human-generated text, finding statistical patterns to replicate human-like language abilities.

To simplify, think of the model first being shown a sentence such as "The teacher teaches the student." Then, we hide the last few words of this sentence (i.e., "teaches the student") and ask the model what the next word should be. The model should learn to predict "teaches" as the next word, "the" as the word after that, and so on. There are various methods of teaching the model, including causal language modeling (CLM) and masked language modeling (MLM). Figure 1.4 shows the idea behind these two techniques.

The training data can have billions of sentences of different kinds. The next token (or word) is chosen from a probability distribution observed in the training data. There are different means and methods to choose the next token from the ones for which a probability has been calculated. Crudely, you can assume that a probability is calculated for all the words in the vocabulary, and one among the high-probability words is selected. Figure 1.5 shows the probability distribution for our example, "The teacher ____ ." The word "teaches" is selected because it has the highest probability. Other words could also have been selected.

In this case, the model is just trying to predict a word in sequence. It is almost magical how LLMs can store knowledge from the data they have been trained on and present that knowledge (in most cases) in a coherent and understandable language. This ability is possible thanks to a neural network architecture based on an attention mechanism known as "transformers." The nuances of transformers' architecture and building LLMs from scratch offer a wide area of study. It is out of the scope of this book, but you're encouraged to find out more about LLM training and transformers.

Returning to the limitations of LLMs, their training process introduces three major characteristic drawbacks.

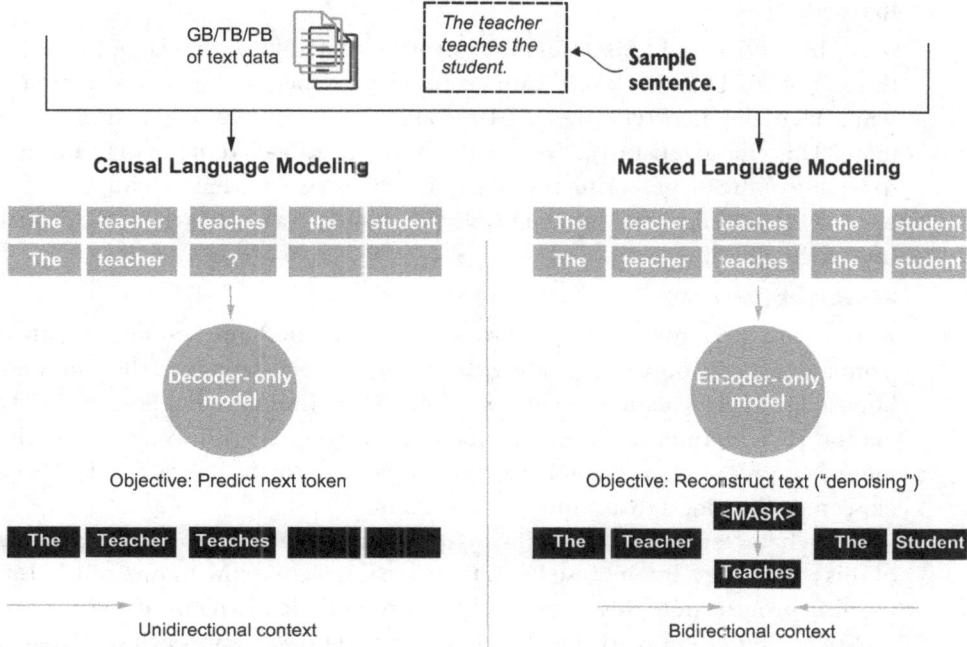

Figure 1.4   Two token prediction techniques: CLM and MLM. In the CLM approach, the model predicts the next token based on the preceding tokens. In MLM, the model predicts the masked token based on both the preceding and the succeeding tokens.

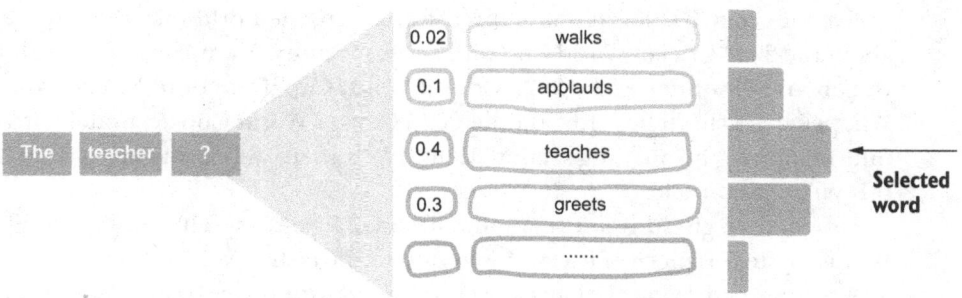

Figure 1.5   Illustrative probability distribution of words after "The teacher"

KNOWLEDGE CUT-OFF DATE

Training an LLM is an expensive and time-consuming process. It takes massive volumes of data and several weeks, or even months, to train an LLM. The data that LLMs are trained on is, therefore, not always up to date. For instance, OpenAI's flagship model, GPT-4.1, released in April 2025, has knowledge only until June 1, 2024. Any event that happened after this knowledge cut-off date is not available to the model.

HALLUCINATIONS

It is observed that LLMs sometimes provide factually incorrect responses. (We saw this in the 2023 Cricket World Cup example at the beginning of this chapter.) Despite being factually incorrect, the LLM responses sound extremely confident and legitimate. This characteristic of "lying with confidence," called hallucinations, has proved to be one of the biggest criticisms of LLMs. The reason for hallucinations can be traced back to LLMs being a next-token prediction model that selects the most probable word from a distribution.

KNOWLEDGE LIMITATION

As you have already seen, LLMs have been trained on large volumes of data obtained from a variety of sources, including the open internet. However, they do not have any knowledge of information that is not public. The LLMs have not been trained on information such as internal company documents, customer information, product documents, confidential personnel information, and so forth. Therefore, LLMs cannot be expected to respond to any query about them.

This characteristic raises significant questions about the general adoption and value of this technology. But if these limitations are inherent to the nature of LLMs and their training process, does this mean the LLM is not usable as a technology?

Not at all! Let's now go ahead and understand how an approach such as RAG comes to the rescue.

1.1.2   *What is RAG?*

Recall the question we used to begin this discussion: "Who won the 2023 Cricket World Cup?" What can be done to improve the response?

Even if ChatGPT doesn't have this information, the world (aka the internet) knows about the 2023 Cricket World Cup with no uncertainty. A simple Google Search will tell you about the winner of the 2023 Cricket World Cup if you don't already know it. The Wikipedia article (figure 1.6) on the 2023 Cricket World Cup accurately provides this information in the opening section itself. If only there were a way to tell the LLM about this Wikipedia article.

How can we give this information to ChatGPT, you ask? The answer is quite simple. We just paste this piece of text with our question (see figure 1.7).

And there it is! ChatGPT has now responded with the correct answer. It was able to comprehend the piece of additional information we provided, distill the information about the winner of the tournament, and respond with a precise and factually accurate answer.

It may appear juvenile, but in an oversimplified manner, this example illustrates the basic concept of RAG. Let's look back at what we did here. We understood that the question is about the winner of the 2023 Cricket World Cup. We searched for information about the question and identified Wikipedia as a source of information. We then copied that information and passed it onto ChatGPT (and the LLM powering it) along with the original question. In a way, we added to ChatGPT's knowledge. As a technique,

Context from External Source

Figure 1.6   Wikipedia article on 2023 Cricket World Cup. Source: https://mng.bz/yN4J.

Figure 1.7   ChatGPT (GPT 3.5) response to the question, augmented with external context. Source: Screenshot of the author's account on https://chat.openai.com.

RAG does the same thing programmatically. It overcomes the limitations of LLMs by providing them with previously unknown information and, consequently, enhances the overall memory of the system.

As the name implies, "retrieval augmented generation" can be explained through three steps:

1 It *retrieves* relevant information from a data source external to the LLMs (Wikipedia, in our example).

2 It *augments* the input to the LLM with that external information.

3 Finally, the LLM *generates* a more accurate result.

A simple definition for RAG, illustrated in figure 1.8, can therefore be as follows:

> *Retrieval Augmented Generation is the technique of retrieving relevant information from an external source, augmenting the input to the LLM with that external information, thereby enabling the LLM to generate a response that is contextual, reliable, and factually accurate.*

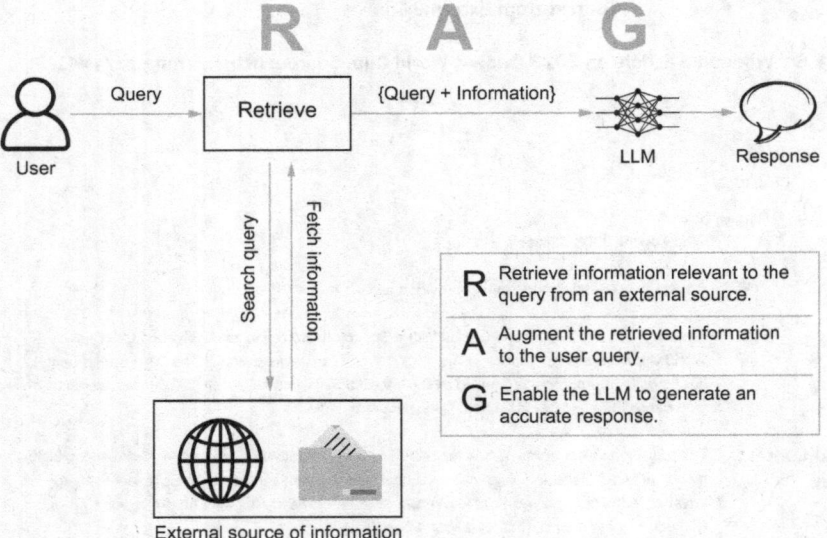

Figure 1.8   RAG (a simple definition): retrieval of information, augmentation with the query, and the generation using an LLM form the three RAG focal points

The example that we have been looking at so far is oversimplified. We manually searched for the external information, and the search was for this one specific question only. In practice, all these processes are automated, which allows the system to scale up to a diverse range of queries and data sources. We will now unravel this idea further.

1.2 The novelty of RAG

The main idea is to provide additional context or knowledge to the LLMs. Essentially, it meant creating a ChatGPT-like system with three main objectives:

- Make LLMs respond with up-to-date information.
- Make LLMs respond with factually accurate information.
- Make LLMs aware of proprietary information.

These objectives can be achieved using diverse techniques. A new LLM can be trained from scratch that includes the new data. An existing model can also be fine-tuned with additional data. However, both approaches require a significant amount of data and computational resources. Furthermore, updating the model with new information at regular intervals is prohibitively costly.

RAG is a cheaper, more effective, and more dynamic technique used to attain the three objectives. LLMs respond with information that is up-to-date and factually accurate, and they are aware of proprietary information, so they have no knowledge gaps.

1.2.1 The RAG discovery

In a paper titled "Retrieval-Augmented Generation for Knowledge-Intensive NLP Tasks" (https://arxiv.org/abs/2005.11401), Patrick Lewis and his coauthors explored the recipe for RAG models, which combine pretrained "parametric" and "non-parametric" memory for language generation. Let's pay some attention to the terms "parametric" and "non-parametric."

Parameters in machine learning parlance refer to the model weights or variables that the model learns during the training process. In simple terms, they are settings or configurations that the model adjusts to perform the assigned task. For language generation, LLMs are trained with billions of parameters (the GPT 4 model is rumored to have over 1 trillion parameters, and the largest Llama 3 model has 405 billion parameters). The ability of an LLM to retain information it has been trained on is based solely on its parameters. It can therefore be said that LLMs store factual information in their parameters. An LLM's internal memory is referred to as "parametric memory." The parametric memory is limited. It depends on the number of parameters and is a factor of the data on which the LLM has been trained.

Conversely, we can provide information to an LLM that it does not have in its parametric memory. We saw in the example of the Cricket World Cup that when we provided information from an external source to ChatGPT, it was able to get rid of the hallucination. This information that is external to the LLM but can be provided to the LLM is termed "non-parametric." If we can gather information from external sources as and when desired and use it with the LLM, it forms the "non-parametric" memory of the system. In the aforementioned paper, Lewis and his coauthors stored Wikipedia data and used a retriever to access the information. They demonstrated that this RAG approach outperformed the parametric-only baseline in generating more specific, diverse, and factual language. We will discuss vector databases and retrievers in chapters 3 and 4.

In 2025, RAG became one of the most used techniques in the LLM domain. With the addition of a non-parametric memory, the LLM responses are more grounded and factual. Let's discuss the advantages of RAG.

1.2.2 How does RAG help?

With the introduction of non-parametric memory, the LLM does not remain limited to its internal knowledge. We can conclude, at least theoretically, that this non-parametric memory can be extended as much as we want. It can store any volume of proprietary documents or data and access all sorts of sources, such as the intranet and the open internet. In a way, through RAG, we open up the possibility of embellishing the LLM with unlimited knowledge. There will always be some effort required to create this non-parametric memory or the knowledge base, and we will look at it in detail later. Chapter 3 is dedicated to the creation of the non-parametric knowledge base.

As a consequence of overcoming the challenge of limited parametric memory, RAG also builds user confidence in the LLM responses. The three advantages of RAG are as follows:

- *Deep contextual awareness*—The added information assists the LLM in generating contextually appropriate responses, and the users can be relatively more confident. For example, if the non-parametric memory contains information about a particular company's products, users can be assured that the LLM will generate responses about those products from the provided sources and not from elsewhere.
- *Source citation*—In addition to being context aware, because the information is being fetched from a known source, these sources can be cited in the response. This makes the responses more reliable since the users have the choice of validating the information from the source.
- *Lesser hallucination*—With contextual awareness, the tendency of LLM responses to be factually inaccurate is greatly reduced. The LLMs hallucinate less in RAG systems.

We have already seen a simple RAG definition. Let's now expand that definition:

> *Retrieval Augmented Generation is the methodological approach of enhancing the parametric memory of an LLM by creating access to an explicit non-parametric memory, from which a retriever can fetch relevant information, augment that information to the prompt, pass the prompt to an LLM to enable the LLM to generate a response that is contextual, reliable, and factually accurate.*

This definition is illustrated in figure 1.9.

RAG has acted as a catalyst in the propagation and acceptance of LLM-powered applications. Before concluding this chapter and getting into the design of RAG systems, let's look at some popular use cases where RAG is being adopted.

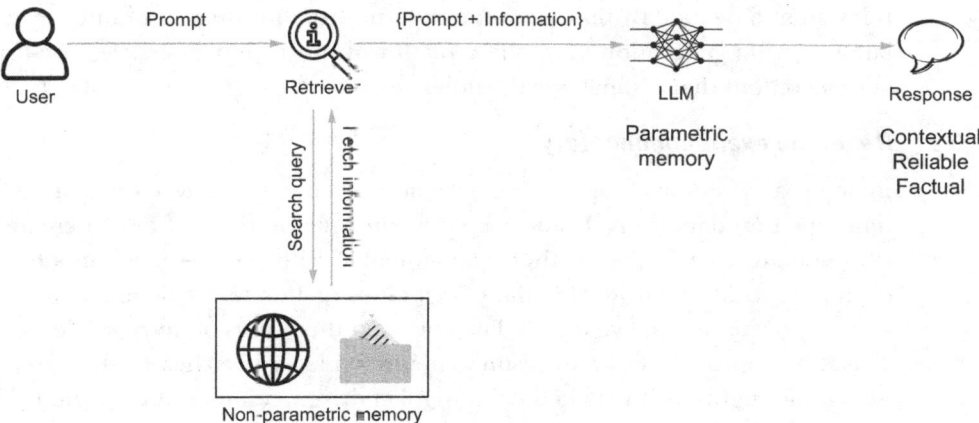

Figure 1.9 RAG enhances the parametric memory of an LLM by creating access to non-parametric memory.

1.3 Popular RAG use cases

RAG is not just a theoretical concept but a technique that is as popular as the LLM technology itself. Software developers started using language models as soon as Google released BERT in 2018. Today, there are thousands of applications that use LLMs to solve language-intensive tasks. Whenever you come across an application using LLMs, it will often have an internal RAG system in some shape or form. Common applications are described in the following sections.

1.3.1 Search Engine Experience

Conventional search results are shown as a list of page links ordered by relevance. Modern search engines integrate RAG to combine live information retrieval with generative answers. Google's Search Generative Experience (SGE) augments queries with relevant results and citations. AI-based search engines such as Perplexity.ai and ChatGPT's search are built on a RAG framework that fetches up-to-date web information and then generates responses with sources attached. By grounding answers in real-time results, these search engines provide more accurate, source-backed answers than standalone LLMs.

1.3.2 Personalized marketing content generation

The widest use of LLMs has probably been in content generation. Content creation tools employ RAG to tailor marketing copy using current data and user-specific context. Yarnit, for instance, uses RAG to generate marketing copy, blog posts, and other content types based on up-to-the-moment information and user inputs. Yarnit can pull in fresh facts or trending material while drafting the text, ensuring the output is relevant and factual. By pulling in the right information (e.g., a brand's style guide or latest stats) at generation time, these platforms produce personalized, on-brand marketing content that resonates with audiences.

1.3.3 *Real-time event commentary*

Imagine an event such as a sport or a news event. A retriever can connect to real-time updates/data via APIs and pass this information to the LLM to create a virtual commentator. These can further be augmented with text-to-speech models. A prime example is IBM's Watson AI at the US Open—it generates audio and text tennis commentary by pulling in live match data and even thousands of news articles for context. This RAG approach allowed Watson to mention player stats, head-to-head records, and match highlights as it narrated, creating fact-driven commentary on the fly. In financial markets, vendors are doing something similar—Bloomberg's AI-driven tools use RAG to ground their insights in up-to-date proprietary data. Bloomberg's platforms explicitly employ a RAG framework so that any generative output (market summaries, answers to trader queries, etc.) is based on recent, authoritative content rather than the model's memory alone.

1.3.4 *Conversational agents*

LLMs can be customized to product/service manuals, domain knowledge, guidelines, and so forth using RAG and serve as support agents, resolving user complaints and problems. These agents can also route users to more specialized agents, depending on the nature of the query. Almost all LLM-based chatbots on websites or as internal tools use RAG. Intercom's Fin AI agent is a notable example—it was specifically designed with a "bespoke and enhanced" RAG architecture to generate answers from a company's support content. Support platforms such as Zendesk follow a similar pattern by retrieving help-center articles to answer customer queries. Industry observers note that these companies use basic RAG to quickly fetch relevant support docs and generate customized responses from them.

1.3.5 *Document question answering systems*

As discussed, one of the LLMs' limitations is that they don't have access to proprietary nonpublic information such as product documents, customer profiles, and similar information specific to an organization. With access to such proprietary documents, a RAG system becomes an intelligent AI system that can answer all questions about the organization. In the legal domain, for example, researchers have highlighted that domain-specific RAG enables far more nuanced and trustworthy answers in tools for legal research. A legal Q&A system can retrieve relevant case law or statutes and feed those into an LLM to answer a question, ensuring the answer cites the correct precedent. This technique was at the heart of products such as ROSS Intelligence, which aimed to answer lawyers' queries by retrieving passages from law databases and then generating an answer. More generally, enterprise knowledge management is being transformed by RAG—instead of relying on an LLM's limited training data, companies can equip AI assistants to search internal documents, wikis, or manuals on the fly.

1.3.6 Virtual assistants

Virtual personal assistants such as Siri, Alexa, and others are beginning to use LLMs to enhance the user's experience. Coupled with more context on user behavior using RAG, these assistants are set to become more personalized. Amazon's next-generation Alexa, for instance, incorporates retrieval techniques, so it can answer with information beyond its core training. By augmenting voice assistant answers with retrieved facts, RAG helps virtual assistants such as Alexa and Google Assistant give far more accurate and current answers to user queries.

1.3.7 AI-powered research

AI agents have been gaining traction in research-intensive fields such as law and finance. RAG has been extensively used to retrieve and analyze case law to assist lawyers. A lot of portfolio management companies are introducing RAG systems to analyze scores of documents to research investment opportunities. ESGReveal is a framework developed by researchers at Alibaba Group that employs RAG to extract and evaluate environmental, social, and governance (ESG) data from corporate reports.

1.3.8 Social media monitoring and sentiment analysis

Analyzing the firehose of social media data is another task suited to RAG. Social listening platforms such as Brandwatch use generative AI to summarize trends and sentiments from millions of posts, but they ground those summaries in the underlying data. Brandwatch's system, for example, scans over 100 million sources, and then its generative AI integration transforms data into easy-to-understand summaries for the user.

1.3.9 News generation and content curation

News organizations have been using RAG to automate and assist in news writing, while maintaining accuracy. Reuters, for instance, offers a solution to feed its trusted news data into generative models so they produce fact-based outputs. By using Reuters' real-time news feeds as the retrieval source, an AI system can generate a news summary or answer questions with the latest verified facts. Reuters asserts that this approach keeps your answers reliable and accurate with a RAG system extracting trusted facts from the latest Reuters stories. The Associated Press (AP) has similarly been a pioneer in automating news: AP has used templates and data to auto-generate sports recaps and earnings reports for years, and now, with generative AI, they are augmenting those systems with LLMs. Thanks to RAG, an AI writer can ingest box score data or financial results and then produce a readable article, grounding every statement in the provided data.

These are only a few select examples. RAG has been extensively used in other domains such as customer support automation, financial market insights, healthcare diagnostics, legal document drafting, learning systems, and supply chain optimization.

This introductory chapter dealt with the RAG concept. Overcoming the limitations of LLMs, RAG addresses these challenges by providing access to a non-parametric knowledge base to the system. With this foundational understanding of RAG, in the next chapter, we take the first step toward understanding how RAG systems are built by looking at the different components of their design.

Summary

- RAG enhances the memory of LLMs by providing access to external information.
- LLMs are next-word (or token) prediction models trained on massive amounts of text data to generate human-like text.
- LLMs face challenges of having a knowledge cut-off date and being trained only on public data. They are also prone to generating factually incorrect information (i.e., hallucinating).
- RAG overcomes the LLM limitations by incorporating non-parametric memory and increases context awareness and reliability of responses.
- Popular use cases of RAG include search engines, document question-answering systems, conversational agents, personalized content generation, virtual assistants, and so forth.

RAG systems
and their design

This chapter covers

- The concept and design of RAG systems
- An overview of the indexing pipeline
- An overview of the generation pipeline
- An initial look at RAG evaluation
- A high-level look at the RAG operations stack

The first chapter explored the core principles behind retrieval-augmented generation (RAG) and the large language model (LLM) challenges addressed by it. To construct a RAG system, several components need to be assembled. This process includes the creation and maintenance of the non-parametric memory, or a knowledge base, for the system. Another pipeline facilitates real-time interaction by sending the prompts to and accepting the response from the LLM, with retrieval and augmentation steps in the middle. Evaluation is yet another critical component, ensuring the effectiveness and accuracy of the system. All these components are supported by layers of the operations stack.

Chapter 2 discusses the design of a RAG system, examining the steps involved and the need for two different pipelines. We will call the pipeline that creates the knowledge base the "indexing pipeline." The other pipeline that allows real-time interaction with the LLM will be referred to as the "generation pipeline." We will discuss their individual components, such as data loading, embeddings, vector stores, retrievers, and more. Additionally, we will get an understanding of how the evaluation of RAG systems is conducted and introduce the RAG operations (RAGOps) stack that powers such systems.

This chapter will introduce you to various components discussed in detail in the coming chapters. By the end of chapter 2, you will have acquired a deep understanding of the components of a RAG system and will be ready to dive deep into the different components. By the end of the chapter, you should

- Be able to understand the several components of the RAG system design.
- Set yourself up for a deeper exploration of the indexing pipeline—the generation pipelines, RAG evaluation methods, and the RAGOps stack.

2.1   *What does a RAG system look like?*

By now, we have come to know that RAG is a vital component of the systems that use LLMs to solve their use cases. But, what is that system like? To illustrate, let's revisit the example used at the beginning chapter 1 ("Who won the 2023 Cricket World Cup?") and lay out the steps we undertook to enable ChatGPT to provide us with the accurate response.

The initial step was asking the question itself: "Who won the 2023 Cricket World Cup?" Following this, we manually searched for sources on the internet that might have information regarding the answer to the question. We found one (Wikipedia, in our example) and extracted a relevant paragraph from the source. Subsequently, we added the relevant paragraph to our original question, pasted the question and the retrieved paragraph together in the prompt to ChatGPT, and got a factually correct response: "Australia won the 2023 Cricket World Cup."

This process can be distilled into five steps, and our system needs to facilitate all of them:

1 User asks a question.
2 The system searches for information relevant to the input question.
3 The information relevant to the input question is fetched, or retrieved, and added to the input question.
4 This question and information are passed to an LLM.
5 The LLM responds with a contextual answer.

If you recall, we have already described this process in chapter 1. Let's visualize it in the context of these five steps as shown in figure 2.1. This workflow will be called the "generation pipeline" since it generates the answer.

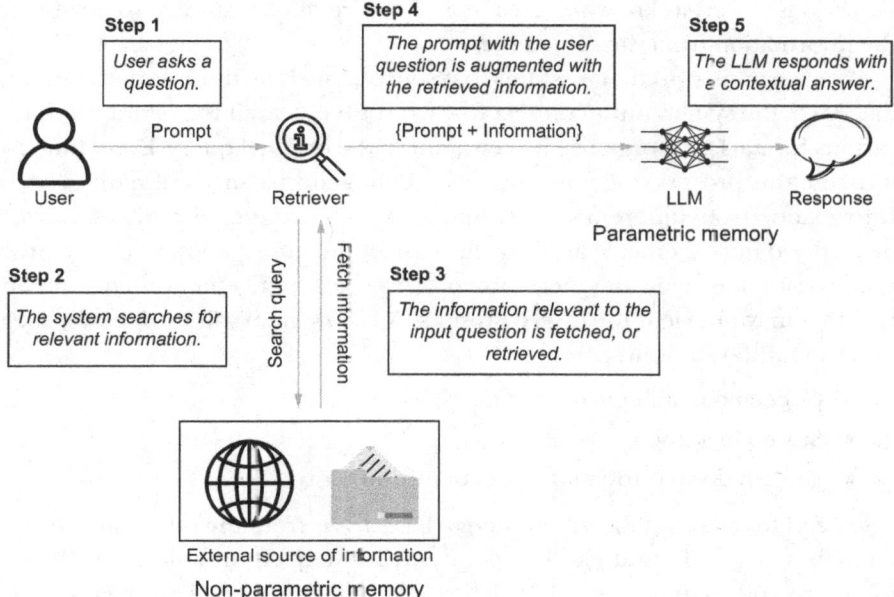

Figure 2.1 Generation pipeline covering the five RAG steps. The journey from query to the response involves search and retrieval, augmentation, and generation.

This pipeline enables real-time contextual interaction with the LLM. There are, of course, several intricacies in each of the five steps needed to create the generation pipeline. Some decisions need to be made about the design of the retriever and the LLM choice. The construction of prompts will also affect the quality of the response. We will discuss prompt construction in chapter 3. We first must address a critical pre-requisite step before this generation pipeline can be put in place. For that, some key questions regarding the external source of information need to be answered. We will also need to know, in advance, where to look and then establish connections to all these disparate sources:

- What is the location of the external source of information?
  - Is it the open internet? Or are there some documents in the company's internal data storage? Is the information present in some third-party databases? Are there multiple sources we want to use?
  - Why is this important?
- What is the nature of the information at the source?
  - Are these Word documents or PDF files? Is the information accessed via an API, and the response is in JSON format? Will we find answers in one document, or is the information distributed in multiple documents?
  - Why is this important?

We will also need to know the format and nature of data storage to be able to extract the information from the source files.

When data is stored across multiple sources, such as the internet and an internal data lake, the system must connect to each source, search for relevant information in various formats, and organize it according to the original query. Every time a question is asked, this process of connecting, extracting, and parsing will have to be repeated. Information from different sources may lead to factual inconsistencies that will have to be resolved in real time. Searching through all the information might be prohibitively time-consuming. This will, therefore, prove to be a highly suboptimal, unscalable process that may not yield the desired results. A RAG system will work best if the information from different sources is

- Collected in a single location.
- Stored in a single format.
- Broken down into small pieces of information.

The need for a consolidated knowledge base arises from the disparate nature of external data sources. To address this requirement, we need to undertake a series of steps to create and maintain a well-structured knowledge base. This, again, is a five-step process:

1 Connect to previously identified external sources.
2 Extract documents and parse text from them.
3 Break down long pieces of text into smaller, manageable pieces.
4 Convert these small pieces into a suitable format.
5 Store this information.

These steps, which facilitate the creation of this knowledge base, form the *indexing pipeline*. The indexing pipeline is shown in figure 2.2.

In addition to creating the knowledge base, the indexing pipeline plays a crucial role in maintaining and updating it with the latest information to ensure its relevance and accuracy. Before the knowledge base is created by the indexing pipeline, there is nowhere for the generation pipeline to search for information. It is the indexing pipeline that lays the foundation for the subsequent operation of the generation pipeline. Therefore, setting up the indexing pipeline comes before the generation pipeline can be activated.

Together, these pipelines form the backbone of a RAG system, enabling seamless interaction with users and delivering contextually relevant responses. Figure 2.3 shows the indexing and generation pipelines working together to form the skeleton of a RAG system.

We have established the flow of a RAG system that includes two pipelines. Conceptually, this is the complete flow. However, to build such systems to be used in the real world, more components are required. The next section reimagines this flow along with other considerations and creates a design for RAG systems.

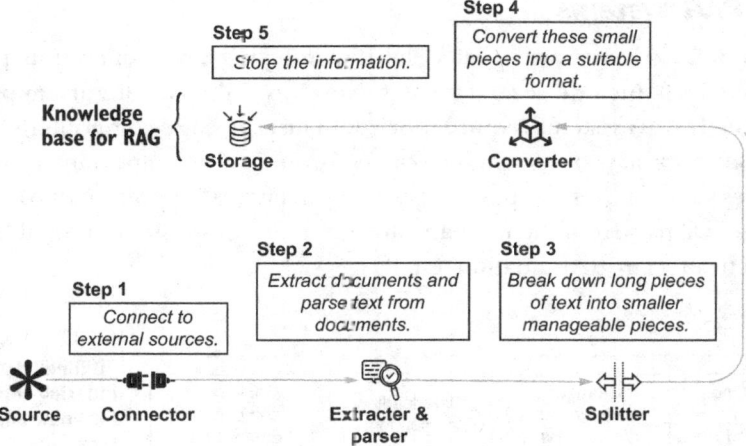

Figure 2.2 Indexing pipeline covering the steps to create the knowledge base for RAG. This involves connecting to the source, parsing, splitting, converting, and storing information.

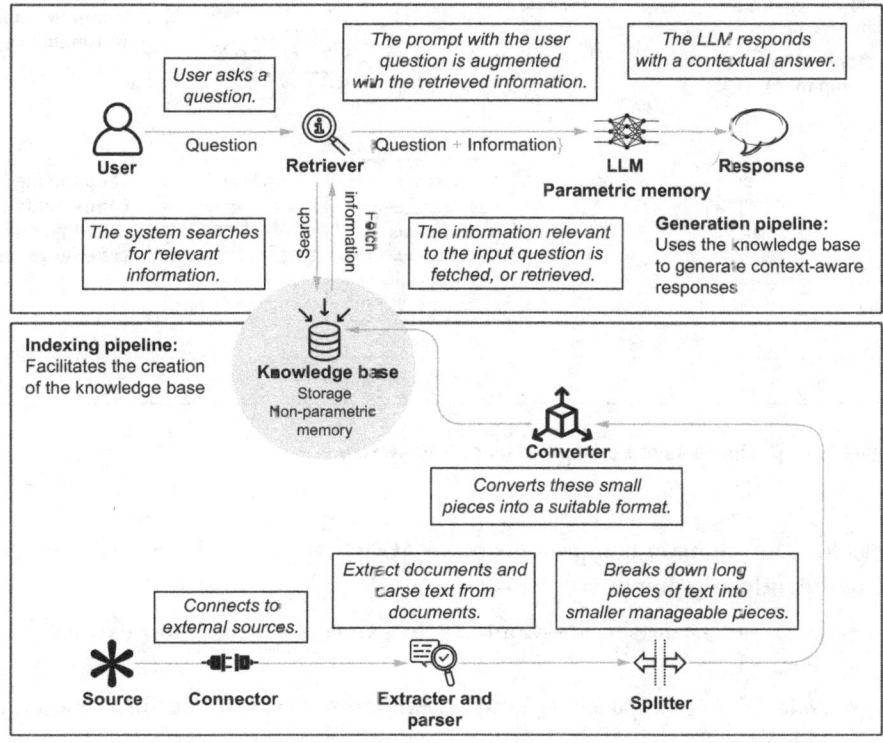

Figure 2.3 The indexing and generation pipelines together make a RAG system. The indexing pipeline is an offline process, while the generation pipeline facilitates real-time interaction with the knowledge base.

2.2   *Design of RAG systems*

We saw how RAG systems are created by the indexing and generation pipelines. These two pipelines include several parts themselves. Like all software applications, production-ready RAG systems require more than just the basic components. We need to think about accuracy, observability, scalability, and other important factors. This book discusses some of these components at length. Figure 2.4 presents a rough layout of a RAG system. Apart from the indexing and generation component, we'll add layers for infrastructure, security, evaluation, etc.

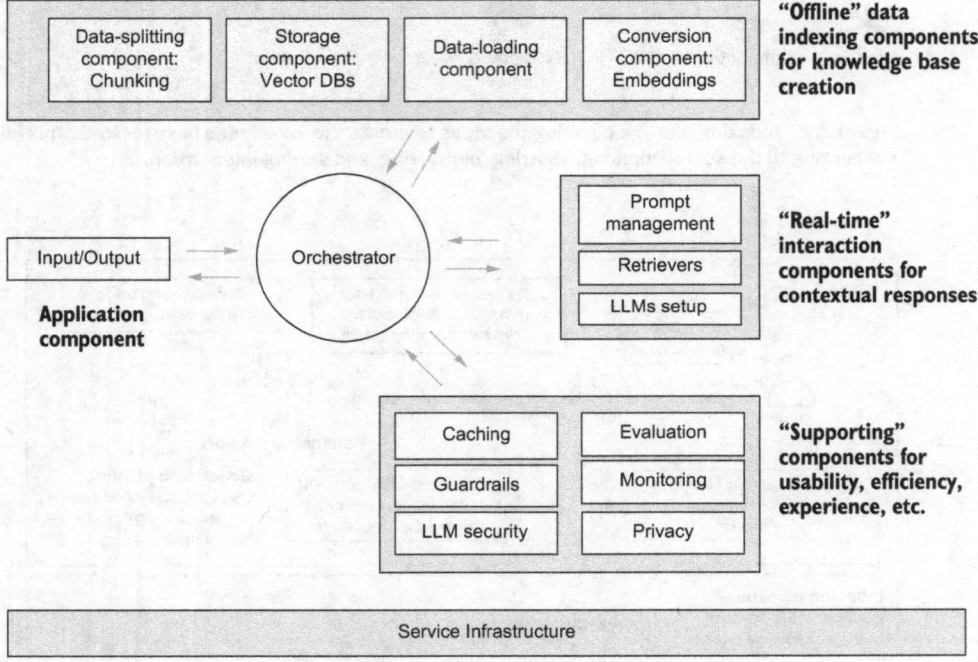

Figure 2.4   Components of a production-ready RAG system

Let's look at the main components of a RAG system. The first four components complete the indexing pipeline:

- *Data-loading component*—Connects to external sources, and extracts and parses data
- *Data-splitting component*—Breaks down large pieces of text into smaller, manageable parts
- *Data conversion component*—Converts text data into a more suitable format
- *Storage component*—Stores the data to create a knowledge base for the system

These next three components complete the generation pipeline:

- *Retrievers*—Responsible for searching and fetching information from the storage
- *LLM setup*—Responsible for generating the response to the input
- *Prompt management*—Enables the augmentation of the retrieved information to the original input

The evaluation component measures the accuracy and reliability of the system before and after deployment. The monitoring component tracks the performance of the RAG system and helps detect failures. Other components include caching, which helps store previously generated responses to expedite retrieval for similar queries; guardrails, to ensure compliance with policy, regulation, and social responsibility; and security, to protect LLMs against breaches such as prompt injection, data poisoning, and similar. All the layers are supported by a service infrastructure.

All these components are managed and controlled by a central orchestration layer, which is responsible for their interaction and sequencing. It provides a unified interface for managing and monitoring workflows and processes.

The following sections provide an overview of these components before we examine them in depth in subsequent chapters.

2.3 Indexing pipeline

We discussed how the indexing pipeline facilitates the creation of the knowledge base used in the real-time generation pipeline. For practical purposes, the indexing pipeline is an offline or asynchronous pipeline. What this means is that the indexing pipeline is not activated in real time when the user is asking a question. Rather, it creates the knowledge base in advance and updates it at predefined intervals. The indexing pipeline comprises four main components, as seen in figure 2.5.

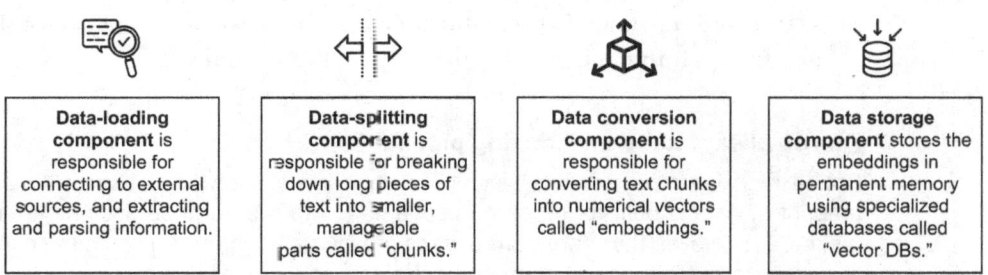

| Data-loading component is responsible for connecting to external sources, and extracting and parsing information. | Data-splitting component is responsible for breaking down long pieces of text into smaller, manageable parts called "chunks." | Data conversion component is responsible for converting text chunks into numerical vectors called "embeddings." | Data storage component stores the embeddings in permanent memory using specialized databases called "vector DBs." |

Figure 2.5 Four components of the indexing pipeline facilitate the creation of the knowledge base.

Let's delve deeper into each:

- *Data loading*—This component is responsible for connecting to different sources where data is present, being able to read the files in these external sources, and extracting and parsing the text from these files. These external sources can be filesystems, data lakes, content management systems, and so forth. The files received from the sources can be in various formats such as PDF, docs, JSON, HTML, and more.

This component, therefore, comprises several connectors (for different external sources), extractors, and parsers (for different file types). In chapter 3, we will look at several examples of such loaders. The data-loading component also involves efficient preprocessing of data for knowledge consistency, removal of irrelevant information and masking of confidential data. Metadata information is another aspect the data-loading component manages. Chapters 3 and 6 discuss how the data loading component is built and enhanced.

- *Data splitting (text splitting)*—Breaking down text into smaller segments enhances the system's ability to process and analyze information efficiently. These smaller pieces in natural language processing (NLP) parlance are commonly referred to as "chunks." The process of splitting large text documents into smaller chunks is called "chunking." We will discuss the need for chunking and various chunking strategies in chapter 3.

- *Data conversion (embeddings)*—Textual data must be converted to a numerical format for search and retrieval computations in RAG systems. There are different ways of implementing this conversion. For all practical purposes, a data format called "embeddings" works best for search and retrieval. You will learn more about embeddings and different embedding models in chapter 3.

- *Data storage*—Once the data is ready in the desired format (embeddings), it needs to be stored in persistent (permanent) memory so that the real-time generation pipeline can access data whenever a user asks a question. Data is stored in specialized databases known as "vector databases," which are best suited for search and retrieval of embeddings. Chapter 3 explores various vector databases and factors influencing their suitability for RAG systems.

Do you always need an indexing pipeline?

Offline indexing pipelines are typically used when a knowledge base with a large amount of data is built for repeated usage (e.g., many enterprise documents, manuals, etc.). However, there are some cases in which the generation pipeline connects to a third-party API to receive information related to the user question.

For example, imagine an application built for users seeking travel advice based on the weather forecast. An important component of this application will be fetching the weather details for the users' location. Suppose the system uses a third-party API service that can respond with a location's weather details when provided with the location in the input. This weather information is then passed to the LLM to generate the advice.

This application can also be thought of as a RAG system. But there is a difference. This system has outsourced the search and retrieval operation to the third-party API. It is the third party that maintains the data. For such systems, the indexing pipeline is not required to be built since the search and retrieval happens outside the system. Another example is applications that ask the user to input external information, like document summarizers. The search operation here is outsourced to the user.

Therefore, systems that use augment external information to the prompts but do not necessarily search and retrieve information themselves, do not warrant the creation of a knowledge base, and therefore, do not have an indexing pipeline. Some will argue that such systems are not RAG systems in the first place.

2.4   *Generation pipeline*

Building on the foundation established by the indexing pipeline, the generation pipeline facilitates real-time interactions in RAG systems. It is the generation pipeline that facilitates the retrieval, augmentation, and generation in the system. When a user asks a question, the generation pipeline processes the query, retrieves relevant information, and generates a response—all without the user directly interacting with the underlying indexing pipeline. The generation pipeline is enabled by three components, as seen in figure 2.6.

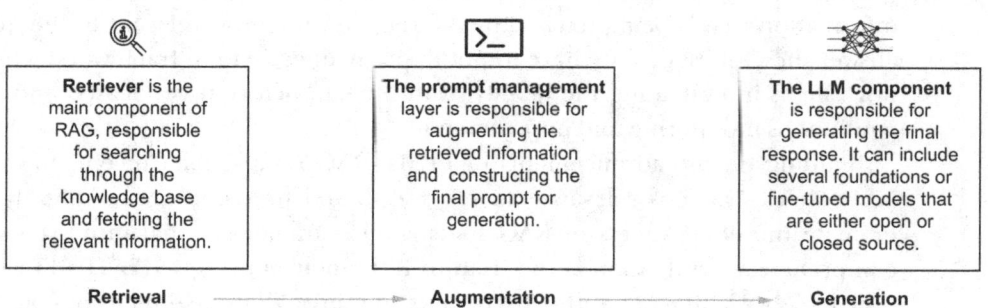

Figure 2.6   Three components of the generation pipeline enable the real-time query-response process of a RAG system.

Let's consider each of these in some more detail:

- *The retriever*—This is arguably the most critical component of the entire system. Using advanced search algorithms, the retriever scans the knowledge base to identify and retrieve the most relevant information based on the user's query. The overall effectiveness of the entire system relies heavily on the accuracy of the retriever. Also, search is a computationally heavy operation and may take time.

Therefore, the retriever also contributes heavily to the overall latency of the system. We will discuss different retrievers and retrieval strategies in chapters 4 and 6.

- *Prompt management*—Once the relevant information is retrieved by the retriever, it needs to be combined, or augmented, with the original user query. Now, this may seem like a simple task at first glance. However, the construction of the prompt makes significant difference to the quality of the generated response. This component also falls in the gambit of prompt engineering. We will explore different prompting and prompt management strategies in chapter 4.

- *LLM setup*—At the end, LLMs are responsible for generating the final response. A RAG system may rely on more than one LLM. The LLMs can be the foundation (base) models that have been pretrained and generally available either open source, like those by Meta or Mistral, or through a managed service, like OpenAI or Anthropic. LLMs can also be fine-tuned for specific tasks. Fine-tuning involves training pre-existing LLMs on specific datasets or tasks to improve performance and adaptability for specialized applications. In rare cases, the developer may decide to train their LLMs. We will discuss LLMs in depth in chapter 4.

2.5   *Evaluation and monitoring*

Indexing and generation pipelines complete the system from a usage perspective. With these two pipelines in place, at least in theory, a user can start interacting with the system and get responses. However, in this case, we have no measure of the system quality. Is the system performing accurately, or is it still prone to hallucinations? Is the information that is being fetched by the retriever the most relevant to the query? To answer these questions, we have to put in place an evaluation framework. This framework helps in evaluating the quality of the system before it is released and then for continuous monitoring and improvement.

Building on the advancements of LLMs, RAG represents a recent innovation in NLP. Metrics such as relevance scores, recall, and precision are commonly used to evaluate the effectiveness of RAG systems. One framework that intuitively guides a comprehensive evaluation is the triad of RAG metrics proposed by TruEra (https://mng.bz/Mw22). It looks at the RAG evaluation through three dimensions, as shown in figure 2.7.

The workflow involves checks in between each step—prompt, context, and answer. Let's take a closer look:

- *Between the retrieved information (context) and the user query (prompt)*—Is the information being searched and retrieved by the retriever the most relevant to the question the user has asked? The consequence of irrelevant information being retrieved is that no matter how good the LLM is, if the information being augmented is not good, the response will be suboptimal.

- *Between the final response (answer) and the retrieved information (context)*—Does the LLM consider all the retrieved information while generating responses? Even

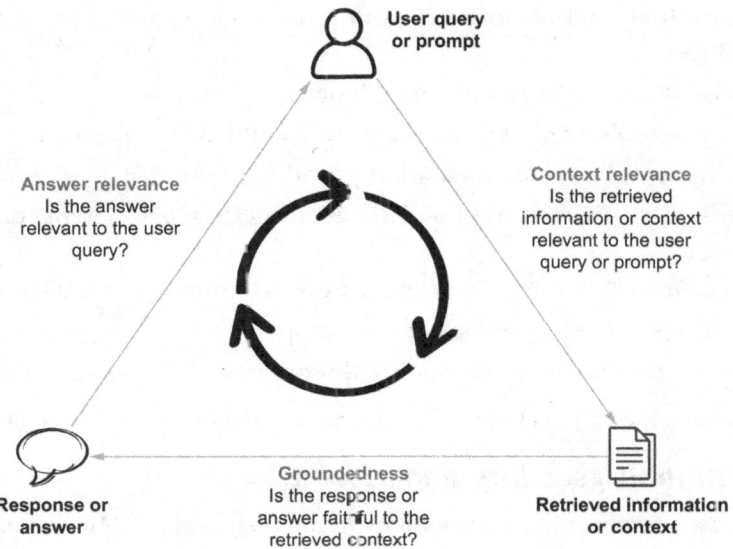

Figure 2.7   The triad of RAG evaluation proposed by TruEra. The three pivotal dimensions of RAG evaluation are the query, context, and response.

though RAG is aimed at reducing hallucinations, the system might still ignore the retrieved information. There are several reasons for it, which will be discussed in subsequent chapters.

- *Between the final response (answer) and the user query (prompt)*—Is the final response in line with the question the user had originally asked? To assess the overall effectiveness of the system, the relevance of the final response to the original question is necessary.

There are several metrics that help assess each of these three dimensions. For some of the metrics, a ground truth dataset is warranted. Ground truth datasets provide a benchmark for evaluating the accuracy and effectiveness of RAG systems by comparing generated responses to manually curated references. We will take a deeper look at these metrics and the ground truth dataset in chapter 5.

Continuous evaluation of metrics during live operation can identify the types of queries the system struggles to answer accurately. Qualitative feedback can also be collected from the user on the generated responses.

2.6   The RAGOps Stack

RAG, and LLM-based apps in general, are being powered by an evolving operations stack. Various providers offer infrastructure components such as data storage platforms, model hosting services, and application orchestration frameworks. The infrastructure can be understood in several layers:

1   *Data layer*—Tools and platforms used to process and store data in the form of embeddings

2   *Model layer*—Providers of proprietary or open source LLMs

3   *Prompt layer*—Tools offering maintenance and evaluation of prompts

4   *Evaluation layer*—Tools and frameworks providing evaluation metrics for RAG

5   *App orchestration*—Frameworks that facilitate invocation of different components of the system

6   *Deployment layer*—Cloud providers and platforms for deploying RAG apps

7   *Application layer*—Hosting services for RAG apps

8   *Monitoring layer*—Platforms offering continuous monitoring of RAG apps

Chapter 7 explores the various layers of infrastructure that support RAG systems.

2.7   *Caching, guardrails, security, and other layers*

Finally, there are certain other components frequently used in RAG systems. These components address the problems of system latency, regulatory and ethical compliances among other aspects.

- *Caching*—Caching is the process in which certain data is stored in cache memory for faster retrieval. LLM caching is slightly different from regular caching. The LLM responses to queries are stored in a semantic cache. Next time a similar query is asked, the response from the cache is retrieved instead of sending the query through the complete RAG pipeline. This approach improves the performance of the system by reducing the time it takes to respond, the cost of LLM inferencing, and the load on the LLM service.

- *Guardrails*—For several use cases, in practice, there will be a set of boundaries within which the output needs to be generated. Guardrails are a predefined set of rules added in the system to comply with policies, regulations, and ethical guidelines.

- *Security*—LLMs and LLM-based applications have witnessed new threats, such as prompt injections, data poisoning, sensitive information disclosure, and others. With evolving threats, the security infrastructure also needs to evolve to address concerns around security and data privacy of RAG systems.

RAGOps has also been evolving fast. Logging and tracing, model versioning, and feedback layers are some of the RAGOps stack components.

This chapter provided an overview of the key components of RAG systems, including the indexing and generation pipelines, evaluation and monitoring, and service infrastructure. By understanding these components, you are now equipped to delve deeper into each of these components and the intricacies of RAG systems in subsequent chapters. In the next chapter, we will start building the indexing pipeline to create a knowledge base of our RAG system.

Summary

- A RAG-enabled system consists of two main pipelines: the indexing and the generation pipeline.

- The indexing pipeline is responsible for creating and maintaining the knowledge base, which involves data loading, text splitting, data conversion (embeddings), and data storage in a vector database.

- The generation pipeline manages real-time interactions by retrieving information, augmenting queries, and generating responses using an LLM.

- Evaluation and monitoring are crucial components for the assessment of system performance, covering the relevance between the retrieved information and query, the final response and retrieved information, and the final response and the original query.

- The service infrastructure for RAG systems includes layers for data, models, prompts, evaluation, app orchestration, deployment, application hosting, and monitoring.

- Additional components such as caching, guardrails, and security measures are often employed to improve performance, ensure compliance, and address potential threats.

Part 2

Creating RAG systems

Now that you are familiar with the fundamental idea of RAG and the components of a RAG system, the second part of the book will guide you through building a basic RAG system with the core pipelines and their evaluation. This part of the book not only offers theoretical details, but also simple code snippets that will provide you with hands-on experience in building a RAG pipeline.

In chapter 3, you'll learn the details of the indexing pipeline and its four components: loading, chunking, embeddings, and vector storage. Each of these components has a variety of techniques to choose from. This chapter also discusses the suitability of these options for different use cases. Step by step, you'll build an indexing pipeline and create the knowledge base for your RAG system.

Chapter 4 talks about retrievers, prompting techniques, and using LLMs for output generation. These elements form the three components of the generation pipeline: retrieval, augmentation, and generation. In this chapter, you will build the generation pipeline that interacts with the knowledge base, created using the indexing pipeline in chapter 3.

Chapter 5 discusses different aspects of evaluating RAG systems, which is a crucial step in AI systems. You will learn about the different metrics used in RAG evaluation for measuring accuracy, relevance, and faithfulness. You will also be introduced to the RAGAs framework to evaluate the pipelines built in chapters 3 and 4, and learn about industry benchmarks popular in comparing different RAG techniques. The chapter closes with a discussion on the limitations and best practices of RAG evaluation.

This part of the book will equip you with all the necessary skills and tools to develop a basic RAG pipeline. By the end of this part, you will be in a good position to further explore the techniques used to optimize any RAG pipeline and the components that are key in building a production-grade system around it.

3
Indexing pipeline: Creating a knowledge base for RAG

This chapter covers

- Data loading
- Text splitting or chunking
- Converting text to embeddings
- Storing embeddings in vector databases
- Examples in Python using LangChain

In chapter 2, we discussed the main components of retrieval-augmented generation (RAG) systems. You may recall that the indexing pipeline creates the knowledge base or the non-parametric memory of RAG applications. An indexing pipeline needs to be set up before the real-time user interaction with the large language model (LLM) can begin.

This chapter elaborates on the four components of the indexing pipeline. We begin by discussing data loading, which involves connecting to the source, extracting files, and parsing text. At this stage, we introduce a framework called LangChain, which has become increasingly popular in the LLM app developer community. Next, we elaborate on the need for data splitting or chunking and discuss chunking strategies.

Embeddings is an important design pattern in the world of AI and ML. We explore embeddings in detail and how they are relevant in the RAG context. Finally, we look at a new storage technique called vector storage and the databases that facilitate it.

By the end of this chapter, you should have a solid understanding of how a knowledge base, or the non-parametric memory of a RAG application, is created. We also embellish this chapter with snippets of Python code, so those of you who are so inclined can try a hands-on development of the indexing pipeline.

By the end of this chapter, you should

- Know how to extract data from sources.
- Get a deeper understanding of text-chunking strategies.
- Learn what embeddings are and how they are used.
- Gain knowledge of vector storage and vector databases.
- Have an end-to-end knowledge of setting up the indexing pipeline.

3.1 Data loading

This section focuses on the first stage of the indexing pipeline. You will read about data loaders, metadata information, and data transformers.

The first step toward building a knowledge base (or non-parametric memory) of a RAG system is to source data from its original location. This data may be in the form of Word documents, PDF files, CSV, HTML, and similar. Furthermore, the data may be stored in file, block, or object stores, in data lakes, data warehouses, or even in third-party sources that can be accessed via the open internet. This process of sourcing data from its original location is called *data loading*. Loading documents from a list of sources may turn out to be a complicated process. Therefore, it is advisable to document all the sources and the file formats in advance.

Before going too deep, let's begin with a simple example. If you recall, in chapter 1, we used Wikipedia as a source of information about the 2023 Cricket World Cup. At that time, we copied the opening paragraph of the article and pasted it in the ChatGPT prompt window. Instead of doing it manually, we will now *connect* to Wikipedia and *extract* the data programmatically, using a very popular framework called LangChain. The code in this chapter and the book can be run on Python notebooks and is available in the GitHub repository of this book (https://mng.bz/a9DJ).

NOTE LangChain is an open source framework developed by Harrison Chase and launched in October 2022. It was written in Python and JavaScript and designed for building applications using LLMs. Apart from being suitable for RAG, LangChain is also suitable for building application use cases such as chatbots, document summarizers, synthetic data generation, and more. Over time, LangChain has built integrations with LLM providers such as OpenAI, Anthropic, and Hugging Face; a variety of vector store providers; cloud storage systems such as AWS, Google, Azure, and SQL and NoSQL databases; and APIs for news, weather, and similar. Although LangChain has received some criticism, it is still a good starting point for developers.

Installing LangChain

To install LangChain (we'll use the version 0.3.19 in this chapter) using `pip`, run

```
%pip install langchain==0.3.19
```

The `langchain-community` package contains third-party integrations. It is automatically installed by LangChain, but in case it does not work, you can also install it separately using `pip`:

```
%pip install langchain-community
```

Now that you have installed LangChain, we will use it to connect to Wikipedia and extract data from the page about the 2023 Cricket World Cup. For this task, we will use the `AsyncHtmlLoader` function from the `document_loaders` library in the `langchain-community` package. To run `AsyncHtmlLoader`, we will have to install another Python package called bs4:

```
#Installing bs4 package
%pip install bs4==0.0.2 --quiet

#Importing the AsyncHtmlLoader
from langchain_community.document_loaders import AsyncHtmlLoader

#This is the URL of the Wikipedia page on the 2023 Cricket World Cup
url="https://en.wikipedia.org/wiki/2023_Cricket_World_Cup"

#Invoking the AsyncHtmlLoader
loader = AsyncHtmlLoader (url)

#Loading the extracted information
html_data = loader.load()
```

The `data` variable in the code now stores the information from the Wikipedia page.

```
print(data)
```

Here is the output (A large section of the text is replaced with periods to save space.)

```
>>[Document(page_content='<!DOCTYPE html>\n<html class="client-nojs vector-
feature-language-in-header-enabled...........................................................................................of
In the knockout stage, India and Australia beat New Zealand and South Africa
respectively to advance to the final, played on 19 November at <a href="/
wiki/Narendra_Modi_Stadium" title="Narendra Modi Stadium">Narendra Modi
Stadium</a>. Australia won by 6 wickets, winning their sixth Cricket World
```

```
Cup title................................................ "datePublished":"2013-06-29T19:20:08Z","dateMo
dified":"2024-05-01T05:16:34Z","image":"https:\\/\\/upload.wikimedia.org\\/
wikipedia\\/en\\/e\\/eb\\/2023_CWC_Logo.svg","headline":"13th edition of the
premier international cricket competition"}</script>\n</body>\n</html>',
metadata={'source': 'https://en.wikipedia.org/wiki/2023_Cricket_World_Cup',
'title': '2023 Cricket World Cup - Wikipedia', 'language': 'en'})]
```

The variable `data` is a list of documents that includes two elements: `page_content` and `metadata`. `page_content` contains the text sourced from the URL. You will notice that the text along with the relevant information also has newline characters (\n) and other HTML tags; however, `metadata` contains another important data aspect.

Metadata is information about the data (e.g., type, origin, and purpose). This can include a data summary; the way the data was created; who created it and why; when it was created; and the size, quality, and condition of the data. Metadata information comes in extremely handy in the retrieval stage. Also, it can be used to resolve conflicting information that can arise due to chronology or origin. In the previous example, while extracting the data from the URL, Wikipedia has already provided the source, title, and language in the metadata information. For many data sources, you will have to add metadata.

Often, a *cleaning* of the source data is required. The data in our example has a lot of new line characters and HTML tags, which requires a certain level of cleanup. We will attempt to clean up the webpage data that we extracted using the `Html2Text-Transformer` function from the `document_transformers` library in the `langchain-community` package. For `Html2TextTransformer`, we will also have to install another package called `html2text`.

```
#Install html2text
%pip install html2text==2024.2.26 –quiet

#Import Html2TextTransformer
from langchain_community.document_transformers import Html2TextTransformer

#Assign the Html2TextTransformer function
html2text = Html2TextTransformer()

#Call transform_documents
html_data_transformed = html2text.transform_documents(data)

print(html_data_transformed[0].page_content)
```

The output of the `page_content` is now free of any HTML tags and contains only the text from the webpage:

```
>>Jump to content  Main menu  Main menu  move to sidebar hide Navigation     *
Main page    * Contents   * Current events   * Random article   * About
Wikipedia   * Contact us   * Donate  Contribute............In the knockout stage,
India and Australia beat New Zealand and South Africa respectively to advance
to the final, played on 19 November at Narendra Modi Stadium. Australia won
by 6 wickets, winning their sixth Cricket World Cup title...... * This page
was last edited on 1 May 2024, at 05:16 (UTC).   * Text is available under
```

The text is more coherent now since we have removed the HTML part of the data. There can be further cleanup, such as removing special characters and other unnecessary information. Data cleaning also removes duplication. Yet another step to include in the data-loading stage can be masking of sensitive information such as PII (Personally Identifiable Information) or company secrets. In some cases, a fact check may also be required.

The source for our data was Wikipedia (more precisely, a web address pointing to a Wikipedia page), and the format was HTML. The source can also be other storage locations such as AWS S3, SQL/NoSQL databases, Google Drive, GitHub, even WhatsApp, YouTube, and other social media sites. Likewise, the data formats can be .doc, .pdf, .csv, .ppt, .eml, and the like. Most of the time, you will be able to use frameworks such as LangChain that have integrations for the sources and the formats already built in. Sometimes, you may have to build custom connectors and loaders.

Although data loading may seem simple (after all, it's just connecting to a source and extracting data), the nuances of adding metadata, document transformation, masking, and similar add complexity to this step. Advanced planning of the sources, a review of the formats, and curation of metadata information are advised for best results.

We have now taken the first step toward building our RAG system. The data-loading process can be further broken down into four sub-steps, as shown in figure 3.1:

1. Connect to the source of data.
2. Extract text from the file.
3. Review and update metadata information.
4. Clean or transform the data.

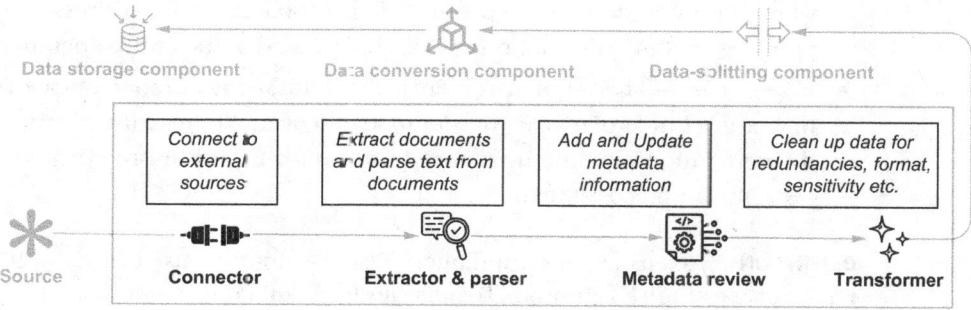

Figure 3.1 Four sub-steps of the data-loading component of the indexing pipeline

We have now obtained data from the source and cleaned it to an extent. This Wikipedia page that we have loaded has more than 8,000 words, alone. Imagine the number of words if we had multiple documents. For efficient management of information, we employ something called data splitting, which will be discussed in the next section.

3.2 Data splitting (chunking)

Breaking down long pieces of text to manageable segments is called *data splitting* or *chunking*. This section discusses why chunking is necessary and the different chunking strategies. We also use functions from LangChain to illustrate a few examples.

3.2.1 Advantages of chunking

In the previous section, we loaded the data from a URL (a Wikipedia page) and extracted the text. It was a long piece of text of approximately 8,000 words. When it comes to overcoming the major limitations of using long pieces of text in LLM applications, chunking offers the following three advantages:

- *Context window of LLMs*—Due to the inherent nature of the technology, the number of tokens (loosely, words) LLMs can work with at a time is limited. This includes both the number of tokens in the prompt (or the input) and in the completion (or the output). The limit on the total number of tokens that an LLM can process in one go is called "the context window size." If we pass an input that is longer than the context window size, the LLM chooses to ignore all text beyond the size. It is thus very important to be careful with the amount of text being passed to the LLM. In our example, a text of 50,000 words will not work well with LLMs that have a smaller context window. The way to address this problem is to break the text down into smaller chunks.

- *Lost-in-the-middle problem*—Even in those LLMs that have a long context window (e.g., Claude 3 by Anthropic has a context window of up to 200,000 tokens), a problem with accurately reading the information has been observed. It has been noticed that accuracy declines dramatically if the relevant information is somewhere in the middle of the prompt. This problem can be addressed by passing only the relevant information to the LLM instead of the entire document.

- *Ease of search*—This is not a problem with the LLM per se, but it has been observed that large chunks of text are harder to search over. When we use a retriever (recall the generation pipeline introduced in chapter 2), it is more efficient to search over smaller pieces of text.

DEFINITION   Tokens are the fundamental semantic units used in natural language processing (NLP) tasks. Tokens can be assumed to be words, but sometimes, a single word can be made up of more than one token. OpenAI suggests one token to be made of four characters or 0.75 words. Tokens are important as most proprietary LLMs are priced based on token usage.

3.2.2 Chunking process

The chunking process can be divided into three steps, as illustrated in figure 3.2:

1 Divide the longer text into compact, meaningful units (e.g., sentences or paragraphs).

2 Merge the smaller units into larger chunks until a specific size is achieved. After that, this chunk is treated as an independent segment of text.

3 When creating a new chunk, include a part of the previous chunk at the start of the new chunk. This overlap is necessary to maintain contextual continuity.

This process is also known as 'small to big" chunking.

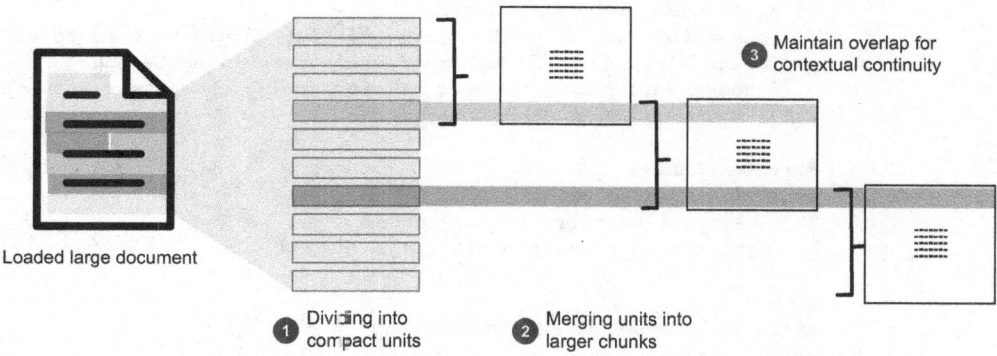

Small to Big Chunking

Figure 3.2 Data-chunking process

3.2.3 Chunking methods

While splitting documents into chunks might sound like a simple concept, multiple methods can be employed to execute chunking. The following two aspects vary across the chunking methodologies:

- The manner of text splitting
- Measuring of the chunk size

FIXED-SIZE CHUNKING

A very common approach is to predetermine the size of the chunk and the amount of overlap between the chunks. The following two methods fall under the *fixed-size chunking* category:

- *Split by character*—Here, we specify a certain character, such as a newline character \n or a special character *, to determine how the text should be split. The text is split into a unit whenever this character is encountered. The chunk size is measured in the number of characters. We must choose the chunk size or the number of characters we need in each chunk. We can also choose the number of characters we need to overlap between two chunks. We will look at an example and demonstrate this method using CharacterTextSplitter from langchain .text_splitters. For this, we will take the same document that we loaded and transformed in the previous section from Wikipedia and store it in the variable html_data_transformed.

```
#import libraries
from langchain.text_splitters import CharacterTextSplitter
#Set the CharacterTextSplitter parameters
text_splitter = CharacterTextSplitter(
    separator="\n",      #The character that should be used to split
    chunk_size=1000,     #Number of characters in each chunk
    chunk_overlap=200,   #Number of overlapping characters between chunks
)


#Create Chunks
chunks=
    text_splitter.create_documents(
    [html_data_transformed[0].page_content]
    )


#Show the number of chunks created
print(f"The number of chunks created : {len(chunks)}")

>>The number of chunks created: 67
```

This method created 64 chunks. But what about the overlap? Let's check two chunks at random, say, chunks 4 and 5. We will compare the last 200 characters of chunk 4 with the first 200 characters of chunk 5:

```
chunks[4].page_content[-200:]

>> 'on was to be played from 9 February to 26 March\n2023.[3][4] In July
2020 it was announced that due to the disruption of the\nqualification
schedule by the COVID-19 pandemic, the start of the tournament'

chunks[5].page_content[:200]

>> '2023.[3][4] In July 2020 it was announced that due to the disruption
of the\nqualification schedule by the COVID-19 pandemic, the start of
the tournament\nwould be delayed to October.[5][6] The ICC rele'
```

Comparing the two outputs, we can observe that there is an overlap between the two consecutive chunks.

Splitting by character is a simple and effective way to create chunks. It is the first chunking method that anyone should try. However, sometimes, it may not be feasible to create chunks within the specified length. This is because the sequential occurrence of the character on which the text needs to be split is far apart. To address this problem, a recursive approach is employed.

- *Recursively split by character*—This method is quite like the split by character but instead of specifying a single character for splitting, we specify a list of characters. The approach initially tries creating chunks based on the first character. In case it is not able to create a chunk of the specified size using the first character, it then uses the next character to further break down chunks to the required size. This method ensures that chunks are largely created within the specified size. This method is recommended for generic texts. You can use `RecursiveCharacter-TextSplitter` from LangChain to use this method. The only difference in `RecursiveCharacterTextSplitter` is that instead of passing a single character in the separator parameter `separator="\n"`, we will need to pass a list `separators=["\n\n","\n", ".", " "]`.

Another perspective to consider with fixed-sized chunking is the use of tokens. As shown at the beginning of this section, tokens are the fundamental units of NLP. They can be understood loosely as a proxy for words. All LLMs process text in the form of tokens. So, it would also make sense to use tokens to determine the size of the chunks. This method is called the *split by token method*. Here, the splitting still happens based on a character, but the size of the chunk and the overlap are determined by the number of tokens instead of the number of characters.

NOTE Tokenizers are used to create tokens from a piece of text. Tokens are slightly different from words. A phrase such as "I'd like that!" has three words; however, in NLP, this text may be parsed as five tokens, that is, "I", "'d", "like", "that", "!". Different LLMs use different methods for creating tokens. OpenAI uses a tokenizer called tiktoken for GPT3.5 and GPT4 models; Llama2 by Meta uses LLamaTokenizer, available in the transformers library by Hugging Face. You can also explore other tokenizers on Hugging Face. NLTK and spaCy are some other popular libraries that can be used as tokenizers.

To use the split by token method, you can use specific methods within the `Recursive-CharacterTextSplitter` and `CharacterTextSplitter` classes, such as `Recursive-CharacterTextSplitter.from_tiktoken_encoder(encoding="cl100k_base",chunk_size=100, chunk_overlap=10)` for creating chunks of 100 tokens with an overlap of 10 tokens using OpenAI's tiktoken tokenizer or `CharacterTextSplitter.from_huggingface_tokenizer(tokenizer, chunk_size=100, chunk_overlap=10)` for creating the same sized chunk using another tokenizer from Hugging Face.

The limitation of fixed-size chunking is that it doesn't consider the semantic integrity of the text. In other words, the meaning of the text is ignored. It works best in scenarios where data is inherently uniform, such as genetic sequences and service manuals, or uniformly structured reports such as survey responses.

SPECIALIZED CHUNKING

Chunking aims to keep meaningful data together. If we are dealing with data in the form of HTML, Markdown, JSON, or even computer code, it makes more sense to split the data based on the structure rather than a fixed size. Another approach to chunking is to consider the format of the extracted and loaded data. A markdown file, for example, is organized by headers, a code written in a programming language such as Python or Java is organized by classes and functions, and likewise, HTML is organized in headers and sections. For such formats, a specialized chunking approach can be employed. LangChain offers classes such as `MarkdownHeaderTextSplitter`, `HTMLHeaderTextSplitter`, and `RecursiveJsonSplitter`, among others, for these formats.

Here is a simple example of a code that splits an HTML document using `HTML-SectionSplitter`. We are using the same Wikipedia article to source the HTML page. We first split the input data based on the sections. Sections in HTML are tagged as `<h1>`, `<h2>`, `<table>`, and so on. It can be assumed that a well-structured HTML document will have similar information. This helps us in creating chunks that have similar information. To use the `HTMLSectionSplitter` library, we must install another Python package called `lxml`:

```
#Installing lxml
%pip install lxml==5.3.1 --quiet

# Import the HTMLHeaderTextSplitter library
from langchain_text_splitters import HTMLSectionSplitter

# Set URL as the Wikipedia page link
url="https://en.wikipedia.org/wiki/2023_Cricket_World_Cup"

loader = AsyncHtmlLoader (url)

html_data = loader.load()

# Specify the header tags on which splits should be made
sections_to_split_on=[
    ("h1", "Header 1"),
    ("h2", "Header 2"),
    ("table ", "Table"),
    ("p", "Paragraph")
]

# Create the HTMLHeaderTextSplitter function
splitter = HTMLSectionSplitter(sections_to_split_on)

# Create splits in text obtained from the URL
Split_content = splitter.split_text(html_data[0].page_content)
```

The advantage of specialized chunking is that chunk sizes are no longer limited by a fixed width. This feature helps in preserving the inherent structure of the data. Because the size of the chunks changes depending on the structure, this method is also sometimes called *adaptive chunking*. Specialized chunking works well in structured scenarios such as customer reviews or patient records where data can be of different lengths but should ideally be in the same chunk.

In the previous example, let's see how many chunks have been created:

```
len(split_content)
```

```
>> 231
```

This method has given us 231 chunks from the URL. Chunking methods do not have to be exclusive. We can further chunk these 231 chunks using a fixed-size chunking method such as RecursiveCharacterTextSplitter.

```
from langchain.text_splitter import RecursiveCharacterTextSplitter

text_splitter = RecursiveCharacterTextSplitter(
separators=["\n\n","\n","."]
chunk_size=1000, chunk_overlap=100,
)

final_chunks = text_splitter.split_documents(split_content)
```

Let's look at how many chunks were created by this combination of techniques:

```
len(chunks)
```

```
>> 285
```

A total of 285 chunks were created by splitting the HTML data from the URL first, using a specialized chunking method followed by a fixed size method. This gave us more chunks than using the fixed size method alone that we saw in the previous section ("split by character" gave us 67 chunks).

You may be wondering about the advantages of having more chunks and the optimal number. Unfortunately, there's no straightforward answer to that. Having many chunks (consequently smaller-sized chunks) means that the information in the chunks is precise. This is advantageous when it comes to providing the LLM with accurate information. In contrast, by chunking into small sizes, you may lose the overall themes, ideas, and coherence of the larger document. The task here is to strike a balance. We will discuss more chunking strategies after we take a cursory look at a novel method that considers the meaning of the text to perform chunking and aims to create chunks that are super-contextual.

SEMANTIC CHUNKING

This idea, proposed by Greg Kamradt, questions two aspects of the previous chunking methods.

- Why should we have a predefined fixed size of chunks?
- Why don't chunking methods take into consideration the actual meaning of content?

To address these problems, a method that looks at semantic similarity (or similarity in the meaning) between sentences is called semantic chunking. It first creates groups of three sentences and then merges groups that are similar in meaning. To find out the similarity in meaning, this method uses embeddings. (We will discuss embeddings in the next section.) This is still an experimental chunking technique. In LangChain, you can use the class `SemanticChunker` from the `langchain_experimental.text_splitter` library. See figure 3.3 for examples of different chunking methods.

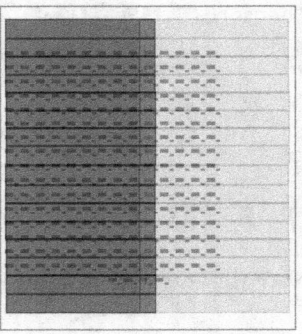 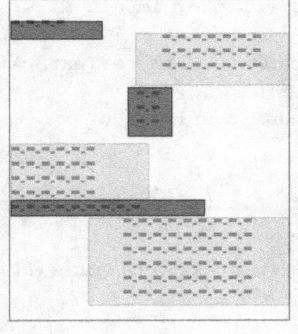 

| **Fixed-size chunking** | **Specialized chunking** | **Semantic chunking** |
| Te length of chunks is uniform and predetermined with some overlap. | Chunking is carried out depending on the structure of the input. | Chunking preserves the semantic integrity or the meaning of the input. |

Figure 3.3   Chunking methods

As the LLM and the generative AI space are evolving fast, chunking methods are also becoming more sophisticated. Simple chunking methods predetermine the size of the chunks and a split by characters. A slightly more nuanced technique is to split the data by tokens. Specialized methods are more suitable for different data formats. Experimental techniques such as semantic chunking and agentic chunking are spearheading the advancements in the chunking space. Now, let's consider the important question of how to select a chunking method.

3.2.4   *Choosing a chunking strategy*

We have seen that there are many chunking methods available. Which chunking method to use (i.e., whether to use a single method or multiple methods) is a question that comes up during the creation of the indexing pipeline. There are no guidelines or rules to answer this question. However, certain features of the application that you're developing can guide you toward an effective strategy.

NATURE OF THE CONTENT

The type of data that you're dealing with can be a guide for the chunking strategy. If your application uses data in a specific format such as code or HTML, a specialized chunking method is recommended. Not only that, whether you're working with long documents such as whitepapers and reports or short-form content such as social media posts, tweets, and so on, can also guide the chunk size and overlap limits. If you're using a diverse set of information sources, then you might have to use different methods for different sources.

EXPECTED LENGTH AND COMPLEXITY OF USER QUERY

The nature of the query that your RAG system is likely to receive also determines the chunking strategy. If your system expects a short and straightforward query, then the size of your chunks should be different when compared to a long and complex query. Matching long queries to short chunks may prove inefficient in certain cases. Similarly, short queries matching large chunks may yield partially irrelevant results.

APPLICATION AND USE CASE REQUIREMENTS

The nature of the use case you're addressing may also determine the optimal chunking strategy. For a direct question-answering system, shorter chunks are likely used for precise results, while for summarization tasks, longer chunks may make more sense. If the results of your system need to serve as an input to another downstream application, that may also influence the choice of the chunking strategy.

EMBEDDINGS MODEL

We are going to discuss embeddings in the next section. For now, you can make a note that certain embeddings models perform better with chunks of specific sizes.

We have discussed chunking at length in this section. From understanding the need and advantages of chunking to different chunking methods and the choice of chunking strategies, you are now equipped to load data from different sources and split them into optimal sizes. Remember, chunking is not an overcomplicated task, and most chunking methods will work. You will, however, have to evaluate and improve your chunking strategy depending on the results you observe.

Now that data has been split into manageable sizes, we need to store it so that it can be fetched later to be used in the generation pipeline. We need to ensure that these chunks can be effectively searched over to match the user query. Turns out that one data pattern is the most efficient for such tasks. This pattern is called "embeddings." Let's explore embeddings and their use in RAG systems in the next section.

3.3   *Data conversion (embeddings)*

Computers, at their very core, do mathematical calculations. Mathematical calculations are done on numbers. Therefore, for a computer to process any kind of nonnumeric data such as text or image, it must be first converted into a numerical form.

3.3.1   *What are embeddings?*

Embeddings is a design pattern that is extremely helpful in the fields of data science, machine learning, and AI. Embeddings are vector representations of data. As a general definition, embeddings are data that has been transformed into *n*-dimensional matrixes. The word *embedding* is a vector representation of words. I explain embeddings by using three words as an example: *dog, bark*, and *fly*.

> **NOTE**   In physics and mathematics, the vector is an object that has a magnitude and a direction, like an arrow in space. The length of the arrow is the magnitude of the quantity and the direction that the arrow points to is the direction of the quantity. Examples of such quantities in physics are velocity, force, acceleration, and so forth. In computer science and machine learning, the idea of a vector is an abstract representation of data, and the representation is an array or list of numbers. These numbers represent the data features or attributes. In NLP, a vector can represent a document, a sentence, or even a word. The length of the array or list is the number of dimensions in the vector. A 2D vector will have two numbers, a 3D vector will have three numbers, and an *n*-dimensional vector will have *n* numbers.

Let's understand embeddings by assigning a number to the three words: Dog = 1, Bark = 2 and Fly = 6, as shown in figure 3.4. We chose these numbers because the word *dog* is closer to the word *bark* and farther from the word *fly*.

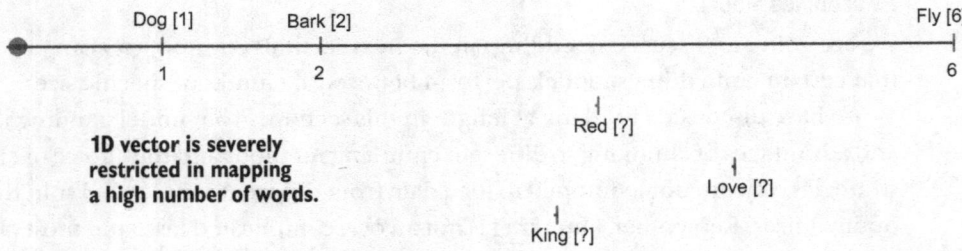

Figure 3.4   Words in a unidimensional vector

Unidimensional vectors are not great representations because we can't plot unrelated words accurately. In our example, we can plot that the words *fly* and *bark*, which are verbs, are far from each other, and bark is closer to a dog because dogs can bark. But how do we plot words such as *love* or *red*? To accurately represent all the words, we need to increase the number of dimensions. See figure 3.5.

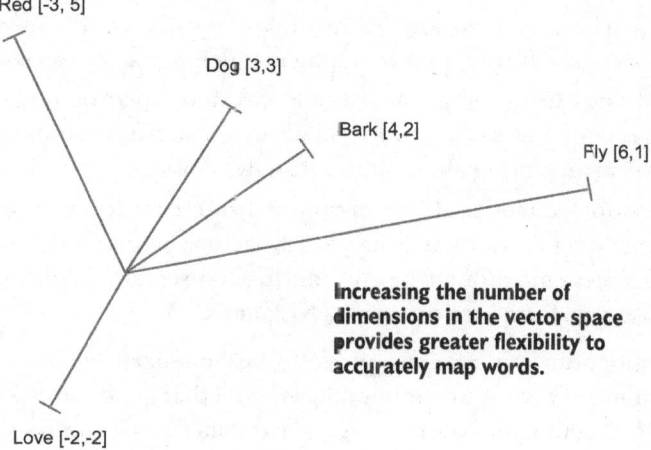

Figure 3.5   Words in a 2D vector space

The goal of an embedding model is to convert words (or sentences/paragraphs) into *n*-dimensional vectors so that the words (or sentences/paragraphs) that are like each other in meaning lie close to each other in the vector space. See figure 3.6.

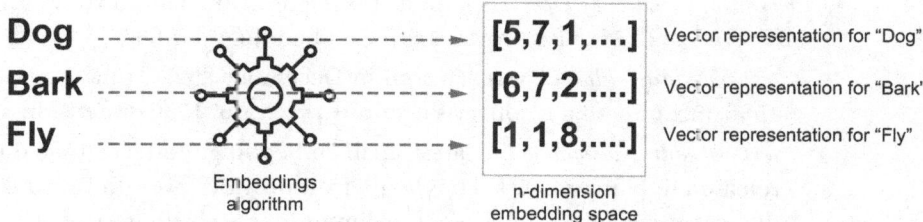

The goal of an embedding model is to convert words (or sentences/paragraphs) into n-dimensional vectors.

Figure 3.6   The process of embedding transforms data (such as text) into vectors and compresses the input information, which results in an embedding space specific to the training data.

An embeddings model can be trained on a corpus of preprocessed text data using an embedding algorithm such as Word2Vec, GloVe, FastText, or BERT:

- *Word2Vec*—Word2Vec is a shallow-neural-network-based model for learning word embeddings, developed by researchers at Google. It is one of the earliest embedding techniques.

- *GloVe*—Global Vectors for Word Representations is an unsupervised learning technique developed by researchers at Stanford University.
- *FastText*—FastText is an extension of Word2Vec developed by Facebook AI Research. It is particularly useful for handling misspellings and rare words.
- *ELMo*—Embeddings from Language Models was developed by researchers at Allen Institute for AI. ELMo embeddings have been shown to improve performance on question answering and sentiment analysis tasks.
- *BERT*—Bidirectional Encoder Representations from Transformers, developed by researchers at Google, is a transformers-architecture-based model. It provides contextualized word embeddings by considering bidirectional context, achieving state-of-the-art performance on various NLP tasks.

Training a custom embeddings model can prove to be beneficial in some use cases where the scope is limited. Training an embeddings model that generalizes well can be a laborious exercise. Collection and preprocessing text data can be cumbersome. The training process can turn out to be computationally expensive too.

3.3.2 *Common pre-trained embeddings models*

The good news for anyone building RAG systems is that embeddings once created can also generalize across tasks and domains. There are a variety of proprietary and open source pre-trained embeddings models available to use. This is also one of the reasons why the usage of embeddings has exploded in popularity across machine learning applications.

- *Embeddings models by OpenAI*—OpenAI, the company behind ChatGPT and the GPT series of LLMs, also provides three embeddings models:
  - *text-embedding-ada-002* was released in December 2022. It has a dimension of 1536, meaning that it converts text into a vector of 1536 dimensions.
  - *text-embedding-3-small* is the latest small embedding model of 1536 dimensions released in January 2024. The flexibility it provides over the ada-002 model is that users can adjust the size of the dimensions according to their needs.
  - *text-embedding-3-large* is a large embedding model of 3072 dimensions, released together with the text-embedding-3-small model. It is the best performing model released by OpenAI yet.

  OpenAI models are closed source and can be accessed using the OpenAI API. They are priced based on the number of input tokens for which embeddings are desired.
- *Gemini Embeddings Model by Google*—*text-embedding-004* (last updated in April 2024) is the model offered by Google Gemini. It offers elastic embeddings size up to 768 dimensions and can be accessed via the Gemini API.
- *Voyage AI*—These embeddings models are recommended by Anthropic, the provider of the Claude series of LLMs. Voyage offers several embedding models such as

- *voyage-large-2-instruct* is a 1024-dimensional embeddings model that has become a leader in embeddings models.
- *voyage-law-2* is a 1024-dimension model optimized for legal documents.
- *voyage-code-2* is a 1536-dimension model optimized for code retrieval.
- *voyage-large-2* is a 1536-dimension general-purpose model optimized for retrieval.

Voyage AI offers several free tokens before charging for using the embeddings models.

- *Mistral AI embeddings*—Mistral is the company behind LLMs such as Mistral and Mixtral. They offer a 1024-dimensional embeddings model known as *mistral-embed*. This is an open source embeddings model.

- *Cohere embeddings*—Cohere, the developers of Command, Command R, and Command R + LLMs also offer a variety of embeddings models, which can be accessed via the Cohere API. Some of these are
  - *embed-english-v3.0* is a 1024-dimension model that works on embeddings for English only.
  - *embed-english-light-v3.0* is a lighter version of the embed-english model, which has 384 dimensions.
  - *embed-multilingual-v3.0* offers multilingual support for over 100 languages.

These five models are in no way recommendations but just a list of the popular embeddings models. Apart from these providers, almost all LLM developers such Meta, TII, and LMSYS also offer pre-trained embeddings models. One place to check out all the popular embeddings models is the MTEB (Massive Text Embedding Benchmark) Leaderboard on Hugging Face (https://huggingface.co/spaces/mteb/leaderboard). The MTEB benchmark compares the embeddings models on tasks such as classification, retrieval, clustering, and more. You now know what embeddings are, but why are they useful? Let's discuss that next with some examples of use cases.

3.3.3 Embeddings use cases

The reason why embeddings are so popular is because they help in establishing semantic relationships between words, phrases, and documents. In the simplest methods of searching or text matching, we use keywords, and if the keywords match, we can show the matching documents as results of the search. However, this approach fails to consider the semantic relationships or the meanings of the words while searching. This challenge is overcome by using embeddings.

HOW IS SIMILARITY CALCULATED

We discussed that embeddings are vector representations of words or sentences. Similar pieces of text lie close to each other. Closeness to each other is calculated by the distance between the points in the vector space. One of the most common measures of similarity is *cosine similarity*. Cosine similarity is calculated as the cosine value of the angle between the two vectors. Recall from trigonometry that the cosine of parallel lines (i.e., angle = 0°) is 1, and the cosine of a right angle (i.e., 90°) is 0. The cosine of the opposite lines (i.e., angle = 180°) is –1. Therefore, the cosine similarity lies between –1 and 1, where unrelated terms have a value close to 0, and related terms have a value close to 1. Terms that are opposite in meaning have a value of –1. See figure 3.7.

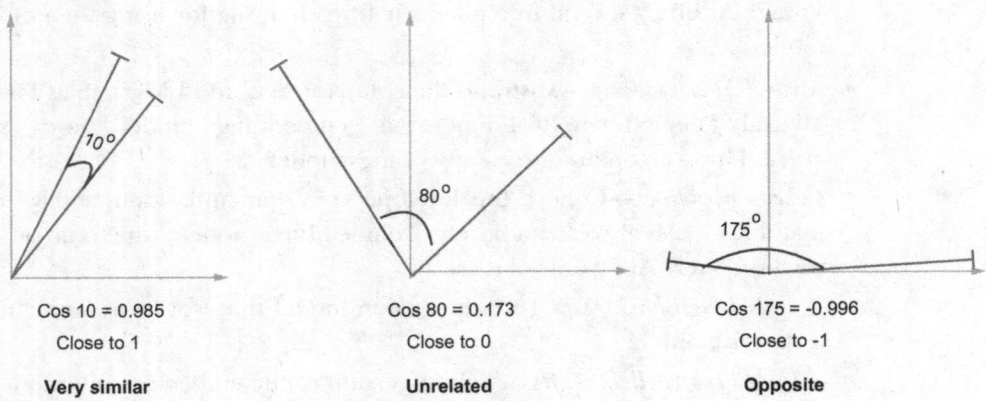

Cos 10 = 0.985	Cos 80 = 0.173	Cos 175 = -0.996
Close to 1	Close to 0	Close to -1
Very similar	**Unrelated**	**Opposite**

Figure 3.7   Cosine similarity of vectors in 2D vector space

Yet another measure of similarity is the *Euclidean distance* between two vectors. Close vectors have a small Euclidean distance. It can be calculated using the following formula:

$$\text{Distance } (A, B) = \text{sqrt}((A_i\text{-}B_i)^2),$$

where i is the i-th dimension of the *n*-dimensional vectors

DIFFERENT USE CASES OF EMBEDDINGS

Here are some different use cases of embeddings:

- *Text search*—Searching through the knowledge base for the right document chunk is a key component of RAG systems. Embeddings are used to calculate similarity between the user query and the stored documents.
- *Clustering*—Categorizing similar data together to find themes and groups in the data can result in valuable insights. Embeddings are used to group similar pieces of text together to find out, for example, the common themes in customer reviews.
- *Machine learning*—Advanced machine learning techniques can be used for different problems such as classification and regression. To convert text data into numerical features, embeddings prove to be a valuable technique.
- *Recommendation engines*—Shorter distances between product features mean greater similarity. Using embeddings for product and user features can be used to recommend similar products.

Since we are focusing on RAG systems, here we examine using embeddings for text search— to find the document chunks that are closest to the user's query. Let's continue with our example of the Wikipedia page on the 2023 Cricket World Cup. In the last section, we created 67 chunks using a combination of specialized and fixed-width chunking. Now we will see how to create embeddings for each chunk. We will see how to use an open source as well as a proprietary embeddings model.

Here is the code example for creating embeddings using an open source embeddings model all-MPnet-base-v2 via Hugging Face:

```
# Import HuggingFaceEmbeddings from embeddings library
from langchain_huggingface import HuggingFaceEmbeddings

# Instantiate the embeddings model. The embeddings model_name can be changed
as desired
embeddings =
    HuggingFaceEmbeddings(
        model_name='sentence-transformers/all-mpnet-base-v2"
        )

# Create embeddings for all chunks
hf_embeddings =
    embeddings.embed_documents(
        [chunk.page_content for chunk in final_chunks]
        )

#Check the length(dimension) of the embedding
len(hf_embeddings [0])
>> 768
```

This model creates embeddings of dimension 768. The list `hf_embeddings` is made up of 285 lists, each containing 768 numbers for each chunk. Figure 3.8 shows the embeddings space of all the chunks.

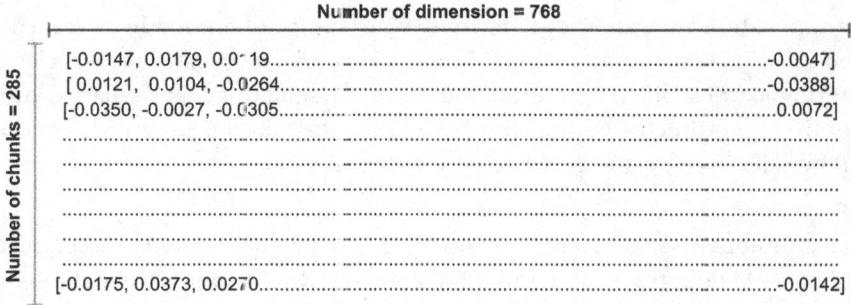

Figure 3.8 Embeddings created for chunks of Wikipedia page using the all-MiniLM-l6-v2 model.

Similarly, we can use a proprietary model such as the text-embedding-3-small model, hosted by OpenAI. The only prerequisite is obtaining an API key and setting up a billing account with OpenAI.

```
# Install the langchain openai library
%pip install langchain-openai==0.3.7 --quiet

# Import OpenAIEmbeddings from the library
from langchain_openai import OpenAIEmbeddings

# Set the OPENAI_API_KEY as the environment variable
import os
os.environ["OPENAI_API_KEY"] = <YOUR_API_KEY>

# Instantiate the embeddings object
embeddings = OpenAIEmbeddings(model="text-embedding-3-small")

# Create embeddings for all chunks
openai_embeddings =
    embeddings.embed_documents(
        [chunk.page_content for chunk in chunks]
        )

#Check the length(dimension) of the embedding
len(openai_embedding[0])
```

```
>> 1536
```

This text-embedding-3-small model creates embeddings for the same chunks of dimension 1536.

There are several embeddings models available, and new ones are being added every day. The choice of embeddings can be dictated by certain factors. Let's look at a few factors.

3.3.4   *How to choose embeddings?*

There are a few major factors that will affect your choice of embeddings.

USE CASE

Your application use case may determine your choice of embeddings. The MTEB leaderboard scores each of the embeddings models across seven use cases: classification, clustering, pair classification, reranking, retrieval, semantic text similarity, and summarization. At the time of writing this book, the SFR-Embedding-Mistral model developed by Salesforce performs the best for retrieval tasks.

COST

Cost is another important factor to consider. To create the knowledge base, you may have to create embeddings for thousands of documents, thus running into millions of tokens.

Embeddings are powerful data patterns that are most effective in finding similarities between texts. In RAG systems, embeddings play a critical role in search and retrieval of data relevant to the user query. Once the embeddings have been created, they need to be stored in persistent memory for real-time access. To store embeddings, a new kind of database called a *vector database* have become increasingly popular.

3.4 Storage (vector databases)

Now we are at the last step of the indexing pipeline. The data has been loaded, split, and converted to embeddings. To use this information repeatedly, we need to store it in memory so that it can be accessed on demand.

3.4.1 What are vector databases?

The evolution of databases can be traced back to the early days of computing. Databases are organized collections of data, designed to be easily accessed, managed, and updated. Relational databases such as MySQL organize structured data into rows and columns. NoSQL databases such as MongoDB specialize in handling unstructured and semi-structured data. Graph databases such as Neo4j are optimized for querying graph data. In the same manner, vector databases are built to handle high-dimensional vectors. These databases specialize in indexing and storing vector embeddings for fast semantic search and retrieval.

Apart from efficiently storing high-dimensional vector data, modern vector databases offer traditional features such as scalability, security, multi-tenancy, versioning and management, and similar. However, vector databases are unique in offering similarity searches based on Euclidean distance or cosine similarity. They also employ specialized indexing techniques.

3.4.2 Types of vector databases

Vector databases started as a specialized database offering, but propelled by the growth in demand for storing vector data, all major database providers have added the vector indexing capability. We can categorize the popular vector databases available today into six broad categories.

- *Vector indexes*—These are libraries that focus on the core features of indexing and search. They do not support data management, query processing, or interfaces. They can be considered a bare-bones vector database. Examples of vector indexes are Facebook AI Similarity Search (FAISS), Non-Metric Space Library (NMSLIB), Approximate Nearest Neighbors Oh Yeah (ANNOY), Scalable Nearest Neighbors (ScaNN), and similar.

- *Specialized vector DBs*—These databases focus on the core feature of high-dimensional vector support, indexing, search, and retrieval such as vector indexes, but also offer database features such as data management, extensibility, security, scalability, non-vector data support, and similar. Examples of specialized vector DBs are Pinecone, ChromaDB, Milvus, Qdrant, Weaviate, Vald, LanceDB, Vespa, and Marqo.

- *Search platforms*—Solr, Elastic Search, Open Search, and Apache Lucene are traditional text search platforms and engines built for full text search. They have now added vector similarity search capabilities to their existing search capabilities.
- *Vector capabilities for SQL databases*—Azure SQL, Postgres SQL(pgvector), SingleStore, and CloudSQL are traditional SQL databases that have now added vector data-handling capabilities.
- *Vector capabilities for NoSQL databases*—Like SQL DBs, NoSQL DBs such as MongoDB have also added vector search capabilities.
- *Graph databases with vector capabilities*—Graph DBs such as Neo4j, have also opened new possibilities by adding vector capabilities, .

Using a vector index such as FAISS is supported by LangChain. To use FAISS, we first must install the `faiss-cpu` library. We will use the chunks already created in section 3.2 and the OpenAI embeddings that we used in section 3.3:

```
# Install FAISS-CPU
%pip install faiss-cpu==1.10.0 --quiet

# Import FAISS class from vectorstore library
from langchain_community.vectorstores import FAISS
from langchain_community.docstore.in_memory import InMemoryDocstore

# Import OpenAIEmbeddings from the library
from langchain_openai import OpenAIEmbeddings

# Set the OPENAI_API_KEY as the environment variable
import os
os.environ["OPENAI_API_KEY"] = <YOUR_API_KEY>

# Chunks from Section 3.3
Final_chunks=final_chunks

# Instantiate the embeddings object
embeddings=OpenAIEmbeddings(model="text-embedding-3-small")

# Instantiate the FAISS object
vector_store = FAISS(
    embedding_function=embeddings,
    index=index,
    docstore=InMemoryDocstore(),
    index_to_docstore_id={},
)

# Add the chunks
vector_store.add_documents(documents=final_chunks)

# Check the number of chunks that have been indexed
vector_store.index.ntotal
```

```
>> 285
```

With this code, the 235 chunks of data have been converted to vector embeddings, and these embeddings are stored in a FAISS vector index. The FAISS vector index can also be saved to memory using the `vector_store.save_local(folder_path,index_name)` and `FAISS.load_local(folder_path,index_name)` functions. Let's now take a cursory look at how a vector store can be used. We will take the original question that we have been asking from the beginning of this book: "Who won the 2023 Cricket World Cup?"

```
# Original Question
query = "Who won the 2023 Cricket World Cup?"

# Ranking the chunks in descending order of similarity
docs = vector_store.similarity_search(query)

# Printing one of the top-ranked chunk
print(docs[0].page_content)
```

Similarity search orders the chunks in descending order of similarity, meaning that the most similar chunks to the query are ranked on top. In the previous example, we can observe that the chunk that speaks about the world cup final has been ranked on top.

FAISS is a stripped-down high-performance vector index that works for many applications. ChromaDB is another user-friendly vector DB that has gained popularity. Pinecone offers managed services and customization. Milvus claims higher performance on similarity search, while Qdrant provides an advanced filtering system. We will now discuss some points on how to choose a vector database that works best for your requirements.

3.4.3 Choosing a vector database

All vector databases offer the same basic capabilities, but each one of them also claims a differentiated value. Your choice should be influenced by the nuance of your use case matching with the value proposition of the database. Here are a few things to consider while evaluating and implementing a vector database:

- *Accuracy vs. speed*—Certain algorithms are more accurate but slower. A balance between search accuracy and query speed must be achieved based on application needs. It will become important to evaluate vector DBs on these parameters.
- *Flexibility vs. performance*—Vector DBs provide customizations to the user. While it may help you in tailoring the DB to your specific requirements, more customizations can add overhead and slow systems down.
- *Local vs. cloud storage*—Assess tradeoffs between local storage speed and access versus cloud storage benefits like security, redundancy, and scalability.
- *Direct access vs. API*—Determine if tight integration control via direct libraries is required or if ease-of-use abstractions like APIs better suit your use case.

- *Simplicity vs. advanced features*—Compare advanced algorithm optimizations, query features, and indexing versus how much complexity your use case necessitates versus needs for simplicity.
- *Cost*—While you may incur regular costs in a fully managed solution, a self-hosted one might prove costlier if not managed well.

We have now completed an end-to-end indexing of a document. We continued with the same question ("Who won the 2023 Cricket World Cup?") and the same external source—the Wikipedia page of the 2023 Cricket World Cup (https://mng.bz/yN4J). In this chapter, we started with the programmatic loading of this Wikipedia page extracting the HTML document and then parsing the HTML document to extract. Thereafter, we divided the text into small-sized chunks using a specialized and fixed-width chunking method. We converted these chunks into embeddings using OpenAI's text-embedding-003-large model. Finally, we stored the embeddings into a FAISS vector index. We also saw how using similarity search on this vector index helped us retrieve relevant chunks.

When several such documents in different formats from different sources are indexed using a combination of methods and strategies, we can store all the information in the form of vector embeddings creating a non-parametric knowledge base for our RAG system.

This concludes our discussion on the indexing pipeline. By now, you must have built a solid understanding of the four components of the indexing pipeline and should be ready to build a knowledge base for a RAG system.

In the next chapter, we will use this knowledge base to generate real-time responses to user queries through the generation pipeline.

Summary

Data loading

- The process of sourcing data from its original location is called *data loading*, and it includes the following four steps: connecting to the source, extracting and parsing text, reviewing and updating metadata, and cleaning and transforming data.
- Loading documents from a list of sources may turn out to be a complicated process. Make sure to plan for all the sources and loaders in advance.
- A variety of data loaders from LangChain can be used.
- Breaking down long pieces of text into manageable sizes is called *data splitting* or *chunking*.
- Chunking addresses context window limits of LLMs, mitigates the lost-in-the-middle problem for long prompts, and enables easier search and retrieval.
- The chunking process involves dividing longer texts into small units, merging small units into chunks, and including an overlap between chunks to preserve contextual continuity.

- Chunking can be fixed size, specialized (or adaptive), or semantic. Newer chunking methods are constantly being introduced.
- Your choice of the chunking strategy should be based on the nature of the content, expected length and complexity of user query, application use case, and the embeddings model being used.
- A chunking strategy can include multiple methods.

Data conversion

- For processing text needs to be converted into a numerical format.
- Embeddings are vector representations of data (words, sentences, documents, etc.).
- The goal of an embedding algorithm is to position similar data points close to each other in a vector space.
- Several pre-trained, open source and proprietary, embedding models are available for use.
- Embeddings models enable similarity search. Embeddings can be used for text search, clustering, ML models, and recommendation engines.
- The choice of embeddings is largely based on the use case and the cost implications.
- Vector databases are designed to efficiently store and retrieve high-dimensional vector data such as embeddings.
- Vector databases provide similarity searches based on distance metrics such as cosine similarity.
- Apart from the similarity search, vector databases offer traditional services such as scalability, security, versioning, and the like.
- Vector capabilities can be offered by standalone vector indexes, specialized vector databases, or legacy offerings such as search platforms, SQL, and NoSQL databases with added vector capabilities.
- Accuracy, speed, flexibility, storage, performance, simplicity, access, and cost are some of the factors that can influence the choice of a vector database.

Generation pipeline: Generating contextual LLM responses

4

This chapter covers

- Retrievers and retrieval methodologies
- Augmentation using prompt engineering techniques
- Generation using LLMs
- Basic implementation of the RAG pipeline in Python

In chapter 3, we discussed the creation of the knowledge base, or the non-parametric memory of retrieval augmented generation (RAG)-based applications, via the indexing pipeline. To use this knowledge base for accurate and contextual responses, we need to create a generation pipeline that includes the steps of retrieval, augmentation, and generation.

This chapter elaborates on the three components of the generation pipeline. We begin by discussing the retrieval process, which primarily involves searching through the embeddings stored in vector databases of the knowledge base and returning a list of documents that closely match the input query of the user. You will also learn about the concept of retrievers and a few retrieval algorithms. Next, we move to the augmentation step. At this point, it is also beneficial to understand different prompt engineering frameworks used with RAG. Finally, as part of the generation step, we discuss a few stages of the LLM life cycle, such as using foundation models versus supervised fine-tuning, models of different sizes, and open source versus proprietary models in the RAG context. In each of these steps, we also highlight the benefits and drawbacks of different methods.

By the end of this chapter, you will be equipped with an understanding of the two foundational pipelines of a RAG system. You should also be ready to build a basic RAG system.

By the end of this chapter, you should

- Know several retrievers used in RAG.
- Get an understanding of augmentation using prompt engineering.
- Learn some details about how LLMs are used in the context of RAG.
- Have an end-to-end knowledge of setting up a basic RAG system.

Let's get started with an overview of the generation pipeline before diving into each component.

4.1 Generation pipeline overview

Recall the generation pipeline introduced in chapter 2. When a user provides an input, the generation pipeline is responsible for providing the contextual response. The retriever searches for the most appropriate information from the knowledge base. The user question is augmented with this information and passed as input to the LLM for generating the final response. This process is illustrated in figure 4.1.

The generation pipeline involves three processes: retrieval, augmentation, and generation. The retrieval process is responsible for fetching the information relevant to the user query from the knowledge base. Augmentation is the process of combining the fetched information with the user query. Generation is the last step, in which the LLM generates a response based on the augmented prompt. This chapter discusses these three processes in detail.

4.2 Retrieval

Retrieval refers to the process of finding and extracting relevant pieces of information from a large corpus or knowledge base. As you saw in chapter 3, the information from various sources is parsed, chunked, and stored as embeddings in vector databases. These stored embeddings are also sometimes referred to as documents, and the knowledge base consists of several volumes of documents. Retrieval, essentially, is a search problem to find the documents that best match the input query.

Searching through the knowledge base and retrieving the right documents is done by a component called the *retriever*. In simple terms, retrievers accept a query as input and return a list of matching documents as output. This process is illustrated in figure

4.2. You can imagine that retrieval is a crucial step since the quality of the retrieved information directly affects the quality of the output that will be generated.

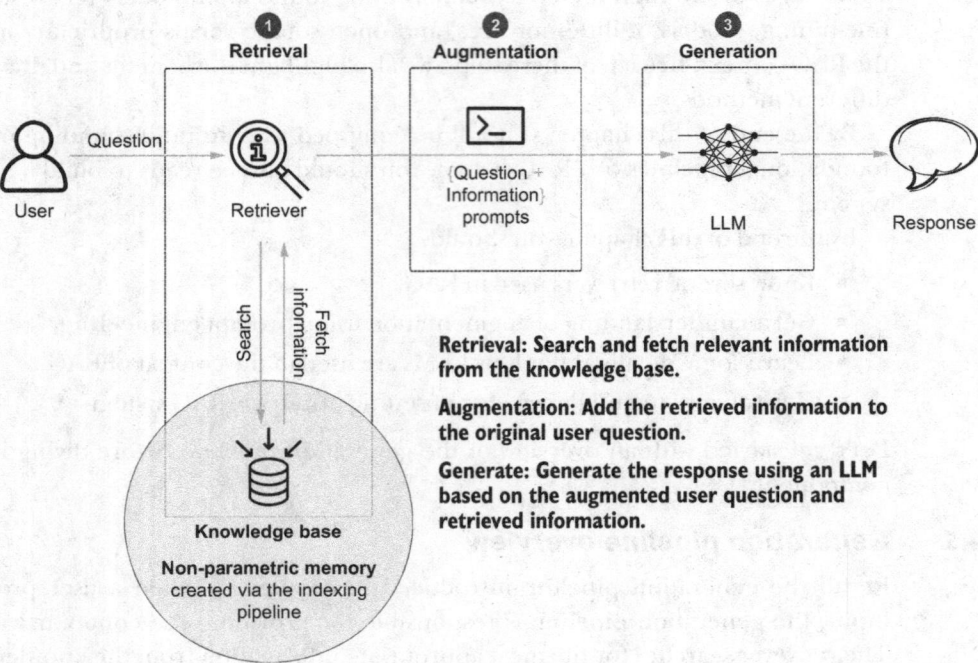

Retrieval: Search and fetch relevant information from the knowledge base.

Augmentation: Add the retrieved information to the original user question.

Generate: Generate the response using an LLM based on the augmented user question and retrieved information.

Figure 4.1   Generation pipeline overview with the three components (i.e., retrieval, augmentation, and generation)

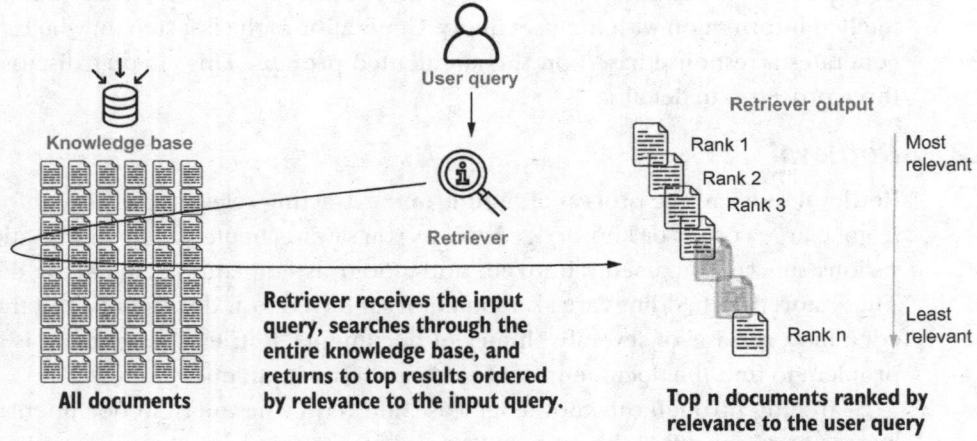

Retriever receives the input query, searches through the entire knowledge base, and returns to top results ordered by relevance to the input query.

Top n documents ranked by relevance to the user query

Figure 4.2   A retriever searches through the knowledge base and returns the most relevant documents.

We have already discussed embeddings in chapter 3 while building the indexing pipeline. Using embeddings, we can find documents that match the user query. Embeddings is one method in which retrieval can happen. There are other methods, too, and it is worth spending some time understanding different types of retrieval methods and the way they calculate the results.

This section on retrievers first discusses different retrieval algorithms and their significance in the context of RAG. In RAG systems, one or more retrieval methods can be used to build the retriever component. Next, we look at a few examples of prebuilt retrievers that can be used directly through a framework (e.g., LangChain). These retrievers are integrated with services such as databases, cloud providers, or third-party information sources. Finally, we will close this section by building a very simple retriever in LangChain using Python. We will continue to demonstrate with this example the augmentation and generation steps, too, so that we have a full implementation of the generation pipeline by the end of this chapter.

NOTE Chapter 3 discussed indexing and how to convert and store data in a numerical form that can be used to retrieve information later. You may recall we discussed embeddings at length in section 3.3. It should be intuitive that since we stored the data in the form of embeddings, to fetch this data, we will also have to work on the search using embeddings. Therefore, the retrieval process is tightly coupled with the indexing process. Whatever we use to index, we will have to use to retrieve.

4.2.1 *Progression of retrieval methods*

Information retrieval, or IR, is the science of searching. Whether you are searching for information in a document or for documents themselves, it falls under the gamut of information retrieval. IR has a rich history in computing, starting from Joseph Marie Jacquard's invention of the Jacquard Loom, the first device that could read punched cards, back in the early 19th century. Since then, IR has evolved leaps and bounds from simple to highly sophisticated search and retrieval. *Boolean retrieval* is a simple keyword-based search (like the one you encounter when you press CTRL/CMD + F on your browser or word processor) where Boolean logic is used to match documents with queries based on the absence or presence of the words. Documents are retrieved if they contain the exact terms in the query, often combined with AND, NOT, and OR operators. *Bag of Words* (BoW) was used quite often in the early days of NLP. It creates a vocabulary of all the words in the documents as a vector indicating the presence or absence of each word. Consider two sentences: "The cat sat on the mat" and "The cat in the hat." The vocabulary is `['the", "cat", "in", "hat", "on", "mat"]` and the first sentence is represented as a vector `[2, 1, 1, 1, 0, 0]`, while the one is `[2, 1, 0, 0, 1, 1]`. While simple, it ignores the context, meaning, and the order of words.

Some of these, although popular in ML and IR space, don't make sense in the context of RAG for a variety of reasons. For our purpose, we focus on a few of the popular retrieval techniques that have been used in RAG.

TERM FREQUENCY-INVERSE DOCUMENT FREQUENCY

Term Frequency–Inverse Document Frequency (TF-IDF) is a statistical measure used to evaluate the importance of a word in a document relative to a collection of documents (corpus). It assigns higher weights to words that appear frequently in a document but infrequently across the corpus. Figure 4.3 illustrates how TF-IDF is calculated for a unigram search term.

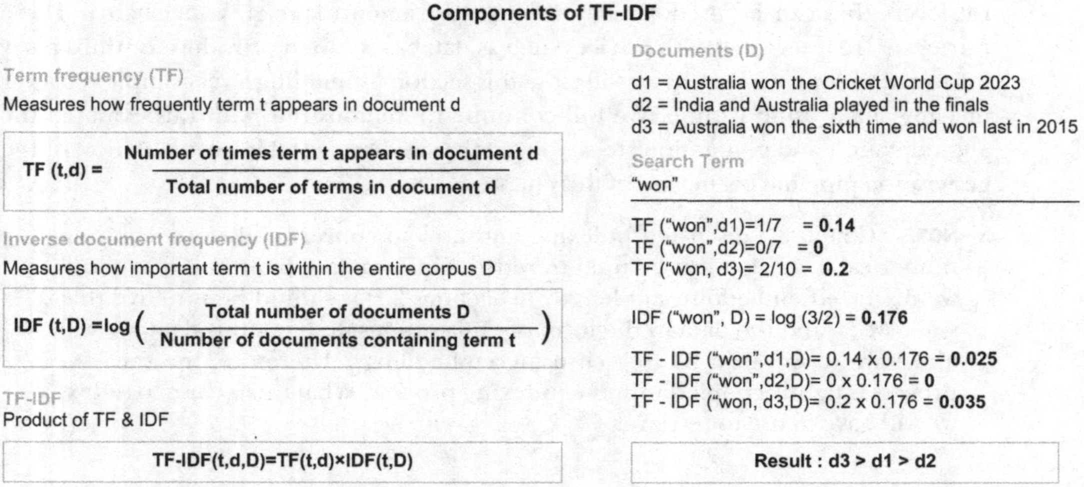

Components of TF-IDF

Term frequency (TF)

Measures how frequently term t appears in document d

$$TF(t,d) = \frac{\text{Number of times term t appears in document d}}{\text{Total number of terms in document d}}$$

Inverse document frequency (IDF)

Measures how important term t is within the entire corpus D

$$IDF(t,D) = \log\left(\frac{\text{Total number of documents D}}{\text{Number of documents containing term t}}\right)$$

TF-IDF

Product of TF & IDF

$$TF\text{-}IDF(t,d,D) = TF(t,d) \times IDF(t,D)$$

Documents (D)

d1 = Australia won the Cricket World Cup 2023
d2 = India and Australia played in the finals
d3 = Australia won the sixth time and won last in 2015

Search Term
"won"

TF ("won",d1)=1/7 = **0.14**
TF ("won",d2)=0/7 = **0**
TF ("won, d3)= 2/10 = **0.2**

IDF ("won", D) = log (3/2) = **0.176**

TF - IDF ("won",d1,D)= 0.14 x 0.176 = **0.025**
TF - IDF ("won",d2,D)= 0 x 0.176 = **0**
TF - IDF ("won, d3,D)= 0.2 x 0.176 = **0.035**

Result : d3 > d1 > d2

Figure 4.3 Calculating TF-IDF to rank documents based on search terms

LangChain also provides an abstract implementation of TF-IDF using retrievers from `langchain_community`, which, in turn, uses `scikit-learn`:

```
# Install or Upgrade Scikit-learn
%pip install --upgrade scikit-learn

# Import TFIDFRetriever class from retrievers library
from langchain_community.retrievers import TFIDFRetriever

# Create an instance of the TFIDFRetriever with texts
retriever = TFIDFRetriever.from_texts(
["Australia won the Cricket World Cup 2023",
 "India and Australia played in the finals",
 "Australia won the sixth time having last won in 2015"]
)

# Use the retriever using the invoke method
result=retriever.invoke("won")

# Print the results
print(result)
```

TF-IDF not only can be used for unigrams, but also for phrases (n-grams). However, even TF-IDF improves on simpler search methods by emphasizing unique words, it still lacks context and word-order consideration, making it less suitable for complex tasks like RAG.

BEST MATCH 25

Best Match 25 (BM25) is an advanced probabilistic model used to rank documents based on the query terms appearing in each document. It is part of the family of probabilistic information retrieval models and is considered an advancement over the classic TF-IDF model. The improvement that BM25 brings is that it adjusts for the length of the documents so that longer documents do not unfairly get higher scores. Figure 4.4 illustrates the BM25 calculation.

Calculating BM25

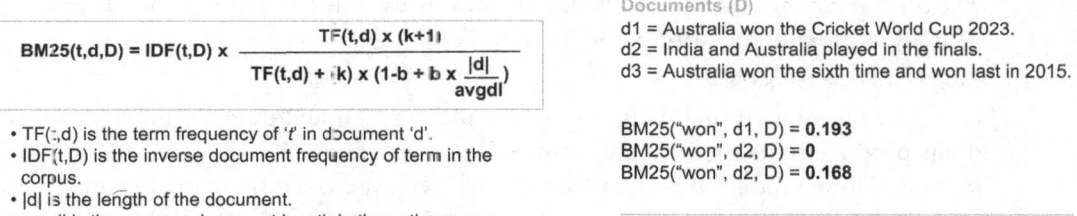

$$BM25(t,d,D) = IDF(t,D) \times \frac{TF(t,d) \times (k+1)}{TF(t,d) + k \times (1 - b + b \times \frac{|d|}{avgdl})}$$

- TF(t,d) is the term frequency of 't' in document 'd'.
- IDF(t,D) is the inverse document frequency of term in the corpus.
- |d| is the length of the document.
- avgdl is the average document length in the entire corpus.
- k and b are free parameters.

Documents (D)
d1 = Australia won the Cricket World Cup 2023.
d2 = India and Australia played in the finals.
d3 = Australia won the sixth time and won last in 2015.

BM25("won", d1, D) = **0.193**
BM25("won", d2, D) = **0**
BM25("won", d2, D) = **0.168**

Result : d1 > d3 > d2

Figure 4.4 BM25 also considers the length of the documents.

Like TF-IDF, LangChain also has an abstract implementation of BM25 (Okapi BM25, specifically) using the `rank_bm25` package:

```
# Install or Upgrade rank_bm25
%pip install --upgrade rank_bm25


# Import BM25Retriever class from retrievers library
from langchain_community.retrievers import BM25Retriever


# Create an instance of the TFIDFRetriever with texts
retriever = BM25Retriever.from_texts(
["Australia won the Cricket World Cup 2023",
 "India and Australia played in the finals",
 "Australia won the sixth time having last won in 2015"]
)


# Use the retriever using the invoke method
result=retriever.invoke("Who won the 2023 Cricket World Cup?")


# Print the results
print(result)
```

For long queries instead of single keywords, the BM25 value is calculated for each word in the query, and the final BM25 value for the query is a summation of the values for all the words. BM25 is a powerful tool in traditional IR, but it still doesn't capture the full semantic meaning of queries and documents required for RAG applications. BM25 is generally used in RAG for quick initial retrieval, and then a more powerful retriever is used to re-rank the results. We will learn about re-ranking later in chapter 6, when we discuss advanced strategies for RAG.

STATIC WORD EMBEDDINGS

Static embeddings such as Word2Vec and GloVe represent words as dense vectors in a continuous vector space, capturing semantic relationships based on context. For instance, "king" – "man" + "woman" approximates "queen." These embeddings can capture nuances such as similarity and analogy, which BoW, TF-IDF, and BM25 miss. However, while they provide a richer representation, they still lack full contextual understanding and are limited in handling polysemy (words with multiple meanings). The term *static* here highlights that the vector representation of words does not change with the context of the word in the input query.

CONTEXTUAL EMBEDDINGS

Generated by models such as BERT or OpenAI's text embeddings, contextual embeddings produce high-dimensional, context-aware representations for queries and documents. These models, based on transformers, capture deep semantic meanings and relationships. For example, a query about "apple" will retrieve documents discussing apple the fruit, or Apple the technology company, depending on the input query. Figure 4.5 illustrates the difference between static and contextual embeddings. Contextual embeddings represent a significant advancement in IR, providing the context and understanding necessary for RAG tasks. Despite being computationally intensive, contextual embeddings are the most widely used retrievers in RAG. Examples of embedding models discussed in section 3.3.2 are contextual embeddings.

Methods such as TF-IDF and BM25 use frequency-based calculations to rank documents. In embeddings (both static and contextual), ranking is done based on a similarity score. Similarity is popularly calculated using the cosine of the angle between document vectors. We discussed cosine similarity calculation in section 3.3.3. Figure 4.6 illustrates the process of retrieval using embeddings.

OTHER RETRIEVAL METHODS

While the discussed methods are most popular in the discourse, other methods are also available. These methods represent more recent developments and specialized approaches and are good to refer to if you want to dive deeper into the world of information retrieval:

- *Learned sparse retrieval*—Generates sparse, interpretable representations using neural networks (examples: SPLADE, DeepCT, and DocT5Quer)
- *Dense retrieval*—Encodes queries and documents as dense vectors for semantic matching (examples: dense passage retriever [DPR], ANCE, RepBERT)

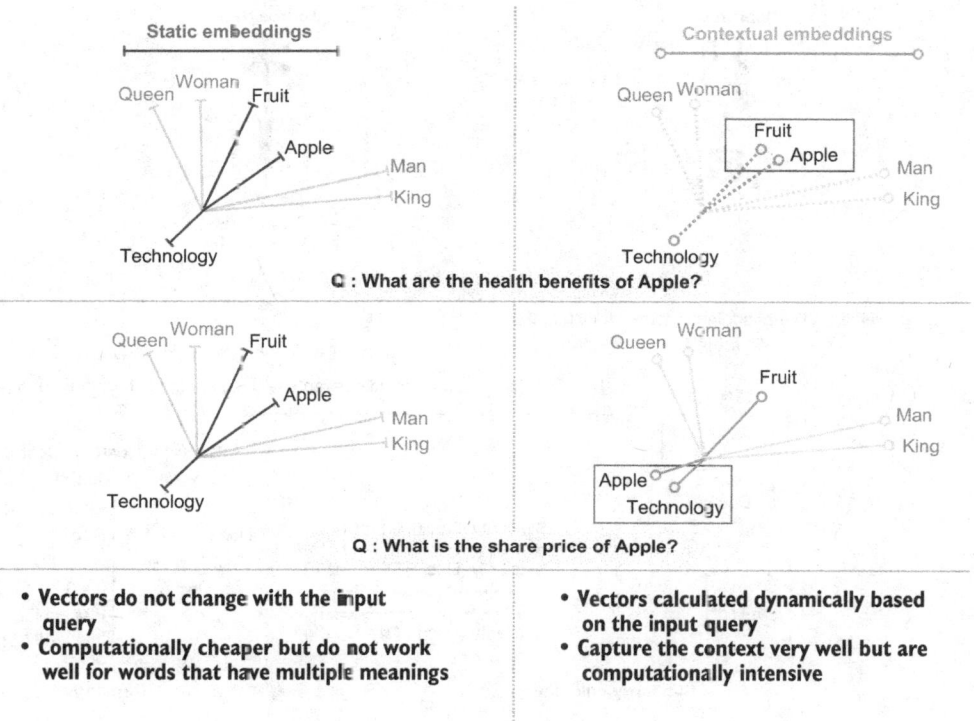

Figure 4.5 Static vs. contextual embeddings

- *Hybrid retrieval*—Combines sparse and dense methods for balanced efficiency and effectiveness (examples: ColBERT, COIL)

- *Cross-encoder retrieval*—Directly compares query-document pairs using transformer models (example: BERT-based re-rankers)

- *Graph-based retrieval*—Uses graph structures to model relationships between documents (examples: TextGraphs, graph neural networks for IR)

- *Quantum-inspired retrieval*—Applies quantum computing principles to information retrieval (example: quantum language models [QLM])

- *Neural IR models*—Encompass various neural network-based approaches to information retrieval (examples: NPRF [neural PRF], KNRM [Kernel-based Neural Ranking Model])

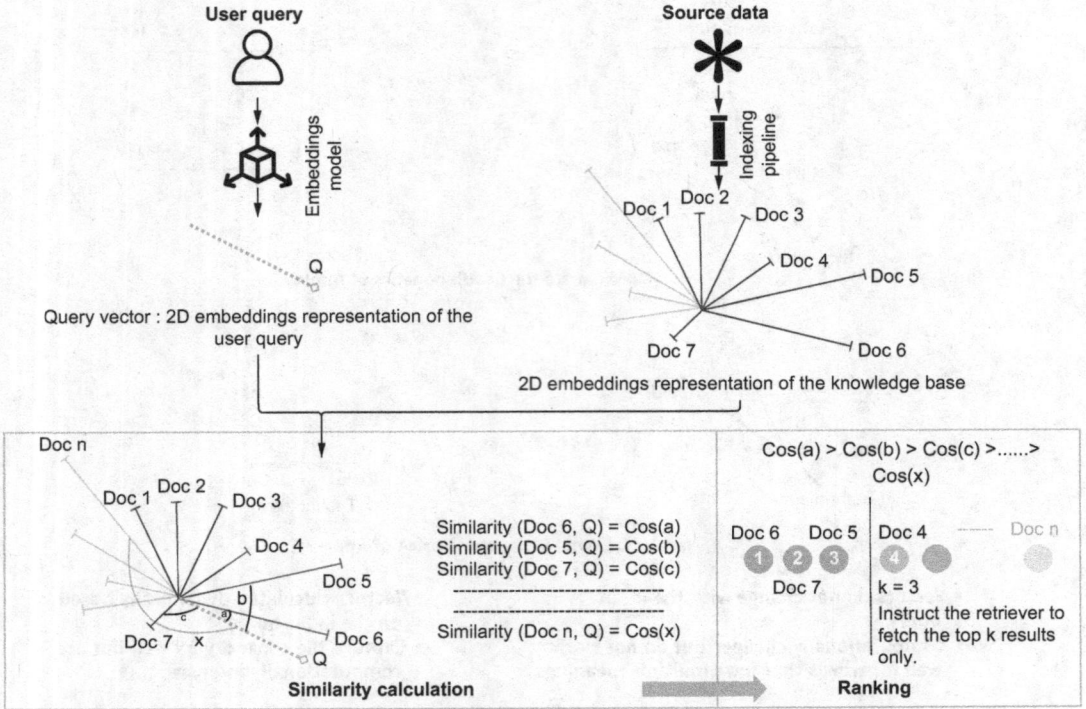

Figure 4.6   Similarity calculation and results ranking in embeddings-based retrieval technique

Table 4.1 notes the weaknesses and strengths of different retrievers. While contextual embeddings are the only ones you need to know to get started with RAG, it is useful to get familiar with other retrievers for further exploration and for cases where you want to improve retriever performance. As we discussed, the implementation of TF-IDF using the `scikit-learn` retriever and BM25 using `rank_bm25` retriever in LangChain, there are many others available that use one of the mentioned methodologies. We will look at some of the popular ones in the next section.

Table 4.1   Comparison of different retrieval techniques for RAG

Technique	Key feature	Strengths	Weaknesses	Suitability for RAG
Boolean retrieval	Exact matching with logical operators	Simple, fast, and precise	Limited relevance ranking; no partial matching	Low: Too rigid
BoW	Unordered word frequency counts	Simple and intuitive	Ignores word order and context	Low: Lacks semantic understanding

Table 4.1 Comparison of different retrieval techniques for RAG (*continued*)

Technique	Key feature	Strengths	Weaknesses	Suitability for RAG
TF-IDF	Term weighting based on document and corpus frequency	Improved relevance ranking over BoW	Still ignores semantics and word relationships	Low–medium: Better than BoW but limited; used in hybrid retrieval
BM25	Advanced ranking function with length normalization	Robust performance; industry standard	Limited semantic understanding	Medium: Good baseline for simple RAG; used in hybrid retrieval.
Static embeddings	Fixed dense vector representations	Captures some semantic relationships	Context-independent; limited in polysemy handling	Medium: Introduces basic semantics
Contextual embeddings	Context-aware dense representations	Rich semantic understanding; handles polysemy	Computationally intensive	High: Excellent semantic capture
Learned sparse retrievers	Neural-network-generated sparse representations	Efficient, interpretable, and has some semantic understanding	May miss some semantic relationships	High: Balances efficiency and semantics
Dense retrievers	Dense vector matching for queries and documents	Strong semantic matching	Computationally intensive; less interpretable	High: Excellent for semantic search in RAG
Hybrid retrievers	Combination of sparse and dense methods	Balances efficiency and effectiveness	Complex to implement and tune	High: Versatile for various RAG needs
Cross-encoder retrievers	Direct query-document comparison	Very accurate relevance assessment	Extremely computationally expensive	Medium–high: Great for reranking in RAG
Graph-based retrievers	Graph structure for document relationships	Captures complex relationships in data	Can be complex to construct and query	Medium–high: Good for structured data in RAG
Quantum-inspired retrievers	Quantum computing concepts in IR	Potential for handling complex queries	Emerging field; practical benefits not fully proven	Low–medium: Potentially promising but not mature
Neural IR models	Various neural network approaches to IR	Flexible; can capture complex patterns	Often require large training data; can be black-box	High: Adaptable to various RAG scenarios

4.2.2 *Popular retrievers*

Developers can build their retrievers based on one or a combination of multiple retrieval methodologies. Retrievers are used not just in RAG but in a variety of search-related tasks.

For RAG, LangChain provides many integrations where the algorithms such as TF-IDF, embeddings and similarity search, and BM25 have been abstracted as retrievers for developers to use. We have already seen the ones for TF-IDF and BM25. Some of the other popular retrievers are described in the following sections.

VECTOR STORES AND DATABASES AS RETRIEVERS

Vector stores can act as the retrievers, taking away the responsibility from the developer to convert the query vector into embeddings by calculating similarity and ranking the results. FAISS is typically used in tandem with a contextual embedding model for retrieval. Other vector DBs such as PineCone, Milvus, and Weaviate provide hybrid search functionality by combining dense retrieval methods such as embeddings and sparse methods such as BM25 and SPLADE.

CLOUD PROVIDERS

Cloud providers Azure, AWS, and Google also offer their retrievers. Integration with Amazon Kendra, Azure AI Search, AWS Bedrock, Google Drive, and Google Vertex AI Search provides developers with infrastructure, APIs, and tools for information retrieval of vector, keyword, and hybrid queries at scale.

WEB INFORMATION RESOURCES

Connections to information resources such as Wikipedia, Arxiv, and AskNews provide optimized search and retrieval from these sources. You can check these retrievers and more in the official LangChain documentation (https://mng.bz/gm4R).

This was a brief introduction to the world of retrievers. If you found the information slightly complex, you can always revisit it. At this stage, the understanding of contextual embeddings will suffice. Contextual embeddings are the most popular technique for basic RAG pipelines, and we will now create a simple retriever using OpenAI embeddings.

4.2.3   *A simple retriever implementation*

Before we move to the next step of the generation pipeline, let's look at a simple example of a retriever. In chapter 3, we were working on indexing the Wikipedia page for the 2023 Cricket World Cup. If you recall, we used embeddings from OpenAI to encode the text and used FAISS as the vector index to store the embeddings. We also stored the FAISS index in a local directory. Let's reuse this index:

```
# Install the langchain openai library
%pip install langchain-openai==0.3.7


# Import FAISS class from vectorstore library
from langchain_community.vectorstores import FAISS


# Import OpenAIEmbeddings from the library
from langchain_openai import OpenAIEmbeddings


# Set the OPENAI_API_KEY as the environment variable
import os
```

```
os.environ["OPENAI_API_KEY"] = <YOUR_API_KEY>

# Instantiate the embeddings object
embeddings=OpenAIEmbeddings(model="text-embedding-3-small")

# Load the database stored in the local directory
vector_store=FAISS.load_local(
folder_path="../../Assets/Data",
index_name="CWC_index",
embeddings=embeddings,
allow_dangerous_deserialization=True
)


# Original Question
query = "Who won the 2023 Cricket World Cup?"

# Ranking the chunks in descending order of similarity
retrieved_docs = vector_store.similarity_search(query, k=2)
```

This `similarity_search ()` function returns a list of matching documents ordered by a score. This score is a quantification of the similarity between the query and the document and is hence called the similarity score. In this example, the vector index's inbuilt similarity search feature was used for retrieval. As one of the retrievers we discussed in section 4.2.2, the vector store itself acted as the retriever. K=2 tells the function to retrieve the top two documents. This is the most basic implementation of a retriever in the generation pipeline of a RAG system, and the retrieval method is enabled by embeddings. We used the text-embedding-3-small from OpenAI. FAISS calculated the similarity score based on these embeddings.

Retrievers are the backbone of RAG systems. The quality of the retriever has a great bearing on the quality of the generated output. In this section, you learned about vanilla retrieval methods. Multiple strategies are used when designing production-grade systems. We will read about these advanced strategies in chapter 6. Now that we have gained an understanding of the retrievers, we will move on to the next important step—augmentation.

4.3 Augmentation

A retriever fetches the information (or documents) that are most relevant to the user query. But, what next? How do we use this information? The answer is quite intuitive. If you recall the discussion in chapter 1, the input to an LLM is a natural language prompt. This information fetched by the retriever should also be sent to the LLM in the form of a natural language prompt. This process of combining the user query and the retrieved information is called *augmentation*.

The augmentation step in RAG largely falls under the discipline of prompt engineering. Prompt engineering can be defined as the technique of giving instructions to an LLM to attain a desired outcome. The goal of prompt engineering is to construct the prompts to achieve accuracy and relevance in the LLM responses to the desired outcome(s). At the first glance, augmentation is quite simple—just add the retrieved information to the query. However, some nuanced augmentation techniques help improve the quality of the generated results. See figure 4.7 for an example of simple augmentation.

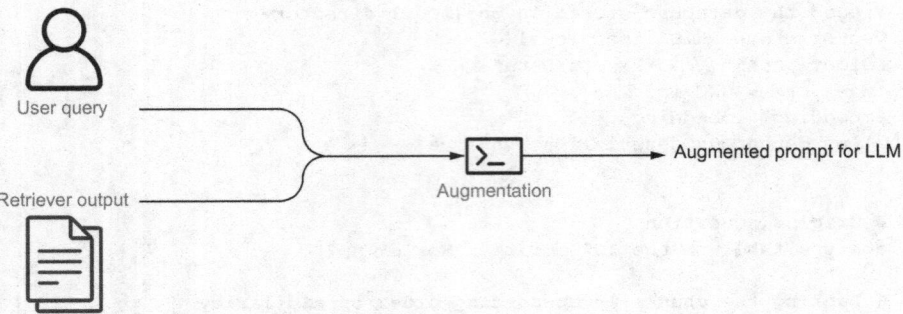

Figure 4.7   Simple augmentation combines the user query with retrieved documents to send to the LLM.

4.3.1   RAG prompt engineering techniques

Prompt engineering as a discipline has, sometimes, been dismissed as being too simple to be called engineering. You may have heard the phrase, "English is the new programming language." Interaction with LLMs is indeed in natural language. However, what is also true is that the principles of programming are not the language in which code is written but the logic in which the machine is instructed. With that in mind, let's examine different logical approaches that can be taken to augment the user query with the retrieved information.

CONTEXTUAL PROMPTING

To understand a simple augmentation technique, let's revisit chapter 1. Recall our example of "Who won the 2023 Cricket World Cup?" We copied an excerpt from the Wikipedia article. This excerpt is the retrieved information. We then added this information to the prompt and provided an extra instruction—"Answer only based on the context provided below." Figure 4.8 illustrates this example.

By adding this instruction, we have set up our generation to focus only on the provided information and not on LLM's internal knowledge (or parametric knowledge). This is a simple augmentation technique that is also referred to as *contextual prompting*. Please note that the instruction can be given in any linguistic construct. For example, we could have added the instruction at the beginning of the prompt as, "Given the context below, answer the question, Who won the 2023 Cricket World Cup. Information: <Wikipedia excerpt>." We can also reiterate the instruction at the end of the prompt—"Remember to answer only based on the context provided and not from any other source.

CONTROLLED GENERATION PROMPTING

Sometimes, the information might not be present in the retrieved document. This happens when the documents in the knowledge base do not have any information

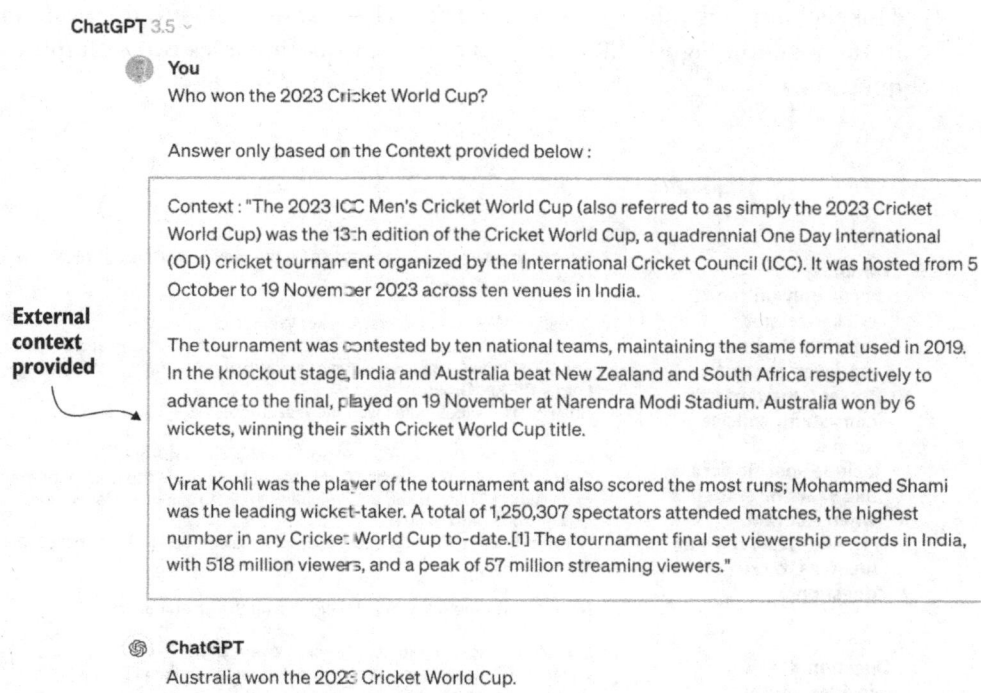

Figure 4.8 Information is augmented to the original question with an added instruction.

relevant to the user query. The retriever might still fetch some documents that are the closest to the user query. In these cases, the chances of hallucination increase because the LLM will still try to follow the instructions for answering the question. To avoid this scenario, an additional instruction is added, which tells the LLM not to answer if the retrieved document does not have proper information to answer the user question (something like, "If the question cannot be answered based on the provided context, say I don't know."). In the context of RAG, this technique is particularly valuable because it ensures that the model's responses are grounded in the retrieved information. If the relevant information hasn't been retrieved or isn't present in the knowledge base, the model is instructed to acknowledge this lack of information rather than attempting to generate a potentially incorrect answer."

FEW-SHOT PROMPTING

It has been observed that while generating responses, LLMs adhere quite well to the examples provided in the prompt. If you want the generation to be in a certain format or style, it is recommended to provide a few examples. In RAG, while providing the retrieved information in the prompt, we can also specify certain examples to help guide the generation in the way we need the retrieved information to be used.

This technique is called *few-shot prompting*. Here "shot" refers to the examples given in the prompt. Figure 4.9 illustrates a prompt that includes two examples with the question.

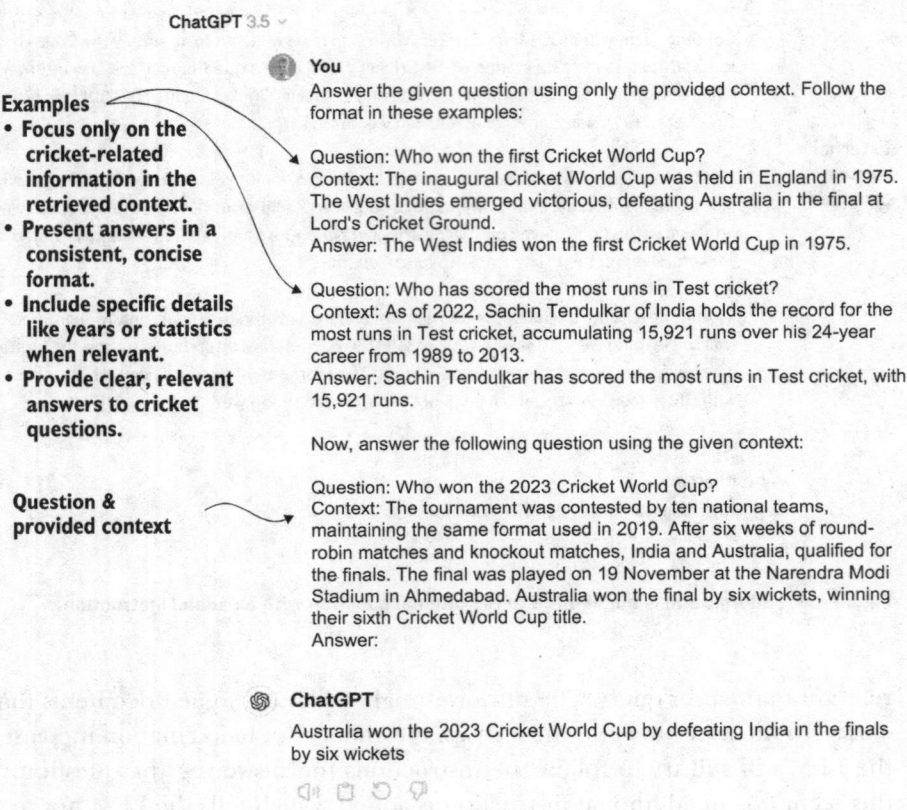

Figure 4.9   Example of few-shot prompting in the context of RAG

You might come across terms such as *one-shot prompting* or *two-shot prompting*, which replaces the word "few" with the number of examples given. Conversely, when no example is given, and the LLM is expected to answer correctly, the technique is also called *zero-shot prompting*.

CHAIN OF THOUGHT PROMPTING

It has been observed that the introduction of intermediate reasoning steps improves the performance of LLMs in tasks requiring complex reasoning, such as arithmetic, common sense, and symbolic reasoning. The same can be applied in the context of RAG. This is called *chain-of-thought*, or CoT, *prompting*. In figure 4.10, I asked ChatGPT to analyze the performance of two teams based on the retrieved information.

ChatGPT 3.5 ∨

 You

Use the provided context to answer the question about team performance in the 2023 Cricket World Cup. Show your reasoning step-by-step, explaining how you use the information to reach your conclusion.

Question —
> Question: Based on the given statistics, which team had the best overall performance in the league stage of 2023 Cricket World Cup, and why?

Retrieved context —
> Context:
> India: Matches played: 9, Wins: 9, Losses: 0, Run rate: +2.57, Highest score: 410/4
> Australia: Matches played: 9, Wins: 7, Wins: 2, Run rate: +0.84, Highest score: 399/8

Reasoning steps —
> Answer the question by following these steps:
> 1. Analyze win-loss record
> 2. Compare run rates
> 3. Consider highest scores
> 4. Evaluate overall tournament progression
> 5. Reach a conclusion

ChatGPT

To determine which team had the best overall performance in the league stage of the 2023 Cricket World Cup, we'll follow the steps outlined:

1. Analyze Win-Loss Record
- India: Played 9 matches, won 9, lost 0.
- Australia: Played 9 matches, won 7, lost 2.

India has a perfect win record, winning all their matches, while Australia lost two matches. Therefore, India has a better win-loss record.

2. Compare Run Rates
- India: Run rate of +2.57
- Australia: Run rate of +0.84

A higher run rate indicates better performance in terms of scoring runs quickly and restricting the opposition. India's run rate is significantly higher than Australia's, showing superior overall performance.

3. Consider Highest Scores
- India: Highest score of 410/4
- Australia: Highest score of 399/8

India's highest score is slightly higher than Australia's. While both teams posted very high scores, India's highest score gives them a slight edge in terms of batting capability.

4. Evaluate Overall Tournament Progression
- India: Undefeated, consistently high performance in every match.
- Australia: Very strong performance but had two losses, indicating moments of vulnerability.

5. Reach a Conclusion
Combining all factors:
- Win-Loss Record: India is undefeated.
- Run Rate: India has a significantly higher run rate.
- Highest Scores: India's highest score is marginally higher.
- Overall Progression: India maintained consistent dominance throughout the league stage.

Conclusion
Based on the win-loss record, run rate, highest scores, and overall consistency, India had the best overall performance in the league stage of the 2023 Cricket World Cup. Their undefeated streak, high run rate, and strong batting performances highlight their dominance in the tournament.

Figure 4.10   Chain-of-thought (CoT) prompting for reasoning tasks

The CoT prompting approach can also be combined with the few-shot prompting technique, where a few examples of reasoning are provided before the final question. Creating these examples is a manually intensive task. In auto-CoT, the examples are also created using an LLM.

OTHER ADVANCED PROMPTING TECHNIQUES

Prompt engineering is becoming an increasingly intricate discipline. Ongoing research constantly presents new improvements in prompting techniques. To dive deeper into prompt engineering, let's check out some of the following techniques:

- *Self-consistency*—While CoT uses a single reasoning chain in CoT prompting, self-consistency aims to sample multiple diverse reasoning paths and use their respective generations to arrive at the most consistent answer.

- *Generated knowledge prompting*—This technique explores the idea of prompt-based knowledge generation by dynamically constructing relevant knowledge chains, using models' latent knowledge to strengthen reasoning.

- *Tree-of-thoughts prompting*—This technique maintains an explorable tree structure of coherent intermediate thought steps aimed at solving problems.

- *Automatic reasoning and tool use* (ART)—The ART framework automatically interleaves model generations with tool use for complex reasoning tasks. ART employs demonstrations to decompose problems and integrate tools without task-specific scripting.

- *Automatic prompt engineer* (APE)—The APE framework automatically generates and selects optimal instructions to guide models. It uses an LLM to synthesize candidate prompt solutions for a task based on output demonstrations.

- *Active prompt*—Active-prompt improves CoT methods by dynamically adapting language models to task-specific prompts through a process involving query, uncertainty analysis, human annotation, and enhanced inference.

- *ReAct prompting*—ReAct integrates LLMs for concurrent reasoning traces and task-specific actions, improving performance by interacting with external tools for information retrieval. When combined with CoT, it optimally utilizes internal knowledge and external information, enhancing the interpretability and trustworthiness of LLMs.

- *Recursive prompting*—Recursive prompting breaks down complex problems into subproblems, solving them by sequentially using prompts. This method aids compositional generalization in tasks such as math problems or question answering, with the model building on solutions from previous steps.

Table 4.2 summarizes different prompting techniques. Prompt engineering for augmentation is an evolving discipline. It is important to note that there is a lot of scope for creativity in writing prompts for RAG applications. Efficient prompting has a significant effect on the generated output. The kind of prompts you use will depend a lot on your use case and the nature of the information in the knowledge base.

Table 4.2 Comparison of prompting techniques for augmentation

Technique	Description	Key advantage	Best use case	Complexity
Contextual prompting	Adds retrieved information to the prompt with instructions to focus on the provided context	Ensures focus on relevant information	General RAG queries	Low
Controlled generation prompting	Instructs the model to say "I don't know" when information is not available	Reduces hallucination risk	When accuracy is critical	Low
Few-shot prompting	Provides examples in the prompt to guide response format and style	Improves output consistency and format adherence	When a specific output format is required	Medium
Chain-of-thought (CoT) prompting	Introduces intermediate reasoning steps	Improves performance on complex reasoning tasks	Complex queries requiring step-by-step analysis	Medium
Self-consistency	Samples multiple diverse reasoning paths	Improves answer consistency and accuracy	Tasks with multiple possible reasoning approaches	High
Generated knowledge prompting	Dynamically constructs relevant knowledge chains	Uses the model's latent knowledge	Tasks requiring broad knowledge application	High
Tree-of-thoughts prompting	Maintains an explorable tree structure of thought steps	Allows for more comprehensive problem-solving	Complex, multistep problem solving	High
Automatic reasoning and tool use (ART)	Interleaves model generations with tool use	Enhances problem decomposition and tool integration	Tasks requiring external tool use	Very High
Automatic prompt engineer (APE)	Automatically generates and selects optimal instructions	Optimizes prompts for specific tasks	Prompt optimization for complex tasks	Very High
Active prompt	Dynamically adapts LMs to task-specific prompts	Improves task-specific performance	Tasks requiring adaptive prompting	High
ReAct prompting	Integrates reasoning traces with task-specific actions	Improves performance and interpretability	Tasks requiring both reasoning and action	High
Recursive prompting	Breaks down complex problems into subproblems	Aids in compositional generalization	Complex, multistep problems	High

We have already built a simple retriever in the previous section. We will now execute augmentation with a simple contextual prompt with controlled generation.

4.3.2   *A simple augmentation prompt creation*

In section 4.2.3, we were able to implement a FAISS-based retriever using OpenAI embeddings. We will now make use of this retriever and create the augmentation prompt:

```
# Import FAISS class from vectorstore library
from langchain_community.vectorstores import FAISS

# Import OpenAIEmbeddings from the library
from langchain_openai import OpenAIEmbeddings

# Set the OPENAI_API_KEY as the environment variable
import os
os.environ["OPENAI_API_KEY"] = <YOUR_API_KEY>

# Instantiate the embeddings object
embeddings=OpenAIEmbeddings(model="text-embedding-3-small")

# Load the database stored in the local directory
vector_store=FAISS.load_local(
folder_path="../../Assets/Data",
index_name="CWC_index",
embeddings=embeddings,
allow_dangerous_deserialization=True
)

# Original Question
query = "Who won the 2023 Cricket World Cup?"

# Ranking the chunks in descending order of similarity
retrieved_docs = vector_store.similarity_search(query, k=2)

# Selecting the first chunk as the retrieved information
retrieved_context= retrieved_docs[0].page_content

# Creating the prompt
augmented_prompt=f"""

Given the context below, answer the question.

Question: {query}

Context : {retrieved_context}

Remember to answer only based on the context provided and not from any other
source.

If the question cannot be answered based on the provided context, say I don't
know.

"""
```

With the augmentation step complete, we are now ready to send the prompt to the LLM for the generation of the desired outcome. You will now learn how LLMs generate text and the nuances of generation.

4.4 Generation

Generation is the final step of this pipeline. While LLMs may be used in any of the previous steps, the generation step relies completely on the LLM. The most popular LLMs are the ones being developed by OpenAI, Anthropic, Meta, Google, Microsoft, and Mistral, among other developers. While text generation is the core capability of LLMs, we are now seeing multimodal models that can handle images and audio along with text. Simultaneously, researchers are developing faster and smaller models.

In this section, we will discuss the factors that can help choose a language model for your RAG system. We will then continue with our example of the retriever and augmented prompt we have built so far and complete it by adding the generation step.

4.4.1 Categorization of LLMs and suitability for RAG

As of June 2024, there are over a hundred LLMs available to use, and new ones are coming out every week. How do we decide then which LLM to choose for our RAG system? To show you the decision-making process, let's discuss three themes under which we can broadly categorize LLMs:

- How they have been trained
- How they can be accessed
- Their size

We will discuss the LLMs under these themes and understand the factors that may influence the LLM choice for RAG.

ORIGINAL VS. FINE-TUNED MODELS

Training an LLM takes massive amounts of data and computational resources. LLMs training is done through an unsupervised learning process. All modern LLMs are autoregressive models and are trained to generate the next token in a sequence. These massive pre-trained LLMs are also called *foundation models*.

The question that you may ask is, if LLMs just predict the next tokens in a sequence, how are we able to ask questions and chat with these models? The answer is in what we call *supervised fine-tuning*, or SFT.

Supervised fine-tuning is a process used to adapt a pre-trained language model for specific tasks or behaviors such as question-answering or chat. It involves further training a pre-trained foundation model on a labeled dataset, where the model learns to map inputs to specific desired outputs. You start with a pre-trained model, prepare a labelled dataset for the target task, and train the model on this dataset, which adjusts the model parameters to perform better on the target task. Figure 4.11 gives an overview of the SFT process.

Supervised fine-tuning adjusts the foundation model weights for specific tasks.

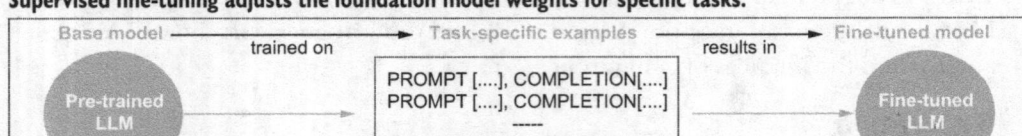

Supervised fine-tuning process is a classification model training.

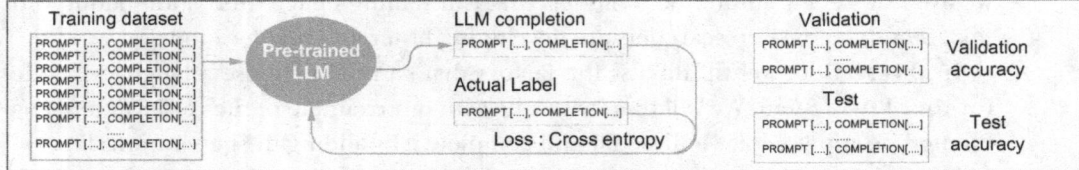

Figure 4.11   Supervised fine-tuning is a classification mode-training process.

While foundation models generalize well for a wide array of tasks, there are several use cases where the need for a fine-tuned model arises. Domain adaptation for specialized fields such as law and healthcare, task specific optimization such as classification and NER (named entity recognition), and conversational AI, personalization are some use cases where you may observe a fine-tuned model performing better.

Specifically, in the context of RAG, some criteria should be considered, while choosing between a foundation model and a fine-tuning one:

- *Domain specificity*—Foundation models have broader knowledge and can handle a wider range of topics and queries for general-purpose RAG systems. If your RAG application is specialized (say, dealing with patient records or instruction manuals for heavy machinery), you may find that fine-tuning the model for specific domains may improve performance.

- *Retrieval integration*—If you observe that a foundation model you are using is not integrating the retrieved information well, a fine-tuned model trained to better utilize information can lead to better quality of generations.

- *Deployment speed*—A foundation model can be quickly deployed since there is no additional training required. To fine-tune a model, you will need to spend time in gathering training data and the actual training of the model.

- *Customization of responses*—For generating results in a specific format or custom-style elements such as tone or vocabulary, a fine-tuned model may result in better adherence to the requirements compared to foundation models.

- *Resource efficiency*—Fine-tuning a model requires more storage and computational resources. Depending on the scale of deployment, the costs may be higher for a fine-tuned model.

- *Ethical alignment*—A fine-tuned model allows for better control over the responses in adherence to ethical guidelines and even certain privacy aspects.

A summary of the criteria is presented in table 4.3.

Table 4.3   Criteria for choosing between foundation and fine-tuned models

Criteria	Better suitability	Explanation
Domain specificity	Fine-tuned models	Better performance for specialized applications (e.g., patient records and instruction manuals)
Retrieval integration	Fine-tuned models	Can be trained to better utilize retrieved information
Deployment speed	Foundation models	Quicker deployment with no additional training required
Customization of responses	Fine-tuned models	Better adherence to specific format, style, tone, or vocabulary requirements
Resource efficiency	Foundation models	Requires less storage and computational resources
Ethical alignment	Fine-tuned models	Allows better control over responses to ethical guidelines and privacy

Fine-tuned models give better control over your RAG systems, but they are costly. There's also a risk of overreliance on retrieval and a potential tradeoff between RAG performance and inherent LLM language abilities. Therefore, whether to use a foundation model or fine-tuning one depends on the improvements you are targeting, availability of data, cost, and other tradeoffs. The general recommendation is to start experimenting with a foundation model and then progress to supervised fine-tuning for performance improvement.

OPEN SOURCE VS. PROPRIETARY MODELS

Software development and distribution are represented by two fundamentally different approaches: open versus proprietary software. The world of LLMs is no different. Some LLM developers such as Meta and Mistral have made the model weights public to foster collaboration and community-driven innovation. In contrast, pioneers such as OpenAI, Anthropic, and Google have kept the models closed, offering support, managed services, and better user experience.

For RAG systems, open source models provide the flexibility of customization, deployment method, and transparency, but warrant the need for the necessary infrastructure to maintain the models. Proprietary model providers might be costlier for high volumes but provide regular updates, ease of use, scalability, and faster development, among other things. Some proprietary model providers such as OpenAI have prebuilt RAG capabilities. Your choice of the type of model you choose may depend on some of the following criteria:

- *Customization*—Open source LLMs are generally considered better for customizations such as deep integration with custom retrieval mechanisms. A better control over fine-tuning is also something that open source LLMs allow for. Customization of proprietary models is limited to API capabilities.

- *Ease of use*—Proprietary models, however, are much easier to use. Some of the models such as OpenAI, Cohere, and similar offer optimized, prebuilt RAG solutions.
- *Deployment flexibility*—Open source models can be deployed according to your preference (private cloud, on-premises), while proprietary models are managed by the providers. This also has a bearing on data security and privacy. Most proprietary model providers are now offering multiple deployment options.
- *Cost*—Open source LLMs may come with upfront infrastructure costs, while proprietary models are priced based on usage. Long-term costs and query volumes are considerations to choose between open source and proprietary models. Large-scale deployments may favor the use of open source models.

The choice between open source and proprietary models for RAG depends on factors such as the scale of deployment, specific domain requirements, integration needs, and the importance of customization in the retrieval and generation process. Apart from these, the need for knowledge updates, transparency, scalability, the structure of data, compliance, and the like will determine the choice of the model. A summary of the discussion is presented in table 4.4

Table 4.4   Criteria for choosing between open source and proprietary models

Criteria	Better suitability	Explanation
Customization	Open source	Allows deeper integration with custom retrieval mechanisms and better control over fine-tuning
Ease of use	Proprietary	Offers optimized, prebuilt RAG solutions and are generally easier to use
Deployment flexibility	Open source	Can be deployed on private cloud or on-premises, offering more options
Cost for large-scale deployment	Open source	May be more cost-effective for large-scale deployments despite upfront infrastructure costs
Data security and privacy	Open source	Offers more control over data, though some private models now offer various deployment options
Regular updates and support	Proprietary	Typically provides regular updates and better support

A hybrid approach is also not ruled out. At a PoC stage, a proprietary model may make sense for quick experimentation.

Here are some examples of popular proprietary models:

- GPT series by OpenAI (https://platform.openai.com/docs/models)
- Claude series by Anthropic (https://www.anthropic.com/claude)

- Gemini series by Google (https://mng.bz/eBnJ)
- Command R series by Cohere (https://cohere.com/command)

Some of open source models are

- Llama series by Meta (https://llama.meta.com/)
- Mistral (https://docs.mistral.ai/getting-started/models/)

MODEL SIZES

LLMs come in various sizes, typically measured by the number of parameters they contain. The size of the model greatly affects the capabilities along with the resource requirements.

Larger models have several billion, even trillions, of parameters. These models exhibit superior performance in reasoning abilities, and language understanding, and have broader knowledge. They can generate more coherent text, and their responses are contextually more accurate. However, these larger models have significantly high computation, storage, and energy requirements.

Smaller models with parameter sizes in millions or a few billion offer benefits such as faster inference times, lower resource usage, and easier deployment on edge devices or resource constrained environments. Researchers and developers continue to explore methods to achieve large-model performance with smaller and more efficient architectures.

For a RAG system, the following should be assessed:

- *Resource constraints*—Small models have a much lower resource usage. Lightweight RAG applications with faster inference can be built with smaller models.
- *Reasoning capability*—On the other spectrum of resource constraints is the language-processing ability of the model. Large models are better suited for complex reasoning tasks and can deal with ambiguity in the retrieved information. Smaller models, therefore, will rely heavily on the quality of retrieved information.
- *Deployment options*—The size of large models makes it difficult to deploy on-edge devices. This is a flexibility that smaller models provide, bringing RAG applications to a wide range of devices and environments.
- *Context handling*—Large models may be better at integrating multiple pieces of retrieved information in RAG systems since they have longer context windows. Large models are also better at handling diverse queries, while small models struggle with out-of-domain queries. Large models might perform better in RAG systems with diverse or unpredictable query types.

In practice, most RAG applications are built on large models. However, smaller models make more sense in the long-term adoption and application of the technology. The various factors are summarized in table 4.5

Table 4.5   Criteria for choosing between small and large models

Criteria	Better suitability	Explanation
Resource constraints	Small models	Lower resource usage; suitable for lightweight RAG applications
Reasoning capability	Large models	Better for complex reasoning tasks and handling ambiguity in retrieved information
Deployment options	Small models	More flexible; can be deployed on edge devices and resource-constrained environments
Context handling	Large models	Better at integrating multiple pieces of retrieved information; longer context windows
Query diversity	Large models	Handle diverse and unpredictable query types better
Inference speed	Small models	Faster inference times; suitable for applications requiring quick responses

Examples of popular small language models are:

- Phi-3 by Microsoft (https://azure.microsoft.com/en-us/products/phi-3)
- Gemma by Google (https://ai.google.dev/gemma)

The choice of the LLM is a core consideration in your RAG system that requires close attention and iterations. The performance of your system may require experimenting and adapting your choice of the LLM.

The list of LLMs has become almost endless. What this means for developers and businesses is that the technology has truly been democratized. While all LLMs have their unique propositions and architecture, for practical applications, there are a wide array of choices available. While simple RAG applications may rely on a single LLM provider, for more complex applications, a multi-LLM strategy may be beneficial.

We have implemented a simple retriever and created an augmented prompt. In the last section of this chapter, we round up the pipeline by creating the generation step.

4.4.2   *Completing the RAG pipeline: Generation using LLMs*

We have built a simple retriever using FAISS and OpenAI embeddings, and we created a simple augmented prompt. Now we will use OpenAI's latest model, GPT-4o, to generate the response:

```
# Import FAISS class from vectorstore library
from langchain_community.vectorstores import FAISS

# Import OpenAIEmbeddings from the library
from langchain_openai import OpenAIEmbeddings

# Set the OPENAI_API_KEY as the environment variable
import os
os.environ["OPENAI_API_KEY"] = <YOUR_API_KEY>

# Instantiate the embeddings object
```

```python
embeddings=OpenAIEmbeddings(model="text-embedding-3-small")

# Load the database stored in the local directory
vector_store=FAISS.load_local(
    folder_path="../../Assets/Data",
    index_name="CWC_index",
    embeddings=embeddings,
    allow_dangerous_deserialization=True
    )

# Original Question
query = "Who won the 2023 Cricket World Cup?"

# Ranking the chunks in descending order of similarity
retrieved_docs = vector_store.similarity_search(query, k=2)

# Selecting the first chunk as the retrieved information
retrieved_context= retrieved_docs[0].page_content

# Creating the prompt
augmented_prompt=f"""

Given the context below, answer the question.

Question: {query}

Context : {retrieved_context}

Remember to answer only based on the context provided and not from any other
source.

If the question cannot be answered based on the provided context, say I don't
know.

"""
# Importing the OpenAI library from langchain
from langchain_openai import ChatOpenAI

# Instantiate the OpenAI LLM
llm = ChatOpenAI(
            model="gpt-4o-mini",
            temperature=0,
            max_tokens=None,
            timeout=None,
            max_retries=2
)
# Make the API call passing the augmented prompt to the LLM
response = llm.invoke (
    [("human",augmented_prompt)]
    )

# Extract the answer from the response object
answer=response.content

print(answer)
```

And there it is. We have built a generation pipeline, albeit a very simple one. It can now fetch information from the knowledge base and generate an answer pertinent to the question asked and rooted in the knowledge base. Try asking a different question to see how well the pipeline generalizes.

We have now covered all three steps—retrieval, augmentation, and generation— of the generation pipeline. With the knowledge of the indexing pipeline (covered in chapter 3) and the generation pipeline, you are now all set to create a basic RAG system. What we have discussed so far can be termed a *naïve RAG implementation.* Naïve RAG can be marred by inaccuracies. It can be inefficient in retrieving and ranking information correctly. The LLM can ignore the retrieved information and still hallucinate. To discuss and address these challenges, in chapter 6, we examine advanced strategies that allow for more complex and better-performing RAG systems.

But before that, the question of evaluating the system arises. Is it generating the responses on the expected lines? Is the LLM still hallucinating? Before trying to improve the performance of the system, we need to be able to measure and benchmark it. That is what we will do in chapter 5. We will look at the evaluation metrics and the popular RAG benchmarks.

Summary

Retrieval

- Retrieval is the process of finding relevant information from the knowledge base based on a user query. It is a search problem to match documents with input queries.
- The popular retrieval methods for RAG include
    - *TF-IDF (Term Frequency-Inverse Document Frequency)*—Statistical measure of word importance in a document relative to a corpus. It can be implemented using LangChain's TFIDFRetriever.
    - *BM25 (Best Match 25)*—Advanced probabilistic model, an improvement over TF-IDF. It adjusts for document length and can be implemented using Lang-Chain's BM25Retriever.
    - *Static word embeddings*—Represent words as dense vectors (e.g., Word2Vec, GloVe) and capture semantic relationships but lack full contextual understanding.
    - *Contextual embeddings*—Produced by models like BERT or OpenAI's text embeddings. They provide context-aware representations and are most widely used in RAG, despite being computationally intensive.
    - *Advanced retrieval methods*—They include learned sparse retrieval, dense retrieval, hybrid retrieval, cross-encoder retrieval, graph-based retrieval, quantum-inspired retrieval, and neural IR models.
- Most advanced implementations will include a hybrid approach.

- Vector stores and databases (e.g., FAISS, PineCone, Milvus, Weaviate), cloud provider solutions (e.g., Amazon Kendra, Azure AI Search, Google Vertex AI Search), and web information resources (e.g., Wikipedia, Arxiv, AskNews) are some of the popular retriever integrations provided by LangChain.
- The choice of retriever depends on factors such as accuracy, speed, and compatibility with the indexing method.

Augmentation

- Augmentation combines the user query with retrieved information to create a prompt for the LLM.
- Prompt engineering is crucial for effective augmentation, aiming for accuracy and relevance in LLM responses.
- Key prompt engineering techniques for RAG include
  - *Contextual prompting*—Adding retrieved information with instructions to focus on the provided context.
  - *Controlled generation prompting*—Instructing the LLM to admit lack of knowledge when information is insufficient.
  - *Few-shot prompting*—Providing examples to guide the LLM's response format or style.
  - *Chain-of-thought (CoT) prompting*—Introducing intermediate reasoning steps for complex tasks.
  - *Advanced techniques*—These include self-consistency, generated knowledge prompting, and tree of thought.
- The choice of augmentation technique depends on the task complexity, desired output format, and LLM capabilities.

Generation

- Generation is the final step in which the LLM produces the response based on the augmented prompt.
- LLMs can be categorized based on how they've been trained, how they can be accessed, and the number of parameters they have.
- Supervised fine-tuning, or SFT, improves context use and domain optimization, enhances coherence, and enables source attribution; however, it comes with challenges such as cost, risk of overreliance on retrieval, and potential tradeoffs with inherent LLM abilities.
- The choice between open source and proprietary LLMs depends on customization needs, long-term costs, and data sensitivity.
- Larger models come with superior reasoning, language understanding, and broader knowledge, and generate more coherent and contextually accurate responses but come with high computational and resource requirements.

Smaller models allow faster inference, lower resource usage, and are easier to deploy on edge devices or resource-constrained environments but do not have the same language understanding abilities as large models.

- Popular LLMs include offerings from OpenAI, Anthropic, Google, and similar, and open source models are available through platforms such as Hugging Face.

- The choice of LLM depends on factors such as performance requirements, resource constraints, deployment environment, and data sensitivity.

- The choice of LLM for RAG systems requires careful consideration, experimentation, and potential adaptation based on performance.

RAG evaluation:
Accuracy, relevance,
and faithfulness

This chapter covers

- The need and requirements for evaluating RAG pipelines
- Metrics, frameworks, and benchmarks for RAG evaluation
- Current limitations and future course of RAG evaluation

Chapters 3 and 4 discussed the development of retrieval-augmented generation (RAG) systems using the indexing and generation pipelines. RAG promises to reduce hallucinations and ground the large language model (LLM) responses in the provided context, which is done by creating a non-parametric memory or knowledge base for the system and then retrieving information from it.

This chapter covers the methods used to evaluate how well the RAG system is functioning. We need to make sure that the components of the two RAG pipelines are performing per the expectations. At a high level, we need to ensure that the information being retrieved is relevant to the input query and that the LLM is generating responses grounded in the retrieved context. To this end, there have been several frameworks developed over time. Here we discuss some popular frameworks and the metrics they calculate.

There is also a second aspect to evaluation. While the frameworks allow for the calculation of metrics, how do you make sure that your RAG pipelines are working better than those developed by other developers? The evaluations cannot be done in isolation. For this purpose, several benchmarks have been established. These benchmarks evaluate the RAG systems on preset data, such as question–answer sets, for accurate comparison of different RAG pipelines. These benchmarks help developers evaluate the performance of their systems vis-à-vis those developed by other developers.

Finally, like RAG techniques, the research on RAG evaluations is still in progress. There are still some limitations in the current set of evaluation parameters. We discuss these limitations and some ideas on the way forward for RAG evaluations.

By the end of this chapter, you should

- Know the fundamentals of RAG evaluations.
- Be aware of the popular frameworks, metrics, and benchmarks for RAG evaluation.
- Understand the limitations and best practices.
- Be able to evaluate the RAG pipeline in Python.

For RAG to live up to the promise of grounding the LLM responses in data, you will need to go beyond the simple implementation of indexing, retrieval, augmentation, and generation. We will discuss these advanced strategies in chapter 6. However, to improve something, you need to first measure the performance. RAG evaluations help in setting up the baseline of your RAG system performance for you to then improve it. First, we look at the fundamental aspects of RAG systems evaluation.

5.1 Key aspects of RAG evaluation

Building a PoC RAG pipeline is not overtly complex. It is achievable through brief training and verification of a limited set of examples. However, to enhance its robustness, thorough testing on a dataset that accurately mirrors the production use case is imperative. RAG pipelines can suffer from hallucinations of their own. This can be because

- The retriever fails to retrieve the entire context or retrieves irrelevant context.
- Despite being provided the context, the LLM does not consider it.
- The LLM picks irrelevant information from the context instead of answering the query.

Retrieval and generation are two processes that need special focus from an evaluation perspective. This is because these two steps produce outputs that can be evaluated. (While indexing and augmentation will have a bearing on the outputs, they do not produce measurable outcomes). Here are several questions we need to ask ourselves about these two processes:

- How good is the retrieval of the context from the knowledge base?
- Is it relevant to the query?
- How much noise (irrelevant information) is present?
- How good is the generated response?
- Is the response grounded in the provided context?
- Is the response relevant to the query?

You can ask many more questions such as these to assess the performance of your RAG system. Contemporary research has discovered certain scores to assess the quality and abilities of a RAG system. The following sections discuss three predominant quality scores and four main abilities.

5.1.1 Quality scores

There are three quality score dimensions prevalent in the discourse on RAG evaluation. They measure the quality of retrieval and generation:

- *Context relevance*—This dimension evaluates how relevant the retrieved information or context is to the user query. It calculates metrics such as the precision and recall with which context is retrieved from the knowledge base.
- *Answer faithfulness (also called groundedness)*—This dimension evaluates whether the answer generated by the system is using the retrieved information.
- *Answer relevance*—This dimension evaluates how relevant the answer generated by the system is to the original user query.

We discuss how these scores are calculated in section 5.2

5.1.2 Required abilities

The quality scores are important for measuring how well the retrieval and the generation components of the RAG system are performing. At an overall level, there are certain critical abilities that a RAG system should possess:

- *Noise robustness*—It is impractical to assume that the information stored in the knowledge base for RAG systems is perfectly curated to answer the questions that can be potentially asked. It is very probable that a document is related to the user query but does not have any meaningful information to answer it. The ability of the RAG system to separate these noisy documents from the relevant ones is termed noise robustness.
- *Negative rejection*—By nature, LLMs always generate text. There may be no information about the user query in the documents in the knowledge base. The ability of the RAG system not to give an answer when there is no relevant information is called negative rejection.

- *Information integration*—To obtain a comprehensive answer to a user query, it is also very likely the information must be retrieved from multiple documents. This ability of the system to assimilate information from multiple documents is called information integration.

- *Counterfactual robustness*—Sometimes the information in the knowledge base might itself be inaccurate. A high-quality RAG system should be able to address this problem and reject known inaccuracies in the retrieved information. This ability is known as counterfactual robustness.

Noise robustness is an ability that the retrieval component should possess, and other abilities are largely related to the generation component.

Apart from these, *latency* is another often-mentioned capability. Although it is a non-functional requirement, it is quite critical in generative AI applications. Latency is the delay that happens between the user query and the response. You may have observed that LLMs themselves have considerable latency before the final response is generated. Add to it the task of retrieval and augmentation, and the latency is bound to increase. Therefore, it is important to monitor how much time your RAG system takes from user input to response.

Ethical considerations are also at the forefront of generative AI adoption. For some RAG applications, it is important to measure the degree of *bias* and *toxicity* in the system responses. This is also influenced by the underlying data in the knowledge base. While it is not specific to RAG, it is important to evaluate the outputs for bias and toxicity.

Another aspect to check is the *robustness* of the system, that is, its ability to handle different types of queries. Some queries may be simple, while others may involve complex reasoning. Some queries may require comparing two pieces of information, while others may involve complex post-processing, like mathematical calculations. We will look at some types of queries when we discuss CRAG, a benchmark, in section 5.4.

Finally, it is important to mention that these are scores and abilities that approach RAG at the core technique level. RAG, after all, is a means to solving the end use case. Therefore, you may have to build a *use case-specific* evaluation criteria for your RAG system. For example, a question-answering system may use an exact match (EM) or F1 score as a metric, and a summarization service may use ROUGE scores. Modern search engines using RAG may look at user interaction metrics, accuracy of source attribution, and similar.

This is the main idea behind evaluating RAG pipelines. The quality scores and the abilities that we discussed before need to be measured and benchmarked. There are two critical enablers of RAG evaluations: frameworks and benchmarks.

Frameworks are tools designed to facilitate evaluation, offering automation of the evaluation process and data generation. They are used to streamline the evaluation process by providing a structured environment for testing different aspects of RAG systems. They are flexible and can be adapted to different datasets and metrics. We will discuss the popular evaluation frameworks in section 5.3.

Benchmarks are standardized datasets and their evaluation metrics used to measure the performance of RAG systems. Benchmarks provide a common ground for comparing different RAG approaches. They ensure consistency across the evaluations by considering a fixed set of tasks and their evaluation criteria. For example, HotpotQA focuses on multi-hop reasoning and retrieval capabilities using metrics such as Exact Match and F1 scores.

Benchmarks are used to establish a baseline for performance and identify strengths/weaknesses in specific tasks or domains. We will discuss a few benchmarks and their characteristics in section 5.4

Developers can use frameworks to integrate evaluation in their development process and use benchmarks to compare their development with established standards. The frameworks and benchmarks both calculate *metrics* that focus on retrieval and the RAG quality scores. We will begin our discussion about the metrics in the next section before moving on to the popular benchmarks and frameworks.

5.2 Evaluation metrics

Metrics quantify the assessment of the RAG system performance. We will classify the evaluation metrics into two broad groups:

- Retrieval metrics that are commonly used in information retrieval tasks
- RAG-specific metrics that have evolved as RAG has found more application

It is noteworthy that there are natural-language-generation-specific metrics such as BLEU, ROUGE, and METEOR that focus on fluency and measure relevance and semantic similarity. They play an important role in analyzing and benchmarking the performance of LLMs. This book discusses metrics specific to retrieval and RAG.

5.2.1 Retrieval metrics

The retrieval component of RAG can be evaluated independently to determine how well the retrievers are satisfying the user query. The primary retrieval evaluation metrics include accuracy, precision, recall, F1-score, mean reciprocal rank (MRR), mean average precision (MAP), and normalized discounted cumulative gain (nDCG).

ACCURACY

Accuracy is typically defined as the proportion of correct predictions (both true positives and true negatives) among the total number of cases examined. In the context of information retrieval, it could be interpreted as

$$\frac{\text{\# of relevant documents retrieved} + \text{\# of irrelevant documents not retrieved}}{\text{Total \# of documents in the knowledge base}}$$

Although accuracy is a simple, intuitive metric, it is not the primary metric for retrieval. In a large knowledge base, a majority of documents are usually irrelevant to any given query, which can lead to misleadingly high accuracy scores. It does not consider the ranking of the retrieved results.

PRECISION

Precision focuses on the quality of the retrieved results. It measures the proportion of retrieved documents relevant to the user query. It answers the question, "Of all the documents that were retrieved, how many were relevant?"

$$\text{Precision} = \frac{\text{Number of relevant documents retrieved}}{\text{Total number of documents retrieved}}$$

A higher precision means that the retriever is performing well and retrieving mostly relevant documents.

PRECISION@K

Precision@k is a variation of precision that measures the proportion of relevant documents among the top 'k' retrieved results. It is particularly important because it focuses on the top results rather than all the retrieved documents. For RAG, it is important because only the top results are most likely to be used for augmentation. For example, if you restrict your RAG system to use only the top five retrieved documents for context augmentation, Precision@5 will be the metric to calculate:

$$\text{Precision@k} = \frac{\text{Number of relevant documents retrieved in top 'k' documents}}{\text{Top 'k' documents retrieved}}$$

where 'k' is a chosen cut-off point. A precision@5 of .8 means that out of the top five retrieved documents, four were relevant.

Precision@k is also useful to compare systems when the total number of results retrieved may be different in different systems. However, the limitation is that the choice of 'k' can be arbitrary, and this metric doesn't look beyond the chosen 'k'.

RECALL

Recall focuses on the coverage that the retriever provides. It measures the proportion of the relevant documents retrieved from all the relevant documents in the corpus. It answers the question, "Of all the relevant documents, how many were retrieved?"

$$\text{Recall} = \frac{\text{Number of relevant documents retrieved}}{\text{Total number of relevant documents in the knowledge base}}$$

Note that, unlike precision, calculation of recall requires prior knowledge of the total number of relevant documents. This requirement can become challenging in large-scale systems, which have many documents in the knowledge base.

Like precision, recall also doesn't consider the ranking of the retrieved documents. It can also be misleading as retrieving all documents in the knowledge base will result in a perfect recall value. Figure 5.1 visualizes various precision and recall scenarios.

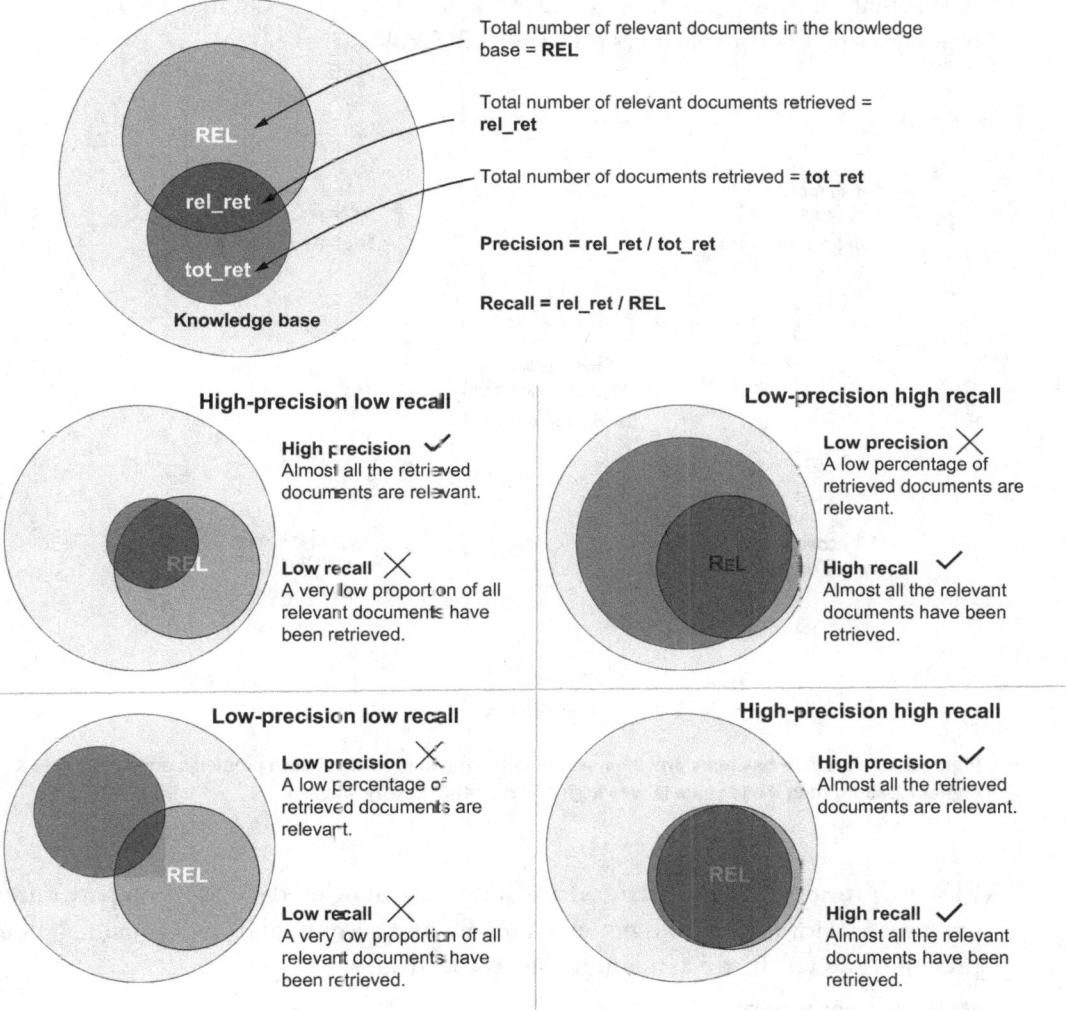

Figure 5.1 Precision and recall

F1-SCORE

F1-score is the harmonic mean of precision and recall. It provides a single metric that balances both the quality and coverage of the retriever:

$$F1 - \text{score} = 2 \times \frac{\text{Precision} \times \text{Recall}}{\text{Precision} + \text{Recall}}$$

The equation is such that the F1-score penalizes either variable having a low score; a high F1 score is only possible when both recall and precision values are high. This means that the score cannot be positively skewed by a single variable. Figure 5.2 illustrates how the F1-score balances precision and recall.

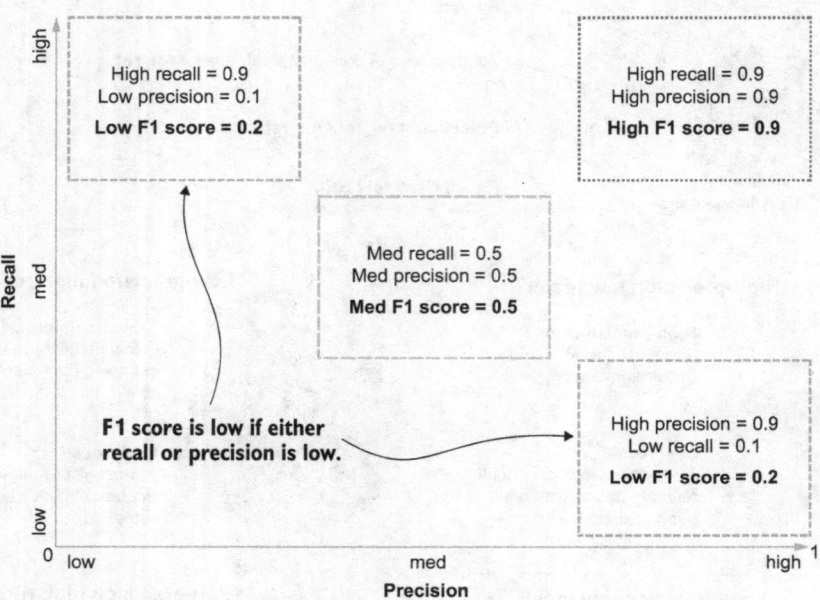

Figure 5.2   F1-score balances precision and recall. A medium value of both precision and recall gets a higher F1-score than if one value is very high and the other is very low.

F1-score provides a single, balanced measure that can be used to easily compare different systems. However, it does not take ranking into account and gives equal weight to precision and recall, which might not always be ideal.

MEAN RECIPROCAL RANK

Mean reciprocal rank, or MRR, is particularly useful in evaluating the rank of the relevant document. It measures the reciprocal of the ranks of the first relevant document in the list of results. MRR is calculated over a set of queries:

$$MRR = \frac{1}{N} \sum_{i=1}^{N} \frac{1}{\text{rank}_i}$$

where N is the total number of queries, and rank$_i$ is the rank of the first relevant document of the i-th query.

MRR is particularly useful when you're interested in how quickly the system can find a relevant document and consider the ranking of the results. However, since it doesn't look at anything beyond the first relevant result, it may not be useful when multiple relevant results are important. Figure 5.3 shows how the mean reciprocal rank is calculated.

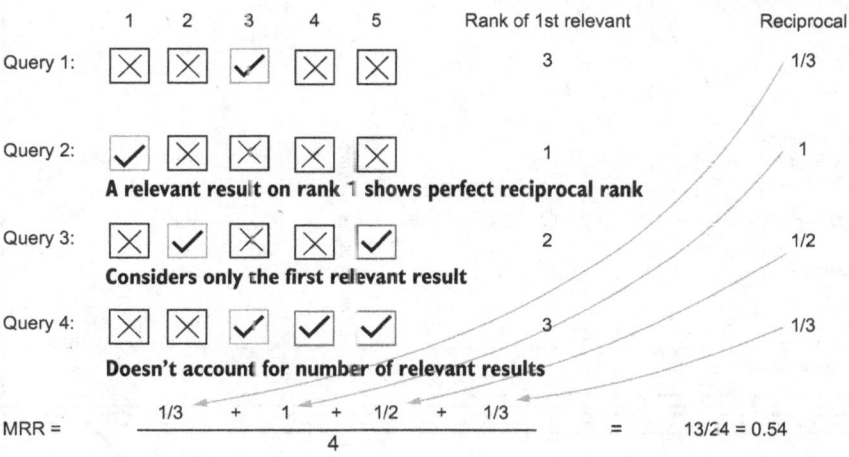

Figure 5.3   MRR considers the ranking but doesn't consider all the documents.

MEAN AVERAGE PRECISION

Mean average precision, or MAP, is a metric that combines precision and recall at different cut-off levels of 'k', that is, the cut-off number for the top results. It calculates a measure called average precision and then averages it across all queries:

$$\text{Average precision for a single query}(i) = \frac{1}{R_i} \sum_{k=1}^{n} \text{Precision@k} \times \text{rel@k}$$

where R^i is the number of relevant documents for query i, Precision@k is the precision at cut-off 'k', and rel@k is a binary flag indicating the relevance of the document at rank k.

Mean average precision is the mean of the average precision over all the N queries:

$$\text{MAP} = \frac{1}{N} \sum_{i=1}^{N} \text{Average precision}(i)$$

MAP provides a single measure of quality across recall levels. It is quite suitable when result ranking is important but complex to calculate. Let's look at an example MAP calculation in figure 5.4.

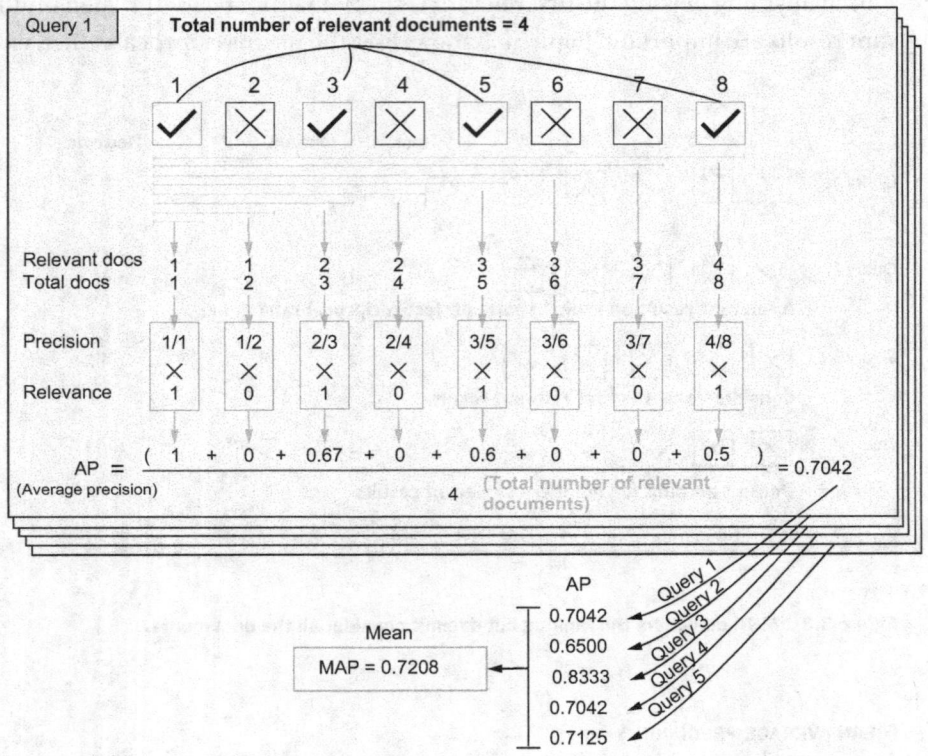

Figure 5.4   MAP considers all the retrieved documents and gives a higher score for better ranking

NORMALIZED DISCOUNTED CUMULATIVE GAIN

Normalized discounted cumulative gain (nDCG) evaluates the ranking quality by considering the position of relevant documents in the result list and assigning higher scores to relevant documents appearing earlier. It is particularly effective for scenarios where documents have varying degrees of relevance. To calculate discounted cumulative gain (DCG), each document in the retrieved list is assigned a relevance score, rel, and a discount factor reduces the weight of documents as their rank position increases:

$$DCG = \sum_{i=1}^{n} \frac{2^{rel_i} - 1}{\log_2(i + 1)}$$

where rel[i] is the graded relevance of the document at position I, and IDCG is the ideal DCG, which is the DCG for perfect ranking.

nDCG is calculated as the ratio between actual DCG and the IDCG:

$$nDCG = \frac{DCG}{IDCG}$$

Figure 5.5 shows an example of nDCG calculation.

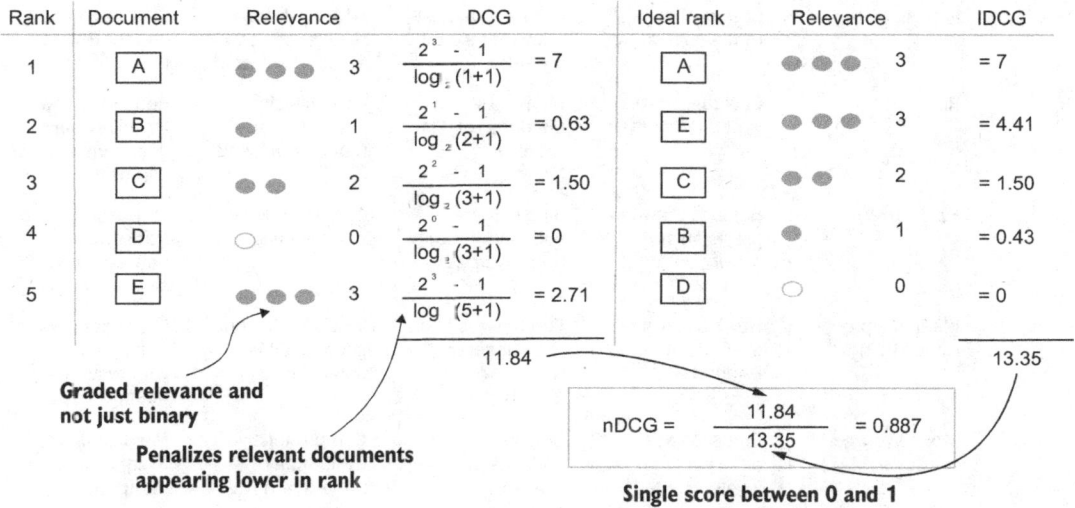

Figure 5.5 nDCG addresses degrees of relevance in documents and penalizes incorrect ranking.

nDCG is a complex metric to calculate. It requires documents to have a relevance score, which may lead to subjectivity, and the choice of the discount factor affects the values significantly, but it accounts for varying degrees of relevance in documents and gives more weight to higher-ranked items.

Retrieval systems are not just used in RAG but also in a variety of other application areas such as web and enterprise search engines, e-commerce product search and personalized recommendations, social media ad retrieval, archival systems, databases, virtual assistants, and more. The retrieval metrics help in assessing and improving the performance to effectively meet user needs. Table 5.1 summarizes different retrieval metrics.

Table 5.1   Retrieval metrics

Metric	What it measures	Strengths	Use cases	Considerations
Accuracy	Overall correctness of retrieval	Simple to understand; includes true negatives	General performance in balanced datasets	Can be misleading in imbalanced datasets; doesn't consider ranking
Precision	Quality of retrieved results	Easy to understand and calculate	General retrieval quality assessment	Doesn't consider ranking or completeness of retrieval
Precision@k	Quality of top k retrieved results	Focuses on most relevant results for RAG	When only top k results are used for augmentation	Choose k based on your RAG system's usage
Recall	Coverage of relevant documents	Measures completeness of retrieval	Assessing if important information is missed	Requires knowing all relevant documents in the corpus
F1-score	Balance between precision and recall	Single metric combining quality and coverage	Overall retrieval performance	May obscure tradeoffs between precision and recall
Mean reciprocal rank (MRR)	How quickly a relevant document is found	Emphasizes finding at least one relevant result quickly	When finding one good result is sufficient	Less useful when multiple relevant results are needed
Mean average precision (MAP)	Precision at different recall levels	Considers both precision and ranking	Comprehensive evaluation of ranked retrieval results	More complex to calculate and interpret
Normalized discounted cumulative gain (nDCG)	Ranking quality with graded relevance	Accounts for varying degrees of relevance and ranking	When documents have different levels of relevance	Requires relevance scoring for documents

Not all retrieval metrics are popular for evaluation. Often, the more complex metrics are overlooked for the sake of explainability. The usage of these metrics depends on the stage of improvement in the evolution of system performance you are in. For example, to start with, you may just be trying to improve precision, while at an evolved stage, you may be looking for better ranking.

While these metrics focus on retrieval in general, some metrics have been created specifically for RAG applications. These metrics focus on the three quality scores discussed in section 5.1.

5.2.2   *RAG-specific metrics*

The three quality scores used to evaluate RAG applications are context relevance, answer relevance, and answer faithfulness. These scores specifically answer the following three questions:

- Is the information retrieval relevant to the user query?
- Is the generated answer rooted in the retrieved information?
- Is the generated answer relevant to the user query?

Let's now take a look at each of these scores.

CONTEXT RELEVANCE

Context relevance evaluates how well the retrieved documents relate to the original query. The key aspects are topical alignment, information usefulness, and redundancy. There are human evaluation methods, as well as semantic similarity measures to calculate context relevance.

One such measure is employed by the Retrieval-Augmented Generation Assessment (RAGAs) framework (further discussed in section 5.3). The retrieved context should contain information only relevant to the query or the prompt. For context relevance, a metric S is estimated, where S is the number of sentences in the retrieved context relevant for responding to the query or the prompt:

$$\text{Context relevance} = \frac{\text{Number of relevant sentences in the retrieved context}}{\text{Total number of sentences in the retrieved context}} \quad (5)$$

Figure 5.6 is an illustrative example of high and low context relevance.

Query : Who won the 2023 ODI Cricket World Cup and when?	
Context 1: High context relevance	**Context 2: Low context relevance**
The 2023 Cricket World Cup, concluded on November 19, 2023, with Australia winning the tournament. The tournament took place in 10 different stadiums, in 10 cities across the country.	*The 2023 Cricket World Cup was the 13th edition of the Cricket World Cup. It was the first Cricket World Cup which India hosted solely. The tournament took place in 10 different stadiums. In the first semi-final India beat New Zealand, and in the second semi-final, Australia beat South Africa.*
Total sentences = 2	**Total sentences = 4**
Relevant sentences = 1	**Relevant sentences = 0**
Context relevance = 0.5 or 50%	**Context relevance = 0**

Figure 5.6 Context relevance evaluates the degree to which the retrieved information is relevant to the query.

The number of relevant sentences is also sometimes customized to the sum of similarity scores of each of the sentences with the query. Context relevance ensures that the generation component has access to appropriate information.

ANSWER FAITHFULNESS

Answer faithfulness is the measure of the extent to which the response is factually grounded in the retrieved context. Faithfulness ensures that the facts in the response do not contradict the context and can be traced back to the source. It also ensures that the LLM is not hallucinating. In the RAGAs framework, faithfulness first identifies the number of claims made in the response and calculates the proportion of those claims present in the context:

$$\text{Answer faithfulness} = \frac{\text{Number of generated claims in the context}}{\text{Total number of claims made in the generated response}}$$

Let's look at an example in figure 5.7

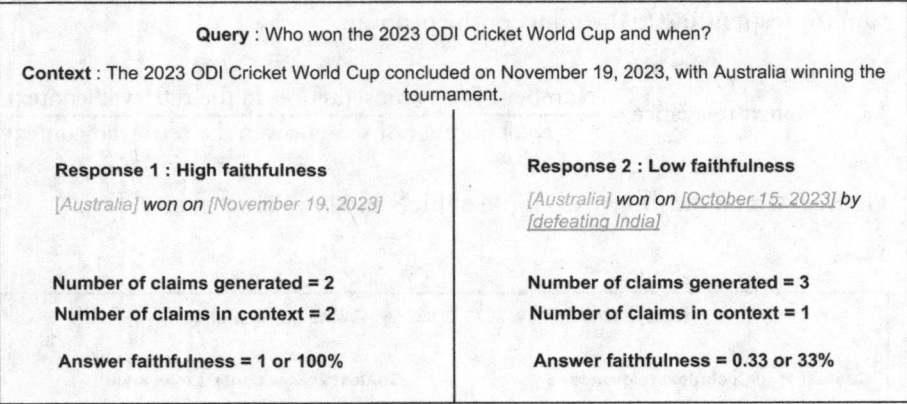

Figure 5.7   Answer faithfulness evaluates the closeness of the generated response to the retrieved context.

Faithfulness is not a complete measure of factual accuracy but only evaluates the groundedness to the context. An inverse metric for faithfulness is also the *hallucination rate,* which can calculate the proportion of generated claims in the response that are not present in the retrieved context.

Another related metric to faithfulness is *coverage*. Coverage measures the number of relevant claims in the context and calculates the proportion of relevant claims present in the generated response. It measures how much of the relevant information from the retrieved passages is included in the generated answer:

$$\text{Coverage} = \frac{\text{Total number of relevant claims from the context in the generated response}}{\text{Total number of relevant claims in the context}}$$

ANSWER RELEVANCE

Like context relevance measures the relevance of the retrieved context to the query, answer relevance is the measure of the extent to which the response is relevant to the query. This metric focuses on key aspects such as the system's ability to comprehend the query, the response being pertinent to the query, and the completeness of the response.

In RAGAs, for this metric, a response is generated for the initial query or prompt. To compute the score, the LLM is then prompted to generate questions for the generated response several times. The mean cosine similarity between these questions and the original one is then calculated. The concept is that if the answer addresses the initial question correctly, the LLM should generate questions from it that match the original question:

$$\text{Answer relevance} = \frac{1}{N} \sum_{i=1}^{N} \text{Similarity(UserQuery, LLMGeneratedQuery}[i])$$

where N is the number of queries generated by the LLM.

Note that answer relevance is not a measure of truthfulness but only of relevance. The response may or may not be factually accurate, but it may be relevant. Figure 5.8 is an illustration of the answer relevance calculation. Can you find the reason why the relevance is not very high? (Hint: The answer may have some irrelevant facts.) Answer relevance ensures that the RAG system provides useful and appropriate responses, enhancing user satisfaction and the system's practical utility.

TRADEOFFS AND OTHER CONSIDERATIONS

These three metrics and their derivatives form the core of RAG quality evaluation. Furthermore, these metrics are interconnected and sometimes involve tradeoffs. High context relevance usually leads to better faithfulness, as the system has access to more pertinent information. However, high faithfulness doesn't always guarantee high answer relevance. A system might faithfully reproduce information from the retrieved passages but fail to directly address the query. Optimizing for answer relevance without considering faithfulness might lead to responses that seem appropriate but contain hallucinated or incorrect information.

We have discussed quite a few metrics in this section. Effective interpretation of these metrics is crucial for performance improvement. As creators of RAG systems, you should use these metrics to compare with similar systems. You can also look at consistent trends to identify the strengths and weaknesses of your system. A low-precision high-recall system may indicate that your system is retrieving a lot of documents, and you may need to make your retriever more selective. A low-precision low-recall system points out fundamental problems with retrieval, and you may need to reassess the indexing pipeline itself. The same problem may be indicated by a low MAP or a low context-relevance score. Similarly, a low MRR or a low nDCG value may indicate a problem with

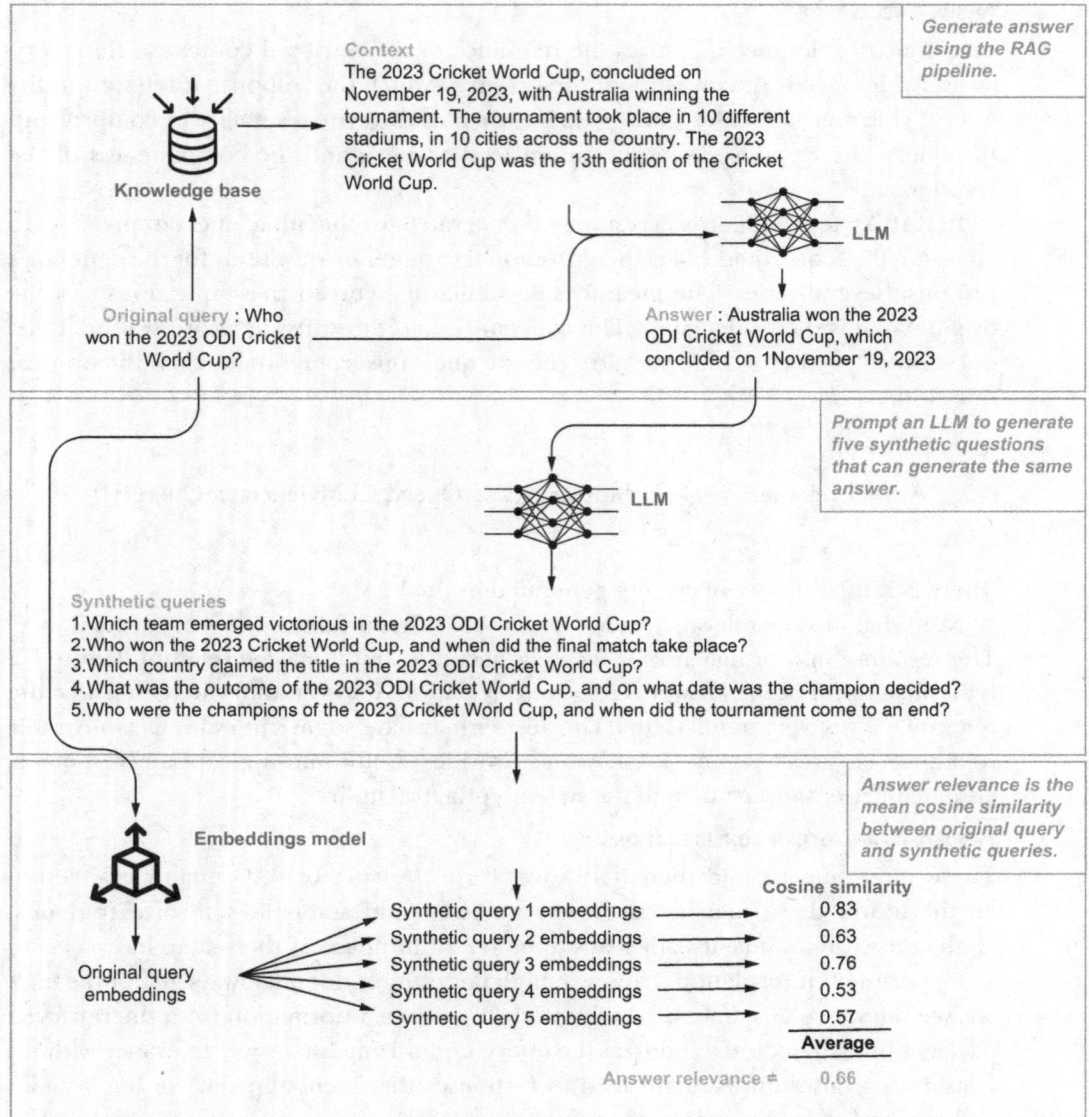

Figure 5.8   Answer relevance is calculated as the mean of cosine similarity between the original and synthetic questions.

the ranking algorithm of the retriever. To address low-answer faithfulness or low-answer relevance, you may need to improve your prompts or fine-tune the LLM.

There may also exist some tradeoffs that you will need to balance. Improving precision often reduces recall and vice-versa. Highly relevant but brief contexts may lead to incomplete answers, and high answer faithfulness may sometimes come at the cost of answer relevance.

The relative importance of each metric will depend on your use case and user requirements. You may need to include other metrics specific to your downstream use case, such as summarization to measure conciseness, and chatbots to emphasize conversation coherence.

Developers can code these metrics from scratch and integrate them in the development and deployment process of their RAG system. However, you'll find evaluation frameworks that are readily available quite handy. We discuss three popular frameworks in the next section.

Human evaluations and ground truth data

Most of the metrics we discussed talk about a concept of relevant documents. For example, precision is calculated as the number of relevant documents retrieved, divided by the total number of retrieved documents. The question that arises is, how does one establish that a document is relevant?

The simple answer is a human evaluation approach. A subject matter expert looks at the documents and determines the relevance. Human evaluation brings in subjectivity, and therefore, human evaluations are done by a panel of experts rather than an individual. But human evaluations are restrictive from a scale and a cost perspective.

Any data that can reliably establish relevance becomes extremely useful consequently. Ground truth is information known to be real or true. In RAG, and the generative AI domain in general, ground truth is a prepared set of prompt–context–response or question–context–response examples, akin to labeled data in supervised machine learning parlance. Ground truth data created for your knowledge base can be used for the evaluation of your RAG system.

How does one go about creating the ground truth data? It can be viewed as a one-time exercise where a group of experts creates this data. However, generating hundreds of QCA (question–context–answer) samples from documents manually can be a time-consuming and labor-intensive task. Additionally, if the knowledge base is dynamic, the ground truth data will also need updates. Questions created by humans may face challenges in achieving the necessary level of complexity for a comprehensive evaluation, potentially affecting the overall quality of the assessment.

LLMs can be used to address these challenges. Synthetic data generation uses LLMs to generate diverse questions and answers from the documents in the knowledge base. LLMs can be prompted to create questions such as simple questions, multi-context questions, conditional questions, reasoning questions, and similar using the documents from the knowledge base as context.

5.3 Frameworks

Frameworks provide a structured approach to RAG evaluations. They can be used to automate the evaluation process. Some go beyond and assist in the synthetic ground truth data generation. While new evaluation frameworks continue to be introduced, there are two popular ones that we discuss here:

- RAGAs (Retrieval-Augmented Generation Assessment)
- ARES (Automated RAG Evaluation System)

5.3.1   RAGAs

Retrieval-Augmented Generation Assessment, or RAGAs, is a framework developed by Exploding Gradients that assesses the retrieval and generation components of RAG systems without relying on extensive human annotations. RAGAs

- Synthetically generate a test dataset that can be used to evaluate a RAG pipeline.
- Use metrics to measure the performance of the pipeline.
- Monitor the quality of the application in production.

We will continue with our example of the Wikipedia page of the 2023 Cricket World Cup, but we first create a synthetic test dataset using RAGAs and then use the RAGAs metrics to evaluate the performance of the RAG pipeline we created in chapters 3 and 4.

SYNTHETIC TEST DATASET GENERATION (GROUND TRUTHS)

Section 5.2 pointed out that ground truths data is necessary to calculate evaluation metrics for assessing the quality of RAG pipelines. While this data can be manually curated, RAGAs provides the functionality of generating this dataset from the documents in the knowledge base.

RAGAs does this using an LLM. It analyses the documents in the knowledge base and uses an LLM to generate seed questions from chunks in the knowledge base. These questions are based on the document chunks from the knowledge base. These chunks act as the context for the questions. Another LLM is used to generate the answer to these questions. This is how it generates a question–context–answer data based on the documents in the knowledge base. RAGAs also has an evolver module that creates more difficult questions (e.g., multi-context, reasoning, and conditional) for a more comprehensive evaluation. Figure 5.9 illustrates the process of synthetic data generation using RAGAs.

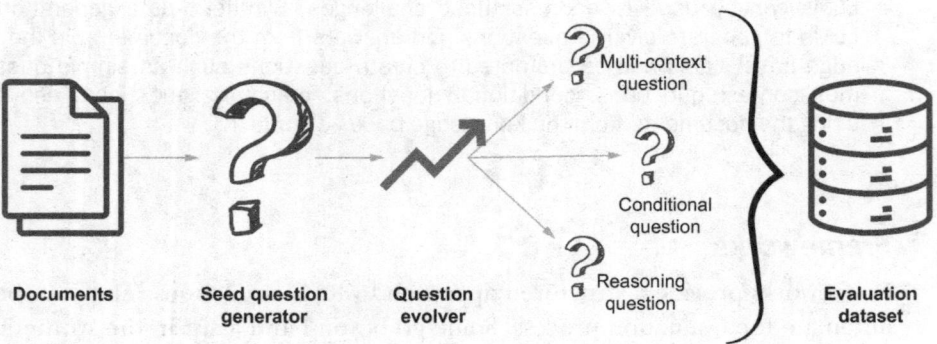

Figure 5.9   Synthetic ground truths data generation using RAGAs

To evaluate our RAG pipeline, let's recreate the documents from the Wikipedia page like we did in chapter 3. Note that we will have to install the packages used in the previous chapters to continue with the following code:

```
#Importing the AsyncHtmlLoader
from langchain_community.document_loaders import AsyncHtmlLoader

#This is the URL of the Wikipedia page on the 2023 Cricket World Cup
url="https://en.wikipedia.org/wiki/2023_Cricket_World_Cup"

#Instantiating the AsyncHtmlLoader
loader = AsyncHtmlLoader (url)

#Loading the extracted information
html_data = loader.load()

from langchain_community.document_transformers import Html2TextTransformer

#Instantiate the Html2TextTransformer function
html2text = Html2TextTransformer()


#Call transform_documents
html_data_transformed = html2text.transform_documents(html_data)
```

The `html_data_transformed` contains the necessary document format of the Wikipedia page. We will use RAGAs library to generate the dataset from these documents. For that, we will first need to install the RAGAs library:

```
%pip install ragas== 0.2.13

# Import necessary libraries
from ragas.llms import LangchainLLMWrapper
from ragas.embeddings import LangchainEmbeddingsWrapper
from ragas.testset import TestsetGenerator
from langchain_openai import ChatOpenAI, OpenAIEmbeddings

# Instantiate the models
generator_llm =
    LangchainLLMWrapper(
        ChatOpenAI(model="gpt-4o-mini")
        )

generator_embeddings =
    LangchainEmbeddingsWrapper(
        OpenAIEmbeddings(model="text-embedding-3-small")
        )

# Create the TestsetGenerator
generator =
    TestsetGenerator(
        llm=generator_llm,
        embedding_model=generator_embeddings
```

```
    )

# Call the generator
testset =
    generator.generate_with_langchain_docs
        (
                html_data_transformed,
        test_size=20,
)
```

The `testset` that we created contains 20 questions based on our document, along with the chunk of the document that the question was based on, and the ground truth answer. A screenshot of the dataset is shown in figure 5.10.

	user_input	reference_contexts	reference	synthesizer_name
0	Why India host Cricket World Cup?	[Cricket World Cup; while India had served as ...	India is hosting the Cricket World Cup solely ...	single_hop_specifc_query_synthesizer
1	How did the BCCI contribute to the 2023 Cricke...	[Cricket World Cup; while India had served as ...	The BCCI provided funding for renovations and ...	single_hop_specifc_query_synthesizer
2	What is the seating capacity of HPCA	[Chennai | M. A. Chidambaram Stadium | 38,200 ...	HPCA Stadium in Dharamshala has a seating	single_hop_specifc_query_synthesizer

Figure 5.10 Synthetic test data generated using RAGAs

We will use this dataset to evaluate our RAG pipeline.

RECREATING THE RAG PIPELINE

From the created test dataset, we use the `question` and the `ground_truth` information. We pass the questions to our RAG pipeline and generate answers. We compare these answers with the `ground_truth` to calculate the evaluation metrics. First, we recreate our RAG pipeline. Again, it is important to note that we will have to install the packages we used in the previous chapters to continue with the code:

```
# Import FAISS class from vectorstore library
from langchain_community.vectorstores import FAISS
# Import OpenAIEmbeddings & ChatOpenAI from the library
from langchain_openai import OpenAIEmbeddings, ChatOpenAI

def rag_function(query, db_path, index_name):

# Instantiate the embeddings object
```

```
embeddings=OpenAIEmbeddings(model="text-embedding-3-small")

# Load the database stored in the local directory

db=FAISS.load_local(
folder_path=db_path,
index_name=index_name,
embeddings=embeddings,
allow_dangerous_deserialization=True
)

# Ranking the chunks in descending order of similarity and selecting the top
2 queries

retrieved_docs = db.similarity_search(query, k=2)

# Keeping text of top 2 retrieved chunks

retrieved_context=[ retrieved_docs[0].page_content
+retrieved_docs[1].page_content]

# Creating the prompt

augmented_prompt=f"""

Given the context below, answer the question.

Question: {query}

Context : {retrieved_context}

Remember to answer only based on the context
provided and not from any other source.

If the question cannot be answered based
on the provided context, say I don't know.

"""

# Instantiate the LLM
llm = ChatOpenAI(
     model="gpt-4o-mini",
    temperature=0,
    max_tokens=None,
    timeout=None,
    max_retries=2
    )

# Create message to send to the LLM

messages=[("human",augmented_prompt)]


# Make the API call passing the message to the LLM
```

```
response = llm.invoke(messages)

# Extract the answer from the response object

answer=response.content

return retrieved_context, answer
```

We can try this pipeline to generate answers.

```
# Location of the stored vector index created by the indexing pipeline
db_path='../../Assets/Data'

# User Question
query="Who won the 2023 cricket world cup?"

# Index Name
index_name="CWC_index"

# Calling the RAG function
rag_function(query, db_path, index_name)
```

Now that we have the RAG pipeline function, we can evaluate this pipeline using the questions that have been synthetically generated.

EVALUATIONS

We first generate answers to the questions in the synthetic test data using our RAG pipeline. We then compare the answers to the ground truth answers. We first generate the answers:

```
# Create Lists for Questions and Ground Truths from testset
sample_queries =
    dataset.to_pandas()['user_input'].to_list()

expected_responses=
    dataset.to_pandas()['reference'].to_list()


# Iterate through the testset to generate responses to questions

dataset_to_eval=[]

for query, reference in zip(sample_queries,expected_responses):

# Call the RAG function
rag_context, rag_answer=rag_function(query,db_path,index_name)

# Create a dictionary of question, answer, context, and ground truth
dataset_to_eval.append(
        {
                "user_input":query,
                "retrieved_contexts":relevant_docs,
                "response":response,
```

```
                    "reference":reference
        }
            )
```

For RAGAs, the evaluation set needs to be in the `Dataset` format:

```
# Import the EvaluationDataset library
from ragas import EvaluationDataset

evaluation_dataset = EvaluationDataset.from_list(dataset_to_eval)
```

Now that we have the complete evaluation dataset, we can invoke the metrics:

```
#Import all the libraries
from ragas import evaluate

from ragas.metrics import (
        LLMContextRecall,
Faithfulness,
FactualCorrectness,
AnswerCorrectness,
ResponseRelevancy)


#Set the judge LLM for evaluation

evaluator_llm =
    LangchainLLMWrapper(
        ChatOpenAI(model="gpt-4o-mini")
        )

# Calculate the metrics for the dataset

result = evaluate(
dataset=evaluation_dataset,
metrics=[
LLMContextRecall(),
Faithfulness(),
AnswerCorrectness(),
ResponseRelevancy(),
FactualCorrectness()],
llm=evaluator_llm)
```

You can also check the official documentation of RAGAs for more information (https://docs.ragas.io/en/stable/). RAGAs calculates a bunch of metrics that are useful for assessing the quality of the RAG pipeline. RAGAs uses an LLM to do this, somewhat subjective, task. For example, to calculate faithfulness for a given question–context–answer record, RAGAs first breaks down the answer into simple statements. Then, for each statement, it asks the LLM whether the statement can be inferred from the context. The LLM provides a 0 or 1 response along with a reason. This process is repeated a couple of times. Finally, faithfulness is calculated as the proportion of statements judged by the LLM as faithful (i.e., 1). Several other metrics are calculated using this LLM-based approach. This approach, where an LLM is used in evaluating a task, is also popularly called *LLM as a judge* approach. An important point to note here is that the accuracy of this evaluation is also dependent on the quality of the LLM being used as the judge.

5.3.2   *Automated RAG evaluation system*

Automated RAG evaluation system, or ARES, is a framework developed by researchers at Stanford University and Databricks. Like RAGAs, ARES uses an LLM as a judge approach for evaluations. Both request a language model to classify answer relevance, context relevance, and faithfulness for a given query. However, there are some differences:

- RAGAs relies on heuristically written prompts sent to the LLM for evaluation. ARES, in contrast, trains a classifier using a language model.
- RAGAs aggregates the responses from the LLM to arrive at a score. ARES provides confidence intervals for the scores using a framework called Prediction-Powered Inference (PPI).
- RAGAs generates a simple synthetic question–context–answer dataset for evaluation from the documents. ARES generate synthetic datasets comprising both positive and negative examples of query–passage–answer triples.

ARES requires more data than RAGAs. To use ARES, you need the following three datasets:

- *In-domain passage set*—This is a collection of passages relevant to the specific domain being evaluated. The passages should be suitable for generating queries and answers. In our case, it will be the documents that we created from the Wikipedia article.
- *Human preference validation set*—A minimum of approximately 150 annotated data points is required. This set is used to validate the preferences of human annotators regarding the relevance of the generated query-passage–answer triples.
- *Few-shot examples*—At least five examples of in-domain queries and answers are needed. These examples help prompt the LLMs during the synthetic data generation process.

The need for a human-preference validation set and fine-tuning of language models for classification makes applying ARES more complex. The application of ARES is out of the scope of this book. However, ARES is a robust framework. It provides a detailed analysis of system performance with statistical confidence intervals, making it suitable for in-depth RAG system evaluations. RAGAs promises a faster evaluation cycle without reliance on human annotations. More details on the ARES application can be found in the official GitHub repository (https://github.com/stanford-futuredata/ARES).

While RAGAs and ARES have gained popularity, there are other frameworks, such as TruLens, DeepEval, and RAGChecker, that have also gotten acceptance amongst RAG developers.

Frameworks provide a standardized method of automating the evaluation of your RAG pipelines. Your choice of the evaluation framework should depend on your use case requirements. For quick and easy evaluations that are widely understood, RAGAs may be your choice. For robustness across diverse domains and question types, ARES might suit better. Most of the proprietary service providers (vector DBs, LLMs, etc.) have their evaluation features you may use. You can also develop your metrics.

Next, we look at benchmarks. Benchmarks are used to compare competing RAG systems with one another.

5.4 Benchmarks

Benchmarks provide a standard point of reference to evaluate the quality and performance of a system. RAG benchmarks are a set of standardized tasks, and a dataset used to compare the efficiency of different RAG systems in retrieving relevant information and generating accurate responses. There has been a surge in creating benchmarks since 2023, when RAG started gaining popularity, but there have been benchmarks on question-answering tasks that were introduced before that. Benchmarks such as Stanford Question Answering Dataset (SQuAD), WikiQA, Natural Question (NQ), and HotpotQA are open domain question-answering datasets that primarily evaluate the retriever component using metrics such as Exact Match (EM) and F1-score. BEIR or benchmarking information retrieval is a comprehensive, heterogeneous benchmark based on 9 IR tasks and 19 question–answer datasets. This section discusses three of the popular RAG-specific benchmarks and their evaluation.

5.4.1 RGB

Retrieval-augmented generation benchmark (RGB) was introduced in a December 2023 paper (https://arxiv.org/pdf/2309.01431). It comprises 600 base questions and 400 additional questions, evenly split between English and Chinese. The corpus was constructed using a multistep process that involved collecting recent news articles, generating questions and answers using ChatGPT, retrieving relevant web pages through Google's API, and selecting the most pertinent text chunks using a dense retrieval model. It is a benchmark that focuses on four key abilities of a RAG system: noise robustness, negative rejection, information integration, and counterfactual robustness, as illustrated in figure 5.11.

RGB focuses on the following metrics for evaluation:

- *Accuracy*—Used for noise robustness and information integration. It is based on the exact matching of the generated text with the correct answer.
- *Rejection rate*—Used for negative rejection. It is measured by exact matching of the model's output with a specific rejection phrase. The rejection rate is also

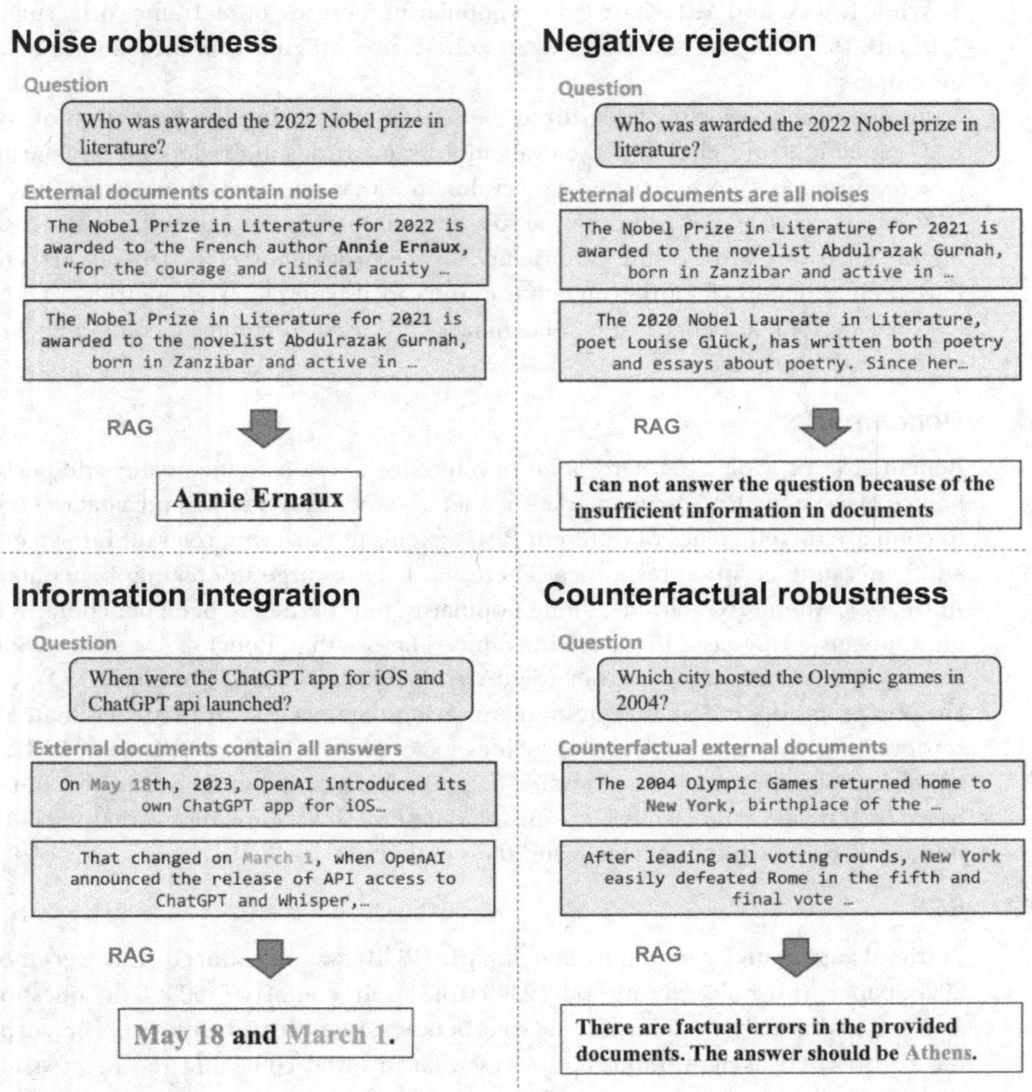

Noise robustness

Question

> Who was awarded the 2022 Nobel prize in literature?

External documents contain noise

> The Nobel Prize in Literature for 2022 is awarded to the French author **Annie Ernaux**, "for the courage and clinical acuity …

> The Nobel Prize in Literature for 2021 is awarded to the novelist Abdulrazak Gurnah, born in Zanzibar and active in …

RAG ⬇

> **Annie Ernaux**

Negative rejection

Question

> Who was awarded the 2022 Nobel prize in literature?

External documents are all noises

> The Nobel Prize in Literature for 2021 is awarded to the novelist Abdulrazak Gurnah, born in Zanzibar and active in …

> The 2020 Nobel Laureate in Literature, poet Louise Glück, has written both poetry and essays about poetry. Since her…

RAG ⬇

> **I can not answer the question because of the insufficient information in documents**

Information integration

Question

> When were the ChatGPT app for iOS and ChatGPT api launched?

External documents contain all answers

> On May 18th, 2023, OpenAI introduced its own ChatGPT app for iOS…

> That changed on March 1, when OpenAI announced the release of API access to ChatGPT and Whisper,…

RAG ⬇

> **May 18 and March 1.**

Counterfactual robustness

Question

> Which city hosted the Olympic games in 2004?

Counterfactual external documents

> The 2004 Olympic Games returned home to New York, birthplace of the …

> After leading all voting rounds, New York easily defeated Rome in the fifth and final vote …

RAG ⬇

> **There are factual errors in the provided documents. The answer should be Athens.**

Figure 5.11 Four abilities required of RAG systems. Source: Benchmarking Large Language Models in Retrieval-Augmented Generation by Chen et al., https://arxiv.org/pdf/2309.0143.

evaluated using ChatGPT to determine whether the responses contain rejection information.

- *Error detection rate*—Used for counterfactual robustness. It is measured by exact matching of the model's output with a specific error-detection phrase and is also evaluated using ChatGPT.

- *Error correction rate*—Used for counterfactual robustness. It measures whether the model can provide the correct answer after identifying errors.

You can use the GitHub repository to implement RGB (https://github.com/chen700564/RGB).

MULTI-HOP RAG

Curated by researchers at HKUST, multi-hop RAG contains 2556 queries, with evidence for each query distributed across two to four documents. The queries also involve document metadata, reflecting complex scenarios commonly found in real-world RAG applications. It contains four types of queries:

- *Inference*—Synthesizing information across multiple sources (e.g., Which report discusses the supply chain risk of Apple—the 2019 annual report or the 2020 annual report?)
- *Comparison*—Comparing facts from different sources (e.g., Did Netflix or Google report higher revenue for the year 2023?)
- *Temporal*—Analyzing the temporal ordering of events (e.g., e.g. Did Apple introduce the AirTag tracking device before or after the launch of the 5th generation iPad Pro?)
- *Null*—Queries not answerable from the knowledge base

Full implementation code is available at https://github.com/yixuantt/MultiHop-RAG.

CRAG

Comprehensive RAG benchmark (CRAG), curated by Meta and HKUST, is a factual question-answering benchmark of 4,409 question–answer pairs and mock APIs to simulate web and knowledge graph (KG) search. It contains eight types (simple, conditions, comparison questions, aggregation questions, multi-hop questions, set queries, post-processing-heavy questions, and false-premise questions, as illustrated in figure 5.12) of queries across five domains (finance, sports, music, movie, and open domain).

For each question in the evaluation set, CRAG labels the answer with one of four classes:

- *Perfect*—The response correctly answers the user's question and contains no hallucinated content (scored as +1).
- *Acceptable*—The response provides a useful answer to the user's question but may contain minor errors that do not harm the usefulness of the answer (scored as +0.5).
- *Missing*—The response is "I don't know", "I'm sorry I can't find ...", a system error such as an empty response, or a request from the system to clarify the original question (scored as 0).
- *Incorrect*—The response provides wrong or irrelevant information to answer the user's question (scored as –1).

Question type	Definition
Simple	Questions asking for simple facts that are unlikely to change overtime, such as the birth date of a person or the authors of a book
Simple w. condition	Questions asking for simple facts with some given conditions, such as stock prices on a certain date or a director's recent movies in a certain genre
Set	Questions that expect a set of entities or objects as the answer (e.g., "What are the continents in the southern hemisphere?")
Comparison	Questions that compare two entities (e.g., "Who started performing earlier, Adele or Ed Sheeran?")
Aggregation	Questions that require aggregation of retrieval results to answer (e.g., "How many Oscar awards did Meryl Streep win?")
Multi-hop	Questions that require chaining multiple pieces of information to compose the answer (e.g., "Who acted in Ang Lee's latest movie?")
Post-processing heavy	Questions that need reasoning or processing of the retrieved information to obtain the answer (e.g., "How many days did Thurgood Marshall serve as a Supreme Court justice?")
False premise	Questions that have a false preposition or assumption (e.g., "What's the name of Taylor Swift's rap album before she transitioned to pop?" (Taylor Swift has not yet released any rap albums.)

Figure 5.12   Eight question types in CRAG

For automatic evaluation, CRAG classifies an answer as perfect if it exactly matches the ground truth. If not, then it asks an LLM to do the classification. It uses two LLM evaluators. You can read more about CRAG at https://arxiv.org/pdf/2406.04744.

Other noteworthy benchmark datasets are MedRAG (https://github.com/Teddy -XiongGZ/MedRAG), which focuses on Medical Information, CRUD-RAG (https:// arxiv.org/pdf/2401.17043), which focuses on the Chinese language, and FeB4RAG (https://arxiv.org/abs/2402.11891), which focuses on federated search. If you're developing an LLM application that has accurate and contextual generation as its core proposition, you'll be able to communicate the quality of your application by showing how it performs on different benchmarks. Table 5.2 compares the different benchmarks.

Table 5.2   RAG benchmarks

Benchmark	Dataset	Task	Metrics	Applicability
SQuAD	Stanford Question Answering Dataset	Open domain QA	Exact match (EM), F1-score	General QA tasks, model evaluation on comprehension accuracy
Natural questions	Real Google search queries	Open domain QA	F1-score	Real-world QA, information retrieval from large corpora

Table 5.2   RAG benchmarks (*continued*)

Benchmark	Dataset	Task	Metrics	Applicability
HotpotQA	Wikipedia-based QA	Multi-hop QA	EM, F1-score	QA involving multiple documents, complex reasoning tasks
BEIR	Multiple datasets	Information retrieval	nDCG@10	Comprehensive IR model evaluation across multiple domains
RGB	News articles, ChatGPT-generated QA	Robust QA	Accuracy, rejection rate, error detection rate, error correction rate	Robustness and reliability of RAG systems
Multi-hop RAG	HKUST-curated queries	Complex QA	Various	RAG applications requiring multi-source synthesis
CRAG	Multiple sources (finance, sports, music, etc.)	Factual QA	Four-class evaluation (perfect, acceptable, missing, and incorrect)	Evaluating factual QA with diverse question types

We have looked frameworks that help in automating the calculation of evaluation metrics and benchmarks that enable comparisons across different implementations and approaches. Frameworks will assist you in improving the performance of your system, and benchmarks will facilitate comparing it with other systems available in the market.

However, as with any evolving field, there are some limitations and challenges to consider. The next section examines these limitations and discusses best practices that have emerged to address them, ensuring a more holistic and nuanced approach to RAG evaluation.

5.5   *Limitations and best practices*

There has been a lot of progress made in the frameworks and benchmarks used for RAG evaluation. The complexity in evaluation arises due to the interplay between the retrieval and generation components. In practice, there's a significant reliance on human judgements, which are subjective and difficult to scale. What follows are a few common challenges and some guidelines to navigate them.

LACK OF STANDARDIZED METRICS

There's no consensus on what the best metrics are to evaluate RAG systems. Precision, recall, and F1-score are commonly measured for retrieval but do not fully capture the nuances of generative response. Similarly, commonly used generation metrics such as BLEU, ROUGE, and similar do not fully capture the context awareness required for RAG. Using RAG-specific metrics such as answer relevance, context relevance, and faithfulness for evaluation brings in the necessary nuances required for RAG evaluation. However, even for these metrics, there's no standard way of calculation and each framework brings in its methodology.

Best practice. Compare the results on RAG specific metrics from different frameworks. Sometimes, it may be warranted to change the calculation method with respect to the use case.

OVERRELIANCE ON LLM AS A JUDGE

The evaluation of RAG-specific metrics (in RAGAs, ARES, etc.) relies on using an LLM as a judge. An LLM is prompted or fine-tuned to classify a response as relevant or not. This adds to the complexity of the LLMs' ability to do this task. It may be possible that the LLM may not be very accurate in judging for your specific documents and knowledge bases. Another problem that arises is that of self-reference. It is possible that if the judge LLM is the same as the generation LLM in your system, you will get a more favorable evaluation.

Best practice. Sample a few results from the judge LLM and evaluate whether the results are in line with commonly understood business practice. To avoid the self-reference problem, make sure to use a judge LLM different from the generation LLM. It may also help if you use multiple judge LLMs and aggregate their results.

LACK OF USE CASE SUBJECTIVITY

Most frameworks have a generalized approach to evaluation. They may not capture the subjective nature of the task relevant to your use case (content generation versus chatbot versus question-answering, etc.)

Best practice. Focus on use-case-specific metrics to assess quality, coherence, usefulness, and similar. Incorporate human judgements in your workflow with techniques such as user feedback, crowd-sourcing, or expert ratings.

BENCHMARKS ARE STATIC

Most benchmarks are static and do not account for the evolving nature of information. RAG systems need to adapt to real-time information changes, which are not currently tested effectively. There is a lack of evaluation for how well RAG models learn and adapt to new data over time. Most benchmarks are domain-agnostic, which may not reflect the performance of RAG systems in your specific domain.

Best practice. Use a benchmark that is tailored to your domain. The static nature of benchmarks is limiting. Do not overly rely on benchmarks, and augment the use of benchmarks with regularly updating data.

SCALABILITY AND COST

Evaluating large-scale RAG systems is more complex than evaluating basic RAG pipelines. It requires significant computational resources. Benchmarks and frameworks also generally do not account for metrics such as latency and efficiency, which are critical for real-world applications.

Best practice. Employ careful sampling of test cases for evaluation. Incorporate workflows to measure latency and efficiency.

Apart from these, you should also carefully consider the aspects of bias and toxicity, focusing on information integration and negative rejection, which the frameworks do not evaluate well. It is also important to keep an eye on how these evaluation frameworks and benchmarks evolve.

In this chapter, we comprehensively examined the evaluation metrics, frameworks, and benchmarks that will help you evaluate your RAG pipelines. We used RAGAs to evaluate the pipeline that we have been building.

Until now, we have looked at building and evaluating a simple RAG system. This also marks the second part 2 of this book. You are now familiar with the creation of the RAG knowledge brain using the indexing pipeline, enabling real-time interaction using the generation pipeline and evaluating your RAG system using frameworks and benchmarks.

In the next part, we will move toward discussing the production aspects of RAG systems. In chapter 6, we will look at strategies and advanced techniques to improve our RAG pipeline, which should also reflect in better evaluation metrics. In chapter 7, we will look at the LLMOps stack that enables RAG in production.

Summary

RAG evaluation fundamentals

- RAG evaluation assesses how well systems reduce hallucinations and ground responses in the provided context.
- Three key quality scores for RAG evaluation are context relevance, answer faithfulness, and answer relevance.
- Four critical abilities required of RAG systems include noise robustness, negative rejection, information integration, and counterfactual robustness.
- Additional considerations include latency, robustness, bias, and toxicity of responses.
- Custom use-case-specific metrics should be developed to evaluate performance.

Evaluation metrics

- Retrieval metrics include precision, recall, F1-score, mean reciprocal rank (MRR), mean average precision (MAP), and normalized discounted cumulative gain (nDCG).
- Accuracy, precision, recall, and F1-score do not consider the ranking order of the results.
- RAG-specific metrics focus on context relevance, answer faithfulness, and answer relevance.
- Human evaluations and ground truth data play a crucial role in RAG assessment.

Evaluation frameworks

- Frameworks such as RAGAs and ARES automate the evaluation process and assist in synthetic data generation.

- RAGAs is an easy-to-implement framework that can be used for quick evaluation of RAG pipelines.

- ARES uses a more complex approach, including classifier training and confidence interval calculations.

Benchmarks

- Benchmarks provide standardized datasets and metrics for comparing different RAG implementations on specific tasks.

- Popular benchmarks such as SQuAD, natural questions, HotpotQA, and BEIR focus on retrieval quality.

- Recent benchmarks such as RGB, multi-hop RAG, and CRAG are more holistic from a RAG perspective.

- Benchmarks focus on different aspects of RAG performance, such as multi-hop reasoning or specific domains.

Limitations and best practices

- Challenges in RAG evaluation include lack of standardized metrics, overreliance on LLMs as judges, and static nature of benchmarks.

- Best practices include using multiple frameworks, incorporating use-case-specific metrics, and regularly updating evaluation data.

- Balancing automated metrics with human judgment and considering use-case-specific requirements is crucial.

- The field of RAG evaluation is evolving, with new frameworks and benchmarks constantly emerging.

- Developers should stay informed about new developments and adapt their evaluation strategies accordingly.

Part 3

RAG in production

You must be confident by now in building and evaluating a core RAG pipeline. Applications such as "chat with your PDF" or question-answering systems based on web pages should no longer be a mystery. This part of the book will guide you in improving your RAG pipeline and also lay out a blueprint for the layers required to build a production-ready RAG system.

In chapter 6, you'll be able to try out different techniques for improving the basic RAG pipeline into a more advanced one. You'll get to know the techniques that improve RAG in three different stages—before, during, and after retrieval. You'll also learn about modularity and how modern RAG systems are made up of replaceable components.

Chapter 7 discusses the operations stack for RAG. You will learn about the critical layers without which any RAG system will fail, the essential layers that improve system performance, and the enhancement layers that focus on usability, scalability, and efficiency of the system.

By the end of this part, you should have the knowledge and skills to start building simple RAG systems and putting them into production. This is also the stage at which you are ready to explore deeper nuances and variations of RAG systems.

Progression of RAG
systems: Naïve, advanced,
and modular RAG

This chapter covers

- Limitations of the naïve RAG approach
- Advanced RAG strategies and techniques
- Modular patterns in RAG

In the first two parts of this book, you learned about the utility of retrieval-augmented generation (RAG), along with the development and evaluation of a basic RAG system. The basic, or the naïve RAG approach that we have discussed is, generally, inadequate when it comes to production-grade systems.

This chapter focuses on more advanced concepts in RAG. We begin by revisiting the limitations and the points of failure of the naïve RAG approach. Next, we discuss the failures at the retrieval, augmentation, and generation stages. Advanced strategies and techniques to address these points of failure will be elaborated on in distinct phases of the RAG pipeline.

Better indexing of the knowledge base leads to better RAG outcomes. We will look at a few data indexing strategies that build on the naïve indexing pipeline to improve the searchability of the knowledge base.

In the generation pipeline, improvements are examined in three stages: pre-retrieval, retrieval, and post-retrieval. Pre-retrieval techniques focus on manipulating and improving the input user query. Retrieval strategies focus on better matching of the user query to the documents in the knowledge base. Finally, in the post-retrieval stage, the focus is on aligning the retrieved context with the desired result and making it suitable for generation.

The last part of the chapter discusses a modular approach to RAG that has been emerging to find applicability in RAG systems. The modular approach is an architectural enhancement to the basic RAG system.

Note that the strategies and techniques for RAG improvement are expansive, and this chapter highlights a few popular ones. The chapter is interspersed with code examples, but for a more exhaustive supporting code, check out the source code repository of this book.

By the end of this chapter, you should

- Understand why the naïve approach to RAG is not suitable for production.
- Be aware of indexing strategies that make the RAG knowledge base more efficient.
- Know some of the popular pre-retrieval, retrieval, and post-retrieval techniques.
- Be familiar with the modular approach to RAG.

RAG powers a variety of AI applications. However, there is a certain aspect of uncertainty when it comes to outcomes. Inaccuracies in retrieval, disjointed context, and incoherence in the LLM outputs need to be addressed before taking RAG to production. In a very short time, researchers and practitioners have experimented with innovative techniques to improve the relevance and faithfulness of RAG systems. But before we look at these techniques, it is important to understand why a naïve RAG approach often doesn't find its way into a production environment.

6.1   *Limitations of naïve RAG*

Naïve RAG can be thought of as the earliest form of RAG, which gained popularity after the release of ChatGPT and the rise of LLM technology. As we have seen so far, it follows a linear process of indexing, retrieving, augmenting, and generation. This process falls in a "retrieve then read" framework, which means that there's a retriever retrieving information and that there's an LLM reading this information to generate the results, as shown in figure 6.1.

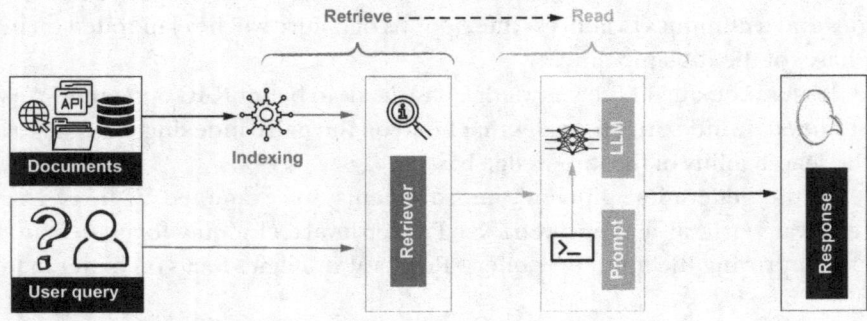

Figure 6.1   Naïve RAG is a sequential "retrieve then read" process.

The naïve RAG approach is marred with drawbacks at each of the three stages:

- *Retrieval*—Naïve retrieval is often observed to have low precision that leads to irrelevant information being retrieved. It also has a low recall, which means that relevant information is missed, which leads to incomplete results.
- *Augmentation*—There is a real possibility of redundancy and repetition when multiple retrieved documents have similar information. Also, when information is sourced from different documents, the context becomes disjointed. There's also the problem of context length of the LLMs that has an effect on the volume of retrieved context that can be passed on to the LLM for generation.
- *Generation*—With the inadequacies of the upstream processes, the generation suffers from hallucination and lack of groundedness of the generated content. The LLM faces challenge in reconciling information. The challenges of toxicity and bias also persist. It is also noticed sometimes that the LLM becomes over-reliant on the retrieved context and forgets to draw from its own parametric memory.

Figure 6.2 summarizes these drawbacks.

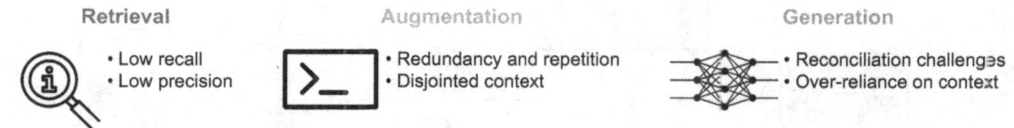

Figure 6.2   Drawbacks of naïve RAG at each stage of the process

In the last few years, a lot of research and experimentation has been done to address these drawbacks. Early approaches involved pre-training language models. Techniques involving fine-tuning of the LLMs, embeddings models, and retrievers have also been tried. These techniques require training data and re-computation of model weights, generally using supervised learning techniques. Since this book is a foundational guide, we will not go into these complex techniques.

This chapter covers some interventions, techniques, and strategies used at different stages of the two RAG pipelines: the indexing and generation pipeline. Although the array of such interventions is endless, some of the more popular ones are highlighted in the subsequent sections.

6.2   *Advanced RAG techniques*

Advanced techniques in RAG have continued to emerge since the earliest experiments with naïve RAG. There are three stages in which we can discuss these techniques:

- *Pre-retrieval stage*—As the name suggests, certain interventions can be employed before the retriever comes into action. This broadly covers two aspects:
  - *Index optimization*—The way documents are stored in the knowledge base

– *Query optimization*—Optimizing the user query so it aligns better with the retrieval and generation tasks

- *Retrieval stage*—Certain strategies can improve the recall and precision of the retrieval process. This goes beyond the capability of the underlying retrieval algorithms discussed in chapter 4.
- *Post-retrieval stage*—Once the information has been retrieved, the context can be further optimized to better align with the generation task and the downstream LLM.

With techniques employed at these three stages, the advanced RAG process follows a "rewrite then retrieve then re-rank then read" frameworks. Two additional components of rewrite and re-rank are added, and the retrieve component is enhanced in comparison with naïve RAG. This structure is presented in figure 6.3.

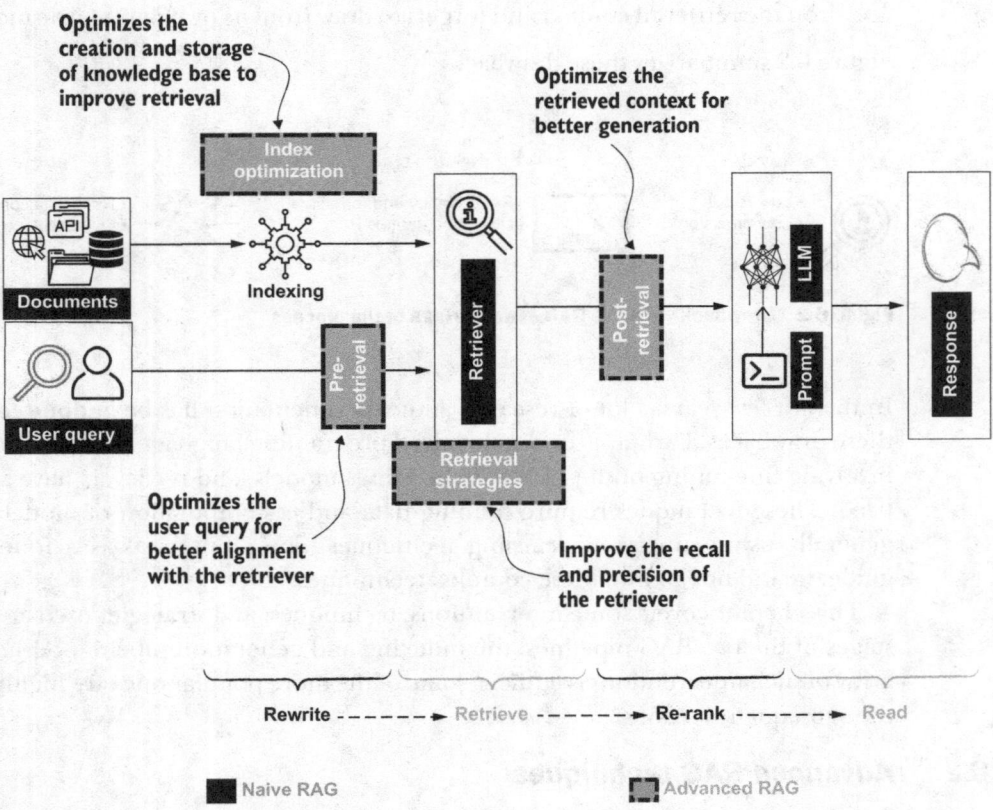

Figure 6.3   Advanced RAG is a rewrite–retrieve–re-rank–read process, as compared to a retrieve–read naïve RAG process.

We now explore these components one by one, beginning with the pre-retrieval stage.

6.3 Pre-retrieval techniques

The primary objective of employing pre-retrieval techniques is to facilitate better retrieval. We have noted that the retrieval stage of naïve RAG suffers from low recall and low precision—irrelevant information is retrieved, and not all relevant information is retrieved. This can happen mainly because of two reasons:

- *Knowledge base is not suited for retrieval.* If the information in the knowledge base is not stored in a manner that is easy to search through, then the quality of retrieval will remain suboptimal. To address this problem, *index optimization* is done in the indexing pipeline for more efficient storage of the knowledge base.

- *Retriever doesn't completely understand the input query.* In generative AI applications, the control over the user query is generally limited. The level of detail a user provides is subjective. The retriever sometimes may misunderstand or not completely understand the context of the user query. *Query optimization* addresses this aspect of the challenge with the naïve RAG.

Both index and query optimizations are carried out before the retriever is invoked. This is the only stage that recommends interventions both in the indexing and generation pipeline. We will look at a few techniques for each of these.

6.3.1 Index optimization

Index optimization is employed in the indexing pipeline. The objective of index optimization is to set up the knowledge base for better retrieval. Some of the popular strategies are as follows.

CHUNK OPTIMIZATION

Chapter 3 discussed the significance of chunking in the indexing pipeline. Chunking large documents into smaller segments plays a crucial role in retrieval and handling the context length limits of LLMs. Certain techniques aim for better chunking and efficient retrieval of the chunks, such as

- *Chunk size optimization*—The size of the chunks can have a significant effect on the quality of the RAG system. While large-sized chunks provide better context, they also carry a lot of noise. Smaller chunks, however, have precise information, but they might miss important information. For instance, consider a legal document that's 10,000 words long. If we chunk it into 1,000-word segments, each chunk might contain multiple legal clauses, making it hard to retrieve specific information. Conversely, chunking it into 200-word segments allows for more precise retrieval of individual clauses, but may lose the context provided by surrounding clauses. Experimenting with chunk sizes can help find the optimal balance for accurate retrieval. The processing time also depends on the chunk size. Chunk size, therefore, has a significant effect on retrieval accuracy, processing speed, and storage efficiency. The ideal chunk size varies with the use case and depends on balancing factors such as document types and structure, complexity of user query, and the desired response time. There is no one-size-fits-all approach to optimizing chunk sizes. Experimentation and evaluation of different chunk sizes on metrics such as faithfulness, relevance, and response time (as discussed in chapter 5) can help in identifying the optimal chunk size for the RAG system. Chunk size optimization may require periodic reassessment as data or requirements change.

- *Context-enriched chunking*—This method adds the summary of the larger document to each chunk to enrich the context of the smaller chunk. This makes more context available to the LLM without adding too much noise. It also improves the retrieval accuracy and maintains semantic coherence across chunks. This feature is particularly useful in scenarios where a more holistic view of the information is crucial. While this approach enhances the understanding of the broader context, it adds a level of complexity and comes at the cost of higher computational requirements, increased storage needs, and possible latency in retrieval. Here is an example of how context enrichment can be done using GPT-4o-mini, OpenAI embeddings, and FAISS:

```
from langchain_community.document_loaders
import AsyncHtmlLoader
from langchain_community.document_transformers
import Html2TextTransformer
url=
https://en.wikipedia.org/wiki/2023_Cricket_World_Cup
loader = AsyncHtmlLoader (url)
data = loader.load()
html2text = Html2TextTransformer()
document_text=data_transformed[0].page_content
```
Loads text from Wikipedia page

```
summary_prompt = f"Summarize the given
document in a single paragraph\n
document: {document_text}"
from openai import OpenAI
client = OpenAI()

response = client.chat.completions.create(
  model="gpt-4o-mini",
  messages= [
    {"role": "user", "content": summary_prompt}
    ]
)

summary=response.choices[0].message.content
```
Generates summary of the text using GPT-4o-mini model

```
from langchain_text_splitters import
RecursiveCharacterTextSplitter
text_splitter = RecursiveCharacterTextSplitter(
chunk_size=1000,
chunk_overlap=200)
```
Creates chunks using recursive character splitter

```
chunks=text_splitter.split_text(
    data_transformed[0].page_content
    )

context_enriched_chunks =
    [answer + "\n" + chunk for chunk in chunks]

embedding = OpenAIEmbeddings(openai_api_key=api_key)
vector_store = FAISS.from_texts(
    context_enriched_chunks,
    embedding
)
```

Enriches chunks with summary data

Creates embeddings and storing in FAISS index

- *Fetch surrounding chunks*—In this technique, chunks are created at a granular level, say, at a sentence level, and when a relevant chunk of text is found in response to a query, the system retrieves not only that chunk but also the surrounding chunks. This makes the search granular but also performs contextual expansion by retrieving adjacent chunks. It is useful in long-form content such as books and reports where information flows across paragraphs and sections. This technique also adds a layer of processing cost and latency to the system. Apart from that, there is a possibility of diluting the relevance as the neighboring chunks may contain noise.

Chunk optimization is an effective step toward better RAG systems. Although it presents challenges such as managing the costs, system latency, and storage efficiency, optimizing chunking can fundamentally improve the retrieval and generation process of the RAG system.

METADATA ENHANCEMENTS

A common way of defining metadata is "data about data." Metadata describes other data. It can provide information such as a description of the data, time of creation, author, and similar. While metadata is useful for managing and organizing data, in the context of RAG, metadata enhances the searchability of data. A few ways in which metadata is crucial in improving RAG systems are

- *Metadata filtering*—Adding metadata such as timestamp, author, category, and similar can enhance the chunks. While retrieving, chunks can first be filtered by relevant metadata information before doing a similarity search. This improves retrieval efficiency and reduces noise in the system. For example, using the timestamp filters can help avoid outdated information in the knowledge base. If a user searches for "latest COVID-19 travel guidelines," metadata filtering by timestamp ensures that only the most recent guidelines are retrieved, avoiding outdated information.

- *Metadata enrichment*—Timestamp, author, category, chapter, page number, and so forth are common metadata elements that can be extracted from documents. However, even more valuable metadata items can be constructed. This can be a summary of the chunk by extracting tags from the chunk. One particularly useful technique is reverse hypothetical document embeddings. It involves using a language model to generate potential queries that could be answered by each document or chunk. These synthetic queries are then added to metadata. During retrieval, the system compares the user's query with these synthetic queries to find the most relevant chunks.

Metadata is a great tool for improving the accuracy of the retrieval system. However, a degree of caution must be exercised when adding metadata to the chunks. Designing the metadata schema is important to avoid redundancies and managing processing and storage costs. Providing improved relevance and accuracy, metadata enhancement has become extremely popular in contemporary RAG systems.

INDEX STRUCTURES

Another important aspect of the knowledge base is how well the information is structured. In the naïve RAG approach, there is no structural order to documents/chunks. However, for a more efficient retrieval, a few indexing structures have become popular and effective:

- *Parent–child document structure*—In a parent–child document structure, documents are organized hierarchically. The parent document contains overarching themes or summaries, while child documents delve into specific details. During retrieval, the system can first locate the most relevant child documents and then refer to the parent documents for additional context if needed. This approach enhances the precision of retrieval, while maintaining the broader context. Simultaneously, this hierarchical structure can present challenges in terms of memory requirements and computational load.

- *Knowledge graph index*—Knowledge graphs organize data in a structured manner as entities and relationships. Using knowledge graph structures not only increases contextual understanding but also equips the system with enhanced reasoning capabilities and improved explainability. Knowledge graph creation and maintenance, however, is an expensive process. Knowledge-graph-powered RAG, also called GraphRAG, is an emerging advanced RAG pattern that has demonstrated significant improvements in RAG performance. We will discuss GraphRAG in detail in chapter 8.

Index structure, perhaps, has the biggest effect on index optimization for retrieval. It, however, introduces storage and memory burden on the system and affects search time performance. Index structure optimization is therefore advised in large scale systems where the true potential of concepts such as GraphRAG and hierarchical index can be realized.

NOTE In the previous chapters, we have discussed that embeddings are a crucial component of RAG. They are used to calculate the semantic similarity between the user query and the documents stored in the knowledge base. Generally available embeddings models have been trained on commonly spoken language. When dealing with domain-specific or specialized content, these models may not yield good results. Fine-tuning embedding models let you optimize vector representations for your specific domain or task, leading to more accurate retrieval of relevant context. Fine-tuning is a slightly complex process since it requires curation of the training dataset and resources for recalculating the embeddings model. In case you're dealing with highly specialized domains where the vocabulary is different from commonly spoken languages, you should consider fine-tuning the embedding model for your domain.

Like the indexing pipeline, index optimization is a periodic process and does not happen in real-time. The objective of index optimization is to set up the knowledge base for better retrieval. One must also be mindful of the added complexity that leads to an increase in computational, memory, and storage requirements. Figure 6.4 is an illustrative workflow of an index-optimized knowledge base.

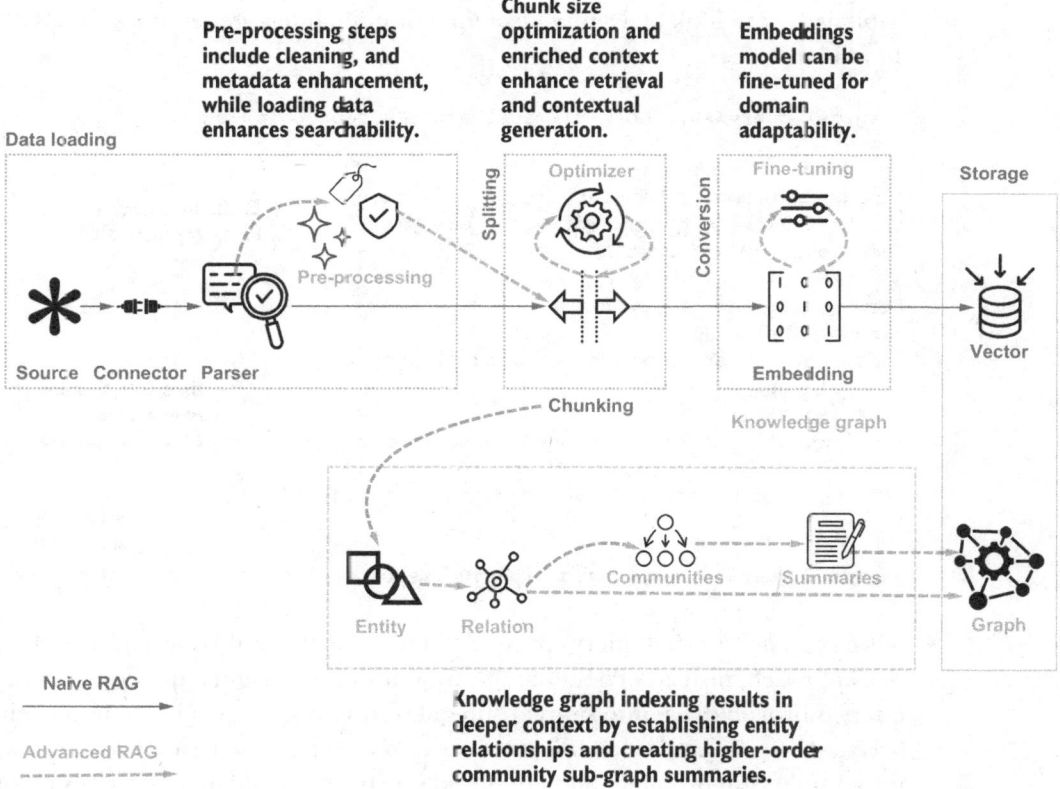

Figure 6.4   Illustration of an index-optimized knowledge base

6.3.2   *Query optimization*

The second stage of pre-retrieval techniques is a part of the generation pipeline. The objective of this stage is to optimize the input user query in a manner that makes it better suited for the retrieval tasks. Some of the popular query optimization strategies are listed in the following sections.

QUERY EXPANSION

In query expansion, the original user query is enriched to retrieve more relevant information. This helps in increasing the recall of the system and overcomes the challenge of incomplete or very brief user queries. Some of the techniques that expand user queries are

- *Multi-query expansion*—In this approach, multiple variations of the original query are generated using an LLM, and each variant query is used to search and retrieve chunks from the knowledge base. For a query "How does climate change affect polar bears?" a multi-query expansion might generate "Impact of global warming on polar bears," "What are the consequences of climate change for polar bear habitats?" Let's look at a simple example of multi-query generation using GPT 4o-mini model:

```
original_query="How does climate change affect polar bears?"
num=5

expansion_prompt=f"Generate {num} variations          Crafts the prompt
of the following query: {original_query}.             for query expansion
Respond in JSON format."

from openai import OpenAI
client = OpenAI()
response = client.chat.completions.create(
  model="gpt-4o-mini",                                Uses GPT 4o-mini
  messages= [                                         to generate
    {"role": "user", "content": expansion_prompt}     expanded queries
      ],
          response_format={ "type": "json_object" }
)                                                      Extracts the
                                                       text from the
expanded_queries=response.choices[0].message.content   response object
```

- *Sub-query expansion*: Subquery approach is quite like the multi-query approach. In this approach, instead of generating variations of the original query, a complex query is broken down into simpler sub-queries. This approach is inspired by the least-to-most prompting technique, where complex problems are broken down into simpler sub-problems and are solved one by one. A sub-query expansion on the same query—"How does climate change affect polar bears?"—may generate "How does melting sea ice influence polar bear hunting and feeding behaviors?" and "What are the physiological and health impacts of climate change on polar bears?" The approach to sub-query is similar to that for multi-query, except for the changes to the prompt:

```
sub_query_expansion_prompt=f" \
    Break down the following \
    query into {num} sub-queries targeting \
    different aspects of the query: {original_query}. \
Respond in JSON format. "
```

- *Step-back expansion*—The term comes from the step-back prompting approach where the original query is abstracted to a higher-level conceptual query. During retrieval, both the original query and the abstracted query are used to fetch chunks. Similar to above example, an abstracted step-back query may be "What are the ecological impacts of climate change on arctic ecosystems?" Here is an example of the prompt that can be used:

```
step_back_expansion_prompt = f" \
    Given the query: {original_query}, \
    generate a more abstract, \
higher-level conceptual query. "
```

While multi-query expansion generates various rephrasing or synonyms of the original query to cast a wider net during retrieval, sub-query expansion breaks down a complex query into simpler, component queries to target specific pieces of information, and step-back expansion abstracts the query to a higher-level concept to capture broader context.

Query expansion also presents its own set of challenges that need to be considered while implementing this strategy. While query expansion may increase recall by matching more documents, it may reduce the precision. The expansion terms need to be carefully selected to avoid contextual drift from the original query. Overexpansion can dilute the focus from the original query. Despite the challenges, query expansion has proved to be an effective technique for improving the recall of retrieval and generating more context aware responses.

QUERY TRANSFORMATION

Compared to query expansion, in query transformation, instead of the original user query, retrieval happens on a transformed query, which is more suitable for the retriever.

- *Rewrite*—Queries are rewritten from the input. The input in quite a few real-world applications may not be a direct query or a query suited for retrieval. Based on the input, a language model can be trained to transform the input into a query that can be used for retrieval. A user's statement like, "I can't send emails from my phone" can be rewritten as "Troubleshooting steps for resolving email sending issues on smartphones," making it more suitable for retrieval.

- *HyDE*—Hypothetical document embedding, or HyDE, is a technique where the language model first generates a hypothetical answer to the user's query without accessing the knowledge base. This generated answer is then used to perform a similarity search against the document embeddings in the knowledge base, effectively retrieving documents that are similar to the hypothetical answer rather than the query itself. Here is an example that generates hypothetical document embeddings:

```
# Original Query
original_query=
    "How does climate change \          Original query
    affect polar bears?"

# Prompts for generating HyDE
system_prompt="You are an expert in \
    climate change and arctic life."       Prompts for
hyde_prompt=f"Generate an answer to the \  generating HyDE
    question: {original_query}"

# Using OpenAI to generate a hypothetical answer

from openai import OpenAI
client = OpenAI()
response = client.chat.completions.create(
  model="gpt-4o-mini",
  messages= [
    {"role": "system", "content": system_prompt},   Uses OpenAI to generate
    {"role": "user", "content": hyde_prompt}         a hypothetical answer
  ]
)

hy_answer=response.choices[0].message.content

# Using OpenAI Embeddings to convert hyde into embeddings
embeddings = OpenAIEmbeddings(
    model="text-embedding-3-large"        Uses OpenAI Embeddings
    )                                     to convert Hyde into
hyde = embeddings.embed_query(hy_answer)  embeddings
```

Challenges similar to query expansion such as drift from original query and maintaining intent also persist in query transformation strategies. Effective rewriting and transformation of the query result in enhancing the context awareness of the system.

QUERY ROUTING

Different queries can demand different retrieval methods. Based on criteria such as intent, domain, language, complexity, source of information, and so forth, queries need to be classified so that they can follow the appropriate retrieval method. This is the idea behind optimizing the user query by routing it to the appropriate workflow. Types of routing techniques include:

- *Intent classification*—A pre-trained classification model is used to classify the intent of the user query to select the appropriate retrieval method. A modification to this technique is prompt-based classification, where instead of a pre-trained classifier, an LLM is prompted to categorize the query into an intent.
- *Metadata routing*—In this approach, keywords and tags are extracted from the user query and then filtering is done on the chunk metadata to narrow down the scope of the search.
- *Semantic routing*—In this approach, the user query is matched with a pre-defined set of queries for each retrieval method. Wherever the similarity between the user query and pre-defined queries is the highest, that retrieval method is invoked.

In customer support chatbots, query routing ensures that technical queries are directed to databases with troubleshooting guides, while billing questions are routed to account information, enhancing user satisfaction.

Implementing query routing takes effort and skill. It introduces a whole new predictive component, bringing uncertainty to the process. Therefore, it must be carefully crafted. Query routing is a must when dealing with source data and query type variability.

Although the universe of pre-retrieval strategies and techniques is expansive and ever-evolving, we have looked at a few of the most popular and effective techniques in this section. Bear in mind that the applicability of the strategies will depend on the nature of the content in the knowledge base and the use case. However, using each of these strategies will result in incremental gains in the RAG system performance. Now that we have set up the knowledge base and the user query for better retrieval, let's discuss important retrieval strategies in the next section.

6.4 Retrieval strategies

Interventions in the pre-retrieval stage can bring significant improvements in the performance of the RAG system if the query and the knowledge base become well aligned with the retrieval algorithm. We have discussed quite a few retrieval algorithms in chapter 4. In this section, we focus on strategies that can be employed for better retrieval.

6.4.1 Hybrid retrieval

Hybrid retrieval strategy is an essential component of production-grade RAG systems. It involves combining retrieval methods for improved retrieval accuracy. This can mean simply using a keyword-based search along with semantic similarity. It can also mean combining all sparse embedding, dense embedding vector, and knowledge graph-based search. The retrieval can be a union or an intersection of all these methods, depending on the requirements of precision and recall. It generally follows a weighted approach to retrieval. Figure 6.5 shows the hybrid retriever querying graph and vector storage.

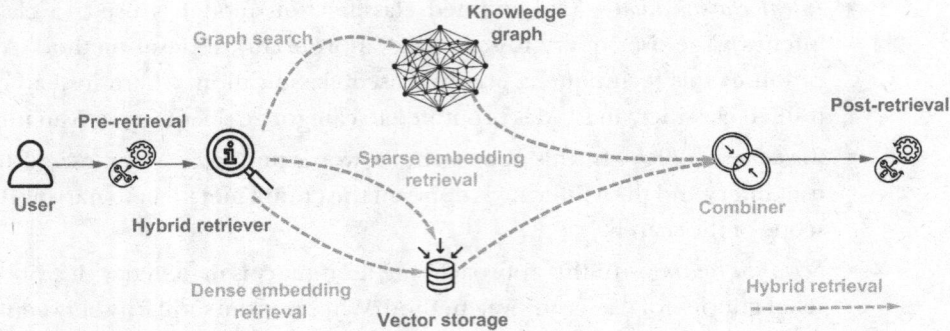

Figure 6.5   Hybrid retriever employs multiple querying techniques and combines the results.

6.4.2   *Iterative retrieval*

Instead of using a retrieve–generate linear process, the iterative retrieval strategy searches the knowledge base repeatedly based on the original query and the generated text, which allows the system to gather more information by refining the search based on initial results. It is useful when solving multi-hop or complex queries. While effective, iterative retrieval can lead to longer processing times and may introduce challenges in managing larger amounts of retrieved information. There are examples of iterative retrieval that have demonstrated remarkably improved performance such as Iter-RetGen, which is an iterative approach that alternates between retrieval and generation steps.

6.4.3   *Recursive retrieval*

The recursive retrieval strategy builds on the idea of iterative retrieval by transforming the query iteratively depending on the results obtained. While the initial query is used to retrieve the chunks, new focused queries are generated based on these chunks. It, therefore, leads to a better ability to find scattered information across document chunks and a more coherent and contextual response. Iterative retrieval chain-of-thought (IRCoT) is a recursive retrieval technique that combines iterative retrieval with CoT prompting.

6.4.4   *Adaptive retrieval*

Adaptive retrieval also follows the approach of repeated retrieval cycles. In adaptive retrieval strategies, an LLM is enabled to determine the most appropriate moment and content for retrieval. The objective of adaptive retrieval is to make the retrieval process more personalized to users and context. It is applied in areas such as adapting queries depending on user behavior or adjusting retrieval based on user performance. FLARE and Self-RAG are two popular examples of adaptive retrieval. Self-RAG introduces "reflection tokens" that enable the model to introspect and decide when additional retrieval is necessary. FLARE (forward-looking active retrieval-augmented generation) predicts future content needs based on the current generation and retrieves relevant information proactively. Adaptive retrieval is a part of a broader trend of agentic AI. Agentic AI refers to AI systems that can make autonomous decisions during tasks, adapting their actions based on the context. In the context of RAG, agentic RAG involves AI agents that dynamically decide when and how to retrieve information, thus enhancing the flexibility and efficiency of the retrieval process. Agentic AI is an important emerging RAG pattern. We will discuss Agentic RAG in detail in chapter 8.

Figure 6.6 compares the three retrieval strategies that focus on repeated retrieval cycles. While recursive and iterative approaches need a threshold to break out of the iterations, in the adaptive approach, a judge model decides on-demand retrieval and generation steps.

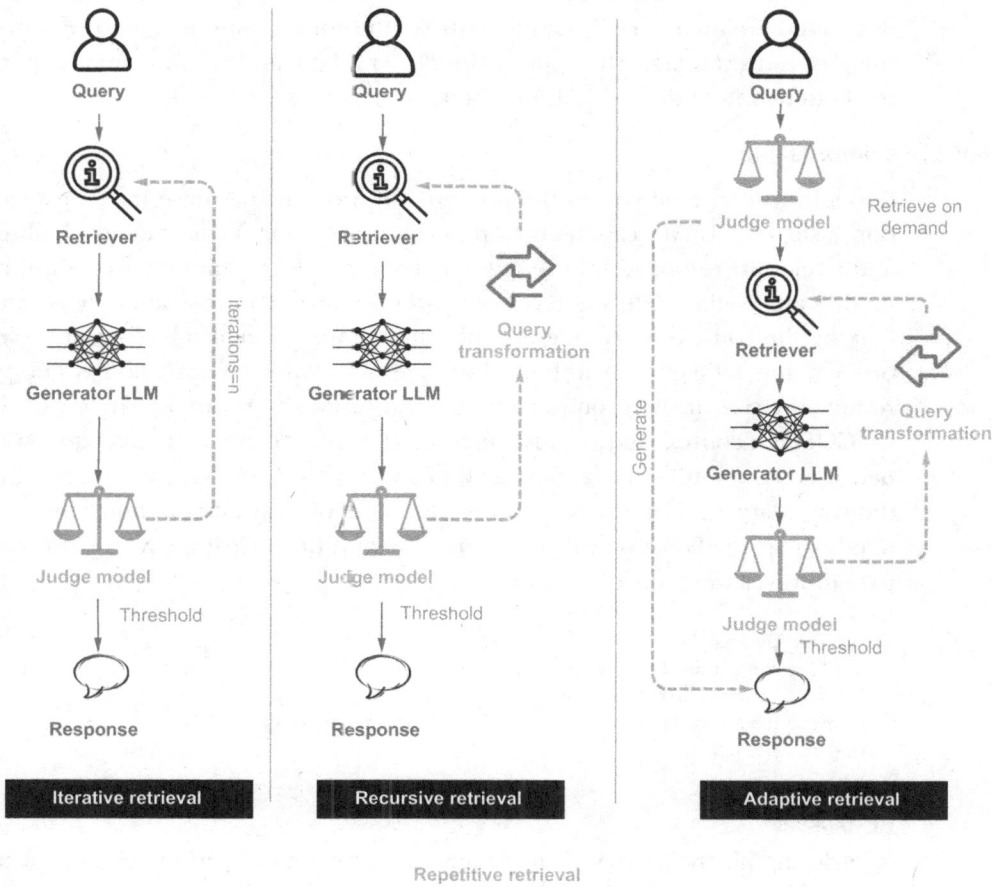

Figure 6.6 Iterative, recursive, and adaptive retrieval incorporate repeated retrieval cycles. Source: Adapted from Gao et al., December 18, 2023. "Retrieval-Augmented Generation for Large Language Models: A Survey."

All the advanced retrieval strategies introduce overheads in terms of computational complexity, and therefore the accuracy must be balanced against the cost and latency of the system.

By employing advanced pre-retrieval techniques and a suitable retrieval strategy, we can expect that richer, deeper, and more relevant context is being retrieved from the knowledge base. Even when the relevant context is retrieved, the LLM may struggle to assimilate all the information. To address this problem, in the next section, we discuss a couple of post-retrieval strategies that help curate the context before augmenting the prompt with the necessary information.

6.5 *Post-retrieval techniques*

Even if the retrieval of the chunks happens in an expected manner, a point of failure still remains. The LLM might not be able to process all the information. This may be due to redundancies or disjointed nature of the context among many other reasons. At the post-retrieval stage, the approaches of re-ranking and compression help in providing better context to the LLM for generation.

6.5.1 *Compression*

Excessively long context has the potential of introducing noise into the system. This diminishes the LLM's capability to process information. Consequently, hallucinations and irrelevant responses to the query may persist. In prompt compression, language models are used to detect and remove unimportant and irrelevant tokens. Apart from making the context more relevant, prompt compression also has a positive influence on cost and efficiency. Another advantage of prompt compression is being able to reduce the size of the prompt so that it can fit into the context window of the LLM. COCOM is a context compression method that compresses contexts into a small number of context embeddings. Similarly, xRAG is a method that uses document embeddings as features. Compression can lead to loss of information, and therefore, there needs to be a balance between compression and performance. A very simple prompt to compress a long-retrieved context is

```
compress_prompt = f"  \
    Compress the following document  \
    into a shorter version,  \
    retaining only the essential information:    \
\n\n{document}"
```

RE-RANKING

Reordering all the retrieved documents ensures that the most relevant information is prioritized for the generation step. It refines retrieval results by prioritizing documents that are more contextually appropriate for the query, improving the overall quality and accuracy of information used for generation. Re-ranking also addresses the question of prioritization when a hybrid approach to retrieval is employed and improves the overall response quality. There are commonly available re-rankers such as multi-vector, Learning to Rank (LTR), BERT-based, and even hybrid re-rankers that can be employed. Specialized APIs such as Cohere Rerank offer pre-trained models for efficient reranking integration.

In this section, we discuss some of the popular advanced RAG strategies and techniques employed at different stages of the RAG pipeline. It is important to also consider the tradeoffs that come with these techniques. Almost any advanced technique will introduce overheads to the system. These can be in the form of computational load, latency in the system, and increased storage and memory requirements. Therefore, these techniques warrant a performance versus overhead assessment catered to specific use cases. Table 6.1 provides a summary of the 12 strategies discussed so far.

Table 6.1 Advanced RAG strategies with their benefits and limitations

Strategy	Description	Benefits	Challenges
Chunk optimization	Adjusting document chunks for optimal size and context	Improves retrieval accuracy, processing speed, and storage	Requires experimentation; optimal chunk varies by use case
Metadata enhancements	Enriching chunks with additional metadata for better filtering and searchability	Improves retrieval efficiency; reduces noise	Requires careful schema design; manages processing costs
Index structures	Organizing data in structured formats for efficient retrieval	Enhances accuracy and context in retrieval	Increases memory and computational load
Query expansion	Enriching the user query to retrieve more relevant information	Increases recall; overcomes brief queries	May reduce precision; risk of contextual drift
Query transformation	Modifying the user query for better retrieval suitability	Enhances context awareness; maintains intent	Potential for misinterpretation; drift from the original query
Query routing	Directing queries to appropriate retrieval methods based on classification	Enhances retrieval by matching method to query type	Introduces uncertainty; requires careful crafting
Hybrid retrieval	Combining multiple retrieval methods (e.g., keyword and semantic)	Improves retrieval accuracy and robustness	Increased complexity; requires method weighting
Iterative retrieval	Repeatedly searching based on initial results and query refinement	Gathers more comprehensive information; refines search	Longer processing times; managing more data
Recursive retrieval	Iteratively transforming the query based on obtained results	Finds scattered information; provides coherent responses	Similar to iterative retrieval; potential for increased load
Adaptive retrieval	LLM decides when and what to retrieve during generation	Personalized and context-aware retrieval; dynamic adaptation	Increased computational complexity; part of agentic AI

Table 6.1   Advanced RAG strategies with their benefits and limitations (*continued*)

Strategy	Description	Benefits	Challenges
Compression	Reducing context length by removing irrelevant information	Fits within LLM context window; reduces noise and costs	Potential loss of important information; needs balance
Reranking	Reordering retrieved documents to prioritize relevance	Enhances response quality; ensures most relevant info is used	Requires additional models; may introduce overhead

Figure 6.7 is an illustrative example of what a generation pipeline looks like after incorporating advanced techniques.

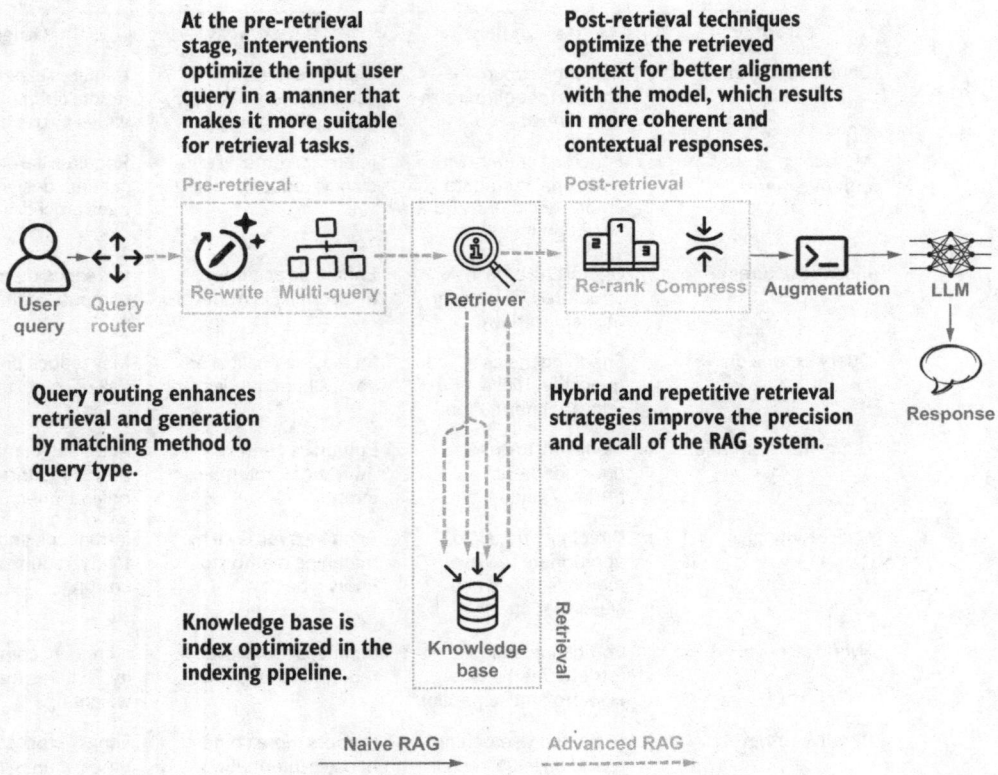

Figure 6.7   Illustrative example of advanced generation pipeline

While these advanced strategies and techniques are extremely useful in improving performance, a RAG system also needs to provide customization and flexibility. This is because we may need to quickly adopt different techniques as the nature of data and queries evolve. A modular RAG approach discussed in the next section aims to provide greater architectural flexibility over the traditional RAG system.

6.6 Modular RAG

AI systems are becoming increasingly complex, demanding more customizable, flexible, and scalable RAG architectures. The emergence of modular RAG is a leap forward in the evolution of RAG systems. Modular RAG breaks down the traditional monolithic RAG structure into interchangeable components. This allows for tailoring of the system to specific use cases. The modular approach brings modularity to RAG components, such as retrievers, indexing, and generation, while also adding more modules such as search, memory, and fusion. We can think of the modular RAG approach in two parts:

- Core components of RAG developed as flexible, interchangeable modules
- Specialized modules to enhance the core features of retrieval, augmentation, and generation

6.6.1 Core modules

The core components of the RAG system (i.e. indexing, retrieval, augmentation and generation), along with the advanced pre- and post-retrieval techniques, are composed as flexible, interchangeable modules in the modular RAG framework.

- *Indexing module*—The indexing module serves as the foundation for building the knowledge base. By modularizing this component, developers can choose from various embedding models for advanced semantic understanding. Vector stores can be interchanged based on scalability and performance needs. Additionally, chunking methods can be adapted to the data structure, whether it's text, code, or multimedia content, ensuring optimal indexing for retrieval.
- *Retrieval module*—The retrieval module enables the use of diverse retrieval algorithms. For instance, developers can switch between semantic similarity search using dense embeddings and traditional keyword-based search such as BM25. This flexibility allows for tailoring retrieval methods to the specific requirements of the application, such as prioritizing speed, accuracy, or resource utilization. For example, a customer support chatbot might use semantic search during off-peak hours for higher accuracy and switch to keyword search during peak hours to handle increased load. The modular retrieval component allows this dynamic interchange of retrieval strategies based on real-time needs.
- *Generation module*—In the generation module, the choice of LLM is modular. Developers can select from models such as GPT-4 for complex language generation or smaller models for cost efficiency. This module also handles prompt engineering for augmentation to guide the LLM in generating accurate and relevant responses.

- *Pre-retrieval module*—Allows flexibility of pre-retrieval techniques to improve the quality of indexed content and user query.
- *Post-retrieval module*—Like the pre-retrieval module, this module allows for flexible implementation of post-retrieval techniques to refine and optimize the retrieved context.

You may note that the first three modules complete the naïve RAG approach, and the addition of the pre-retrieval and post-retrieval modules enhances the naïve RAG into an advanced RAG implementation. It can also be said that naïve RAG is a special (and limited) case of advanced RAG.

6.6.2   *New modules*

The modular RAG framework has introduced several new components to enhance the retrieval and generation capabilities of naïve and advanced RAG approaches. Some of these components/modules are

- *Search*—The search module is aimed at performing searches on different data sources. It is customized to different data sources and aimed at increasing the source data for better response generation.
- *Fusion*—RAG fusion improves traditional search systems by overcoming their limitations through a multi-query approach. The fusion module enhances retrieval by expanding the user's query into multiple, diverse perspectives using an LLM. It then conducts parallel searches for these expanded queries, fuses the results by reranking and selecting the most relevant information, and presents a comprehensive answer. This approach captures both explicit and implicit information, uncovering deeper insights that might be missed with a single query.
- *Memory*—The memory module uses the inherent memory of the LLM, meaning the knowledge encoded within its parameters from pre-training. This module uses the LLM to recall information without explicit retrieval, guiding the system on when to retrieve additional data and when to rely on the LLM's internal knowledge. It can involve techniques such as using reflection tokens or prompts that encourage the model to introspect and decide if more information is needed. For example, when answering a query about historical events, the memory module can decide to rely on the LLM's knowledge about World War II to provide context, only retrieving specific dates or figures as needed. This approach reduces unnecessary retrieval and uses the model's pre-trained knowledge.
- *Routing*—Routing in the RAG system navigates through diverse data sources, selecting the optimal pathway for a query, whether it involves summarization, specific database searches, or merging different information streams.
- *Task adapter*—This module makes RAG adaptable to various downstream tasks allowing the development of task-specific end-to-end retrievers with minimal examples, demonstrating flexibility in handling different tasks. The task adapter module allows the RAG system to be fine-tuned for specific tasks like

summarization, translation, or sentiment analysis. By incorporating a small number of task-specific examples or prompts, the module adjusts the retrieval and generation components to produce outputs tailored to the desired task, enhancing versatility without extensive retraining.

You may observe that advanced RAG is a special case within the modular RAG framework. You also saw earlier that naïve RAG is a special case of advanced RAG. This means that the RAG approaches (i.e., naïve, advanced, and modular) are not competing but progressive. You may start by trying out a naïve implementation of RAG and move to a more modular approach. Figure 6.8 shows the progression of RAG systems.

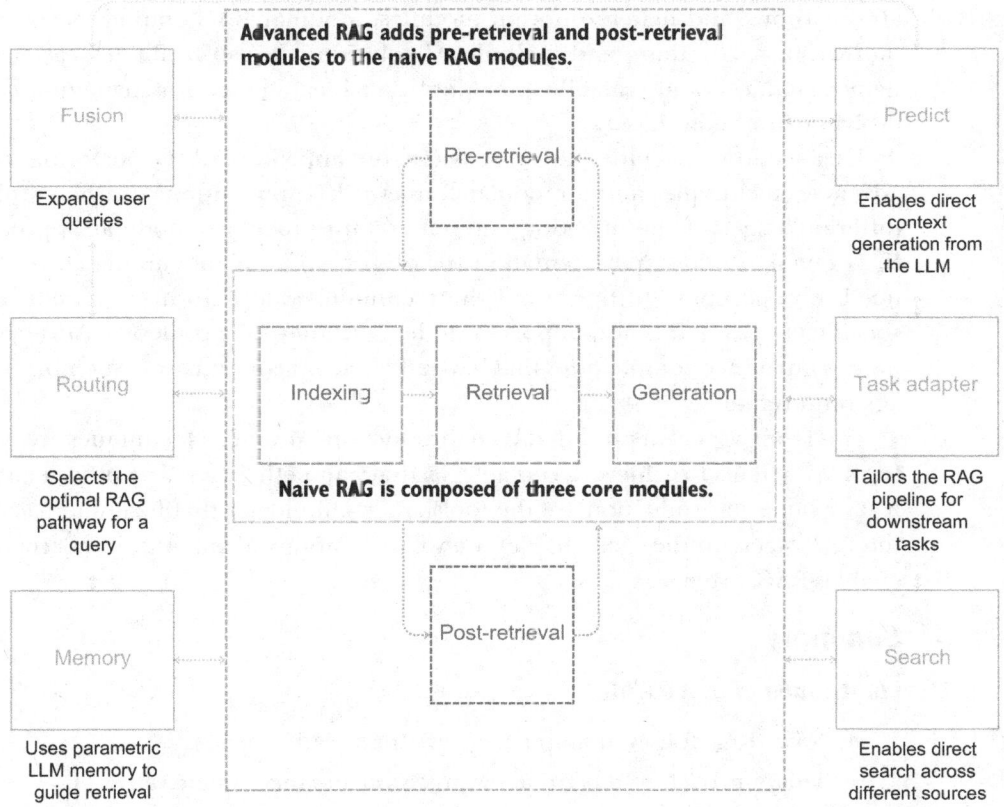

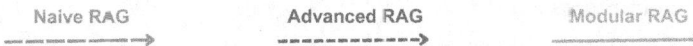

Figure 6.8 Naïve, advanced, and modular approaches to RAG are progressive. Naïve RAG is a sub-component of advanced RAG, which is a sub-component of modular RAG.

While building a modular RAG system, remember that each module should be designed to work independently. This requires defining clear inputs and outputs. Along with the independent modules, the orchestration layer should be flexible to allow mixing and matching of modules. One should also bear in mind that a modular approach introduces complexity in the process. Managing interfaces, dependencies, configurations, and versions of modules can be complex. Ensuring compatibility and consistency between modules can be challenging. Testing each module independently and collectively requires a robust evaluation strategy. Extra modules may also add latency and inference costs to the system.

Despite the added complexities, the modular approach toward RAG is state-of-the-art in large-scale RAG systems. It enables rapid experimentation, efficient optimization, and seamless integration of new technologies as they emerge. By offering the ability to mix and match different modules, modular RAG empowers you to build more robust, accurate, and versatile AI solutions. It also facilitates easier maintenance, updates, and scalability, making it an ideal choice for managing complex, evolving knowledge bases.

This section concludes the discussion on improving RAG performance using advanced techniques and a modular framework. Interventions can be employed at different stages of the indexing and generation pipelines. Modular approaches to RAG enable rapid experimentation, flexibility, and scalable architecture. You will need to experiment to figure out the techniques that help in improving RAG for specific use cases. It is also important to be mindful of the tradeoffs. Advanced techniques introduce complexities that have an effect on computation, memory, and storage requirements.

This is one aspect of putting RAG in production. Advanced techniques are necessary for RAG systems to achieve acceptable accuracy and efficiency. The other enablers for RAG systems in production are the tools and technologies that form the backbone of the RAG stack. In the next chapter, we will look at this technology infrastructure that enables RAG systems.

Summary

Limitations of naïve RAG

- Naïve RAG follows a simple "retrieve then read" process.
- This approach suffers from low precision and incomplete retrieval.
- Retrieval often misses relevant information and pulls in irrelevant content.
- At the augmentation stage, there is often redundancy from similar retrieved documents.
- Context can become disjointed when sourced from multiple documents.
- The generation stage faces hallucinations and biased outputs.
- The model can overly rely on retrieved data and ignore its internal knowledge.

Advanced RAG techniques

- The advanced RAG process follows a "rewrite then retrieve then re-rank then read" framework, where the query is optimized through rewriting, retrieval is enhanced for better precision, results are re-ranked to prioritize relevance, and the most relevant information is used for generating the final response.
- Pre-retrieval techniques include
  - *Index optimization*—Improves document storage for better searchability
  - *Chunk optimization*—Balances chunk sizes to avoid losing context or introducing noise
  - *Context-enriched chunking*—Adds summaries to each chunk to improve retrieval
  - *Metadata enhancements*—Adds tags and metadata like timestamps or categories for better filtering
  - *Query optimization*—Expands or rewrites user queries for improved retrieval accuracy
- Retrieval techniques include
  - *Hybrid retrieval*—Combines keyword-based and semantic searches
  - *Iterative retrieval*—Refines searches by repeatedly querying based on initial results
  - *Recursive retrieval*—Generates new queries based on retrieved chunks to gather more relevant information
- Post-retrieval techniques include
  - *Compression*—Reduces unnecessary context to remove noise and fit within the model's context window
  - *Re-ranking*—Reorders retrieved documents to prioritize the most relevant ones

Modular RAG framework

- Core modules include
  - *Indexing module*—Allows flexible embedding models and vector store options
  - *Retrieval module*—Supports switching between dense and keyword-based retrieval methods
  - *Generation module*—Offers flexibility in selecting language models based on complexity and cost
- New modules include
  - *Search module*—Tailors search to specific data sources for better results
  - *Fusion module*—Expands user queries into multiple forms and combines retrieved results for deeper insights
  - *Memory module*—Uses the model's internal knowledge to reduce unnecessary retrieval, retrieving only when needed

- *Routing module*—Dynamically selects the best path for handling different types of queries
- *Task adapter module*—Adapts the system for different downstream tasks like summarization or translation

Tradeoffs and best practices

- Advanced techniques improve RAG accuracy but add complexity.
- Techniques such as hybrid retrieval or re-ranking can increase computational costs and latency.
- Modular RAG offers flexibility but requires careful management of interfaces and module compatibility.
- Testing each module independently and as a whole is important to ensure system stability and performance.
- Tradeoffs between performance, cost, and system complexity should be carefully assessed.

7

Evolving RAGOps stack

This chapter covers

- The design of RAG systems
- Available tools and technologies that enable
  a RAG system
- Production best practices for RAG systems

So far, we have discussed the indexing pipeline, generation pipeline, and evaluation of a retrieval-augmented generation (RAG) system. Chapter 6 also covered some advanced strategies and techniques that are useful when building production-grade RAG systems. These strategies help improve the accuracy of retrieval and generation and, in some cases, reduce the system latency. With all this information, you should be able to stitch together a RAG system for your use cases. Chapter 2 briefly laid out the design of a RAG system. This chapter elaborates on that design.

A RAG system is composed of standard application layers, as well as layers specific to generative AI applications. Stacked together, these layers create a robust RAG system.

These layers are supported by a technology infrastructure. We delve into these layers and the available technologies and tools offered by popular service providers that can be used in crafting a RAG system. Some providers have started offering managed end-to-end RAG solutions, which we touch upon in this chapter.

We wrap up the chapter with some learnings and best practices for putting RAG systems in production. Chapter 7 also marks the end of part 3 of the book.

By the end of this chapter, you should

- Understand the details of the layers in a RAG (RAGOps) stack.
- Be familiar with a host of service providers and the tools and technologies they offer for RAG systems.
- Know some of the pitfalls and best practices of putting RAG systems in production.

A RAG system includes a lot of additional components compared to traditional software applications. Vector stores and embeddings models are essential components of the indexing pipeline. Knowledge graphs are becoming increasingly popular indexing structures. The generation component can have different kinds of language models. In addition, prompt management is becoming increasingly complex. The production ecosystem for RAG and LLM (large language models) applications is still evolving, but early tooling and design patterns have emerged. RAGOps refers to the operational practices, tools, and processes involved in deploying, maintaining, and optimizing RAG systems in production environments.

7.1   *The evolving RAGOps stack*

This section describes different components required to build a RAG system in layers. These layers come together to form the operations stack for RAG. We will also take this opportunity to revise the workflow of the RAG system discussed in this book.

It should be noted that RAG, like generative AI in general, is an evolving technology, and therefore, the operations stack continues to evolve. You may find varying definitions and structures. This chapter provides a holistic view and discusses the components from the perspective of their criticality to the RAG system. We look at the layers divided into the following three categories:

- Critical layers that are fundamental to the operation of a RAG system. A RAG system is likely to fail if any of these layers are missing or are incomplete.
- Essential layers that are important for performance, reliability, and safety of the system. These essential components bring the system to a standard that provides value to the user.
- Enhancement layers that improve the efficiency, scalability, and usability of the system. These components are used to make the RAG system better and are selected based on the end requirements.

7.1.1 Critical layers

The indexing pipeline and the generation pipeline (discussed in detail in chapters 3 and 4) form the core of a RAG system. Figure 7.1 illustrates the indexing pipeline that facilitates the creation of the knowledge base for RAG systems and the generation pipeline that uses the knowledge base to generate context-aware responses.

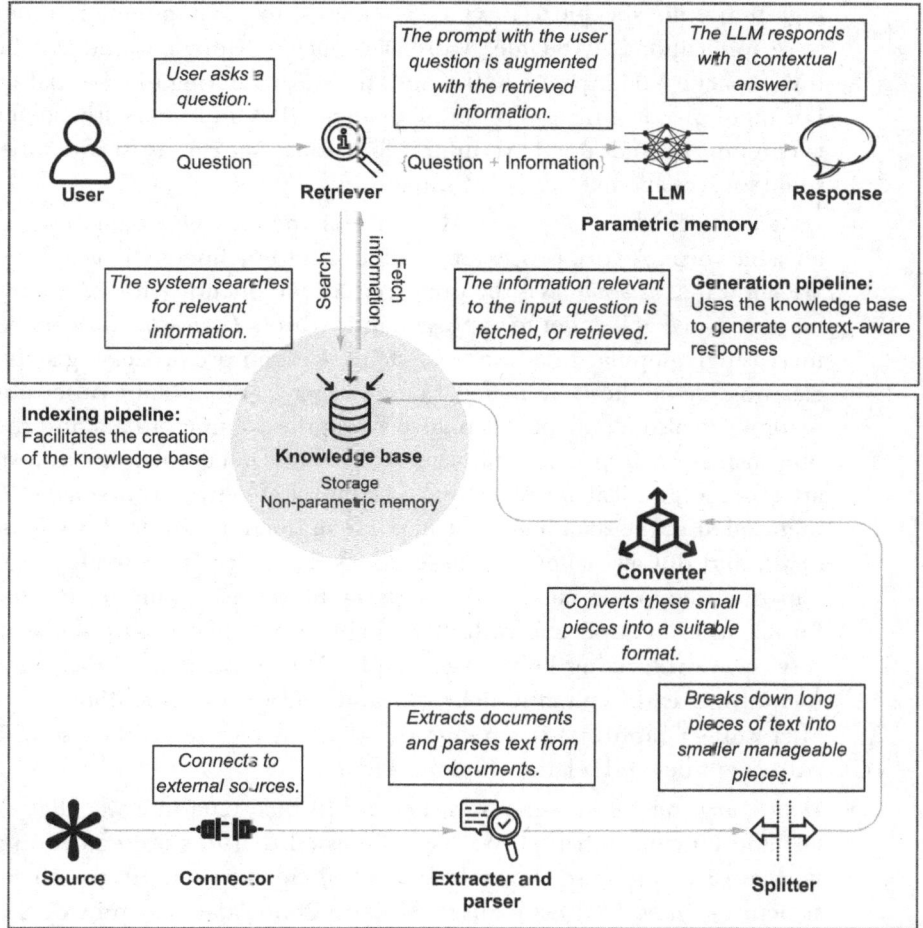

Figure 7.1   Indexing and generation pipelines forming the core of a RAG system

Layers enabling these two pipelines form the critical layers of the RAGOps stack.

DATA LAYER

The data layer serves the critical role of creating and storing the knowledge base for RAG. It is responsible for collecting data from source systems, transforming it into a usable format, and storing it for efficient retrieval. Here are some components of the data layer:

- *Data ingestion component*—It collects data from source systems such as databases, content management systems, file systems, APIs, devices, and even the internet. The data can be ingested in batches or as a stream, depending on the use case. For ingesting data, your choice of tool can depend on factors such as data volume, types of data source, ingestion frequency, cost, and ease of setup. Data ingestion is not specific to RAG but is a mainstream component in modern software applications. AWS Glue, Azure Data Factory, Google Cloud Dataflow, Fivetran, Apache NiFi, Apache Kafka, and Airbyte are among tools available for use. For rapid prototyping and proof of concepts (PoCs), frameworks such as LangChain and LlamaIndex have inbuilt functions that can assist in connecting to some sources and extracting information.

- *Data transformation component*—It converts the ingested data from a raw to a usable form. A core process in the indexing pipeline is the *chunking* of data. We know that *embeddings* is the preferred format of choice for RAG applications because it makes it easier to apply semantic search. *Graph structures* are becoming increasingly popular in advanced systems. Certain pre-processing steps such as cleaning, de-duplication, metadata enrichment, and masking of sensitive information are also a part of this phase. While the volume of data and the nature of transformation play an important role in any data-transformation step, they are especially critical in RAG systems. All the extract–transform–load (ETL) tools mentioned in the data ingestion step in conjunction with tools such as Apache Spark and dbt also allow transformations. However, if we focus just on RAG, Unstructured.io specializes in processing and transforming unstructured data for use in LLM applications. It offers open source libraries as well as managed services. Constructing knowledge graphs from unstructured data has evolved today from early semantic networks and ontologies into robust frameworks. Microsoft's GraphRAG is a framework that has pioneered the use of LLMs to extract entities and relationships from text.

- *Data storage component*—It stores the transformed data in a way that allows for fast and efficient retrieval. We have discussed that to store embeddings, *vector databases* are widely used because they are efficient in similarity search. For graph structures, *graph databases* are used. Most traditional database providers are incorporating vector search capabilities into their systems. Cost, scale, and speed are the primary drivers in the choice of data storage. We have used a vector index such as FAISS in this book. Pinecone is a fully managed cloud-native service. Milvus, Qdrant, and Chroma are among the open source vector databases. Weviate is another database that also has a GraphQL-based interface for knowledge graphs. Neo4j is a leading graph database for storing and querying graph data. A comparison of popular vector databases is available at https://www.superlinked .com/vector-db-comparison.

The flow from source systems to data storage via the ingestion and transformation components that lead to the creation of the knowledge base is shown in figure 7.2.

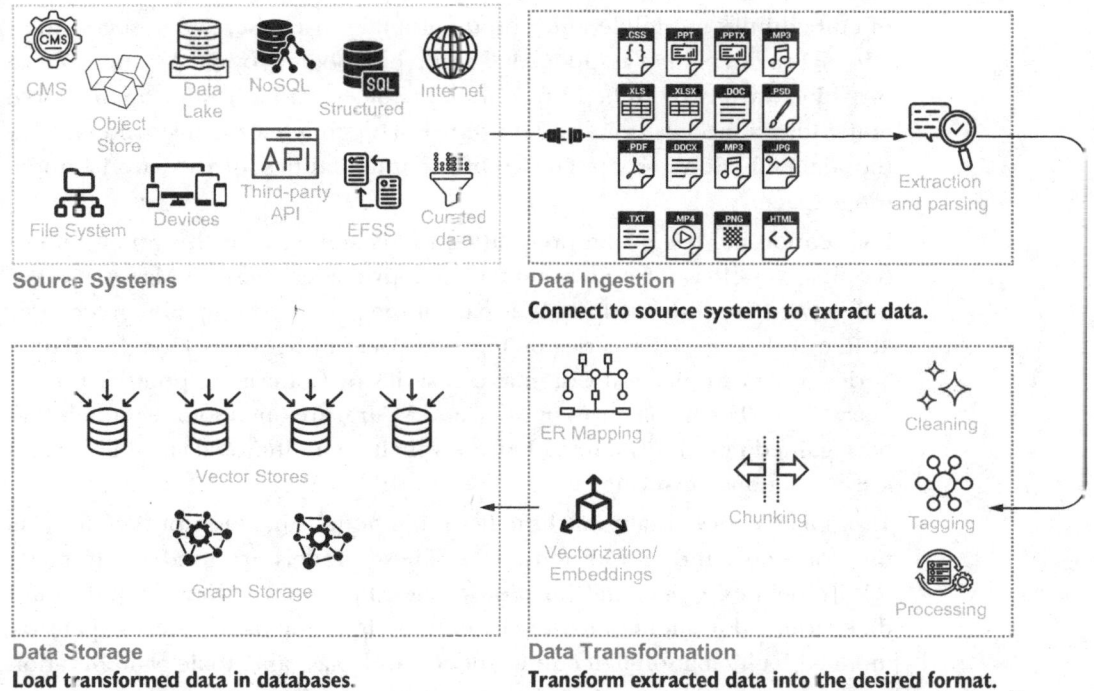

Source Systems

Data Ingestion
Connect to source systems to extract data.

Data Storage
Load transformed data in databases.

Data Transformation
Transform extracted data into the desired format.

Figure 7.2   Data layer: Creating the knowledge base by extracting, transforming, and loading (ETL) data from source systems

A strong data layer is the foundation of an efficient RAG system. The data layer also comes in handy when there is a need for fine-tuning of models. We discuss this feature briefly later in the chapter. Next, we look at the model layer, which includes the embeddings models used to transform text into vectors and the LLMs used in generation.

MODEL LAYER

Predictive models enable generative AI applications. Some models are provided by third parties, and some need to be custom trained or fine-tuned. Generating quick and cost-effective model responses is also an important aspect of using predictive models. The model layer includes the following three components:

- *Model library*—It contains the list of models that have been chosen for the application. The most popular models are the LLMs that generate text and other generative models that can generate images, video, and audio. We saw that in the data layer, raw text is transformed into vector embeddings, and this is done using embeddings models. Apart from this, there are other models used in RAG systems:

- Embeddings models are used to transform data into vector format. We have discussed embeddings models in detail in chapter 3. Recall that the choice of embeddings model depends on the domain, use case, and cost considerations. Providers such as OpenAI, Gemini by Google, Voyage AI, and Cohere provide a variety of embeddings model choices, and a host of open source embeddings models can also be used via Hugging Face transformers. Multimodal embeddings map data of different modalities into a shared embeddings space.

- Foundation models or the pre-trained LLMs are used for the generation of outputs, as well as for evaluation and adaptive tasks where LLMs are used to judge. We have discussed LLMs as part of the generation pipeline in chapter 4. Recall that the GPT series by OpenAI, Gemini Series by Google, Claude Series by Anthropic, and Command R series by Cohere are popular proprietary LLMs. The llama series by Meta and Mistral are open source models that have gained popularity. Most LLMs now include multimodal capabilities and are continuously evolving.

- Task-specific models are machine learning models that are not core to RAG but come in handy for various tasks. These models are used in advanced RAG pipelines. Query classification models for efficient routing and intent detection, NER models to detect entities for metadata, query-expansion models, hallucination-detection models, and bias- and toxicity-moderation models are some examples of task-specific models useful in RAG systems. While task-specific models are generally custom trained, providers such as OpenAI, Hugging Face, and Google also offer these services.

- *Model training and fine-tuning component*—This component is responsible for building custom models and fine-tuning foundation models on custom data. In chapter 4, we discussed that fine-tuning of LLMs is sometimes required for domain adaptation. Fine-tuning can also be done for embeddings models. Additionally, the task-specific models can be trained on custom data. This component supports the algorithms used for training and fine-tuning the models. For training data, this component interacts with the data layer where the training data can be created and managed. A regular MLOps layer is also recommended for the development and maintenance of the models. This is enabled via ML platforms such as Hugging Face, AWS SageMaker, Azure ML, and similar.

- *Inference optimization component*—This component is responsible for generating responses quickly and cost-effectively, which can be done by employing a variety of methods such as quantization, batching, KV(Key Value)-caching, and similar. ONNX and NVIDIA TensorRT-LLM are popular frameworks that optimize inferencing.

Figure 7.3 illustrates different components of the model layer. It shows how the model layer helps in deciding which models to use in the RAG system, facilitates training and fine-tuning of the model, and optimizes the models for efficient serving.

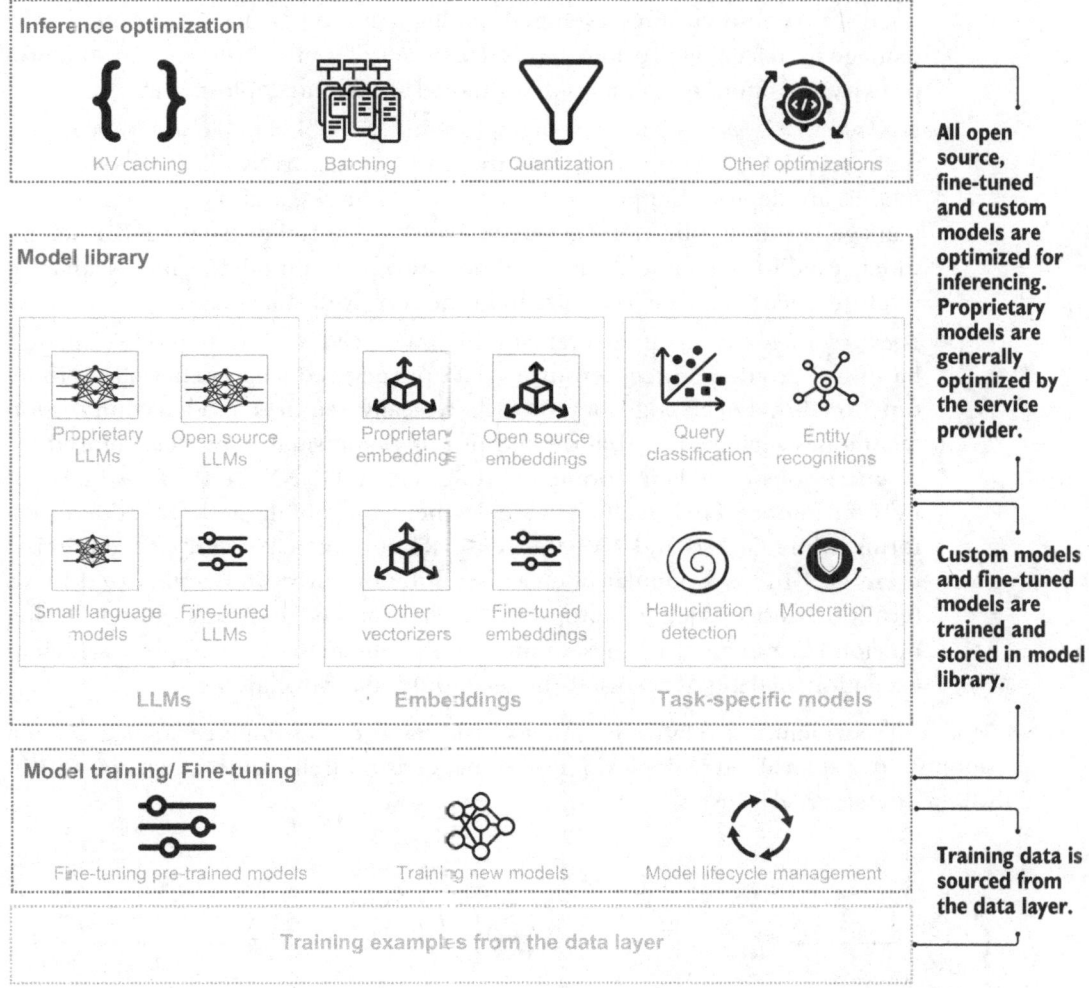

Figure 7.3   The model layer: The model library is the store for all models selected for the application, model training and fine-tuning interact with the data layer to source training data and train custom models, while the inference optimization component is responsible for efficient serving of the model.

MODEL DEPLOYMENT

This layer is responsible for making the RAG system available to the application layer. It handles the infrastructure of the models. It also ensures that the models can be accessed reliably. There are four main methods by which the models can be deployed:

- *Fully managed deployment*—It can be provided by proprietary model providers such as OpenAI, Google, Anthropic, and Cohere, where all infrastructure for model deployment, serving, and scaling is managed and optimized by these providers. Services such as AWS SageMaker, Google Vertex AI, Azure Machine Learning, and Hugging Face offer platforms to deploy, serve, and monitor both open source and custom-developed models. Amazon Bedrock is another fully managed service that provides access to a variety of foundation models, both proprietary and open source, simplifying model access and deployment.

- *Self-hosted deployment*—This type of deployment is enabled by cloud VM providers such as AWS, GCP, Azure, and hardware providers such as Nvidia. In this scenario, models are deployed in private clouds or on-premises, and the infrastructure is managed by the application developer. Tools such as Kubernetes and Docker are widely used for containerization and orchestration of models, while Nvidia Triton Inference Server can optimize inference on Nvidia hardware.

- *Local/edge deployment*—It involves running optimized versions of models on local hardware or edge devices, ensuring data privacy, reduced latency, and offline functionality. Local/edge deployment typically requires model compression techniques such as quantization and pruning, and smaller models tailored for resource-constrained environments. Tools such as ONNX, TensorFlow Lite, and PyTorch Mobile enable efficient deployment on mobile and embedded platforms, while GGML and NVIDIA TensorRT support CPU and GPU optimizations. GPT4All is a popular open source solution for running quantized LLMs locally on devices such as laptops, IoT devices, and edge servers without relying on cloud infrastructure. These frameworks facilitate low-latency, power-efficient execution, making AI accessible in decentralized environments.

Model deployment is a relatively complex task that requires engineering skills when self-hosted and local/edge deployment is done. Figure 7.4 illustrates the three ways in which models are deployed.

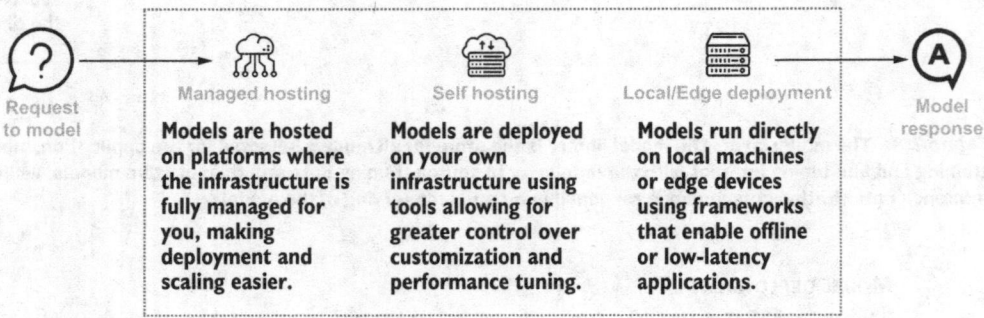

Figure 7.4   The model deployment layer manages the infrastructure for hosting and deployment for efficient serving of all the models in the RAG system.

With the data and the model layers, the most essential components of the RAG system are in place. Now we need a layer that manages the co-ordination between the data and the models. This is the responsibility of the application orchestration layer.

APPLICATION ORCHESTRATION LAYER

When we hear the term *orchestration,* a musical conductor leading a group of musicians in an orchestra comes to mind. An application orchestration layer is somewhat similar. It is responsible for managing the interactions among the other layers in the system. It is a central coordinator that enables communication between data, retrieval systems, generation models, and other services. The major components of the orchestration layer are

- *Query orchestration component*—Responsible for receiving and orchestrating user queries. All pre-retrieval query optimization steps such as query classification, expansion, and rewriting are orchestrated by this component. The query orchestration layer may coordinate with the end application layer to receive the input, and the model layer to access the models required for the query optimization. This component will generally pass on the processed query to the retrieval coordination and the generation coordination components.

- *Retrieval coordination component*—Hosts the various retrieval logics. Depending on the input from the query orchestration module, it selects the appropriate retrieval method (dense retrieval or hybrid retrieval) and interacts with the data layer. Depending on the retrieval strategy, it may also interact with the model layer if any recursive or adaptive retrieval method is invoked.

- *Generation coordination component*—Receives the query and the context from the previous components and coordinates all the post-retrieval steps. Its primary function is to interact with the model layer and prompt the LLM to generate the output. Apart from generation, all the post-retrieval steps such as re-ranking and contextual compression are coordinated by this component. Post-generation tasks such as reflection, fact-checking, and moderation can be coordinated by the generation component. This component can also be made responsible for passing the output to the application layer.

These are the three primary components of the orchestration layer. There are two additional components to consider:

- *Multi-agent orchestration component*—Used for agentic RAG where multiple agents handle specific tasks. We will take a deeper look at agentic RAG in chapter 8. The orchestration layer is responsible for managing agent interactions and coordination.

- *Workflow automation component*—Sometimes employed for managing the flow and the movement of data between different components. This component is not specific to RAG systems but is commonly employed in data products. Apache Airflow and Dagster are popular tools used for workflow automation.

Figure 7.5 illustrates the orchestration layer components interacting with the application layer, which is supported by the model deployment and data layer.

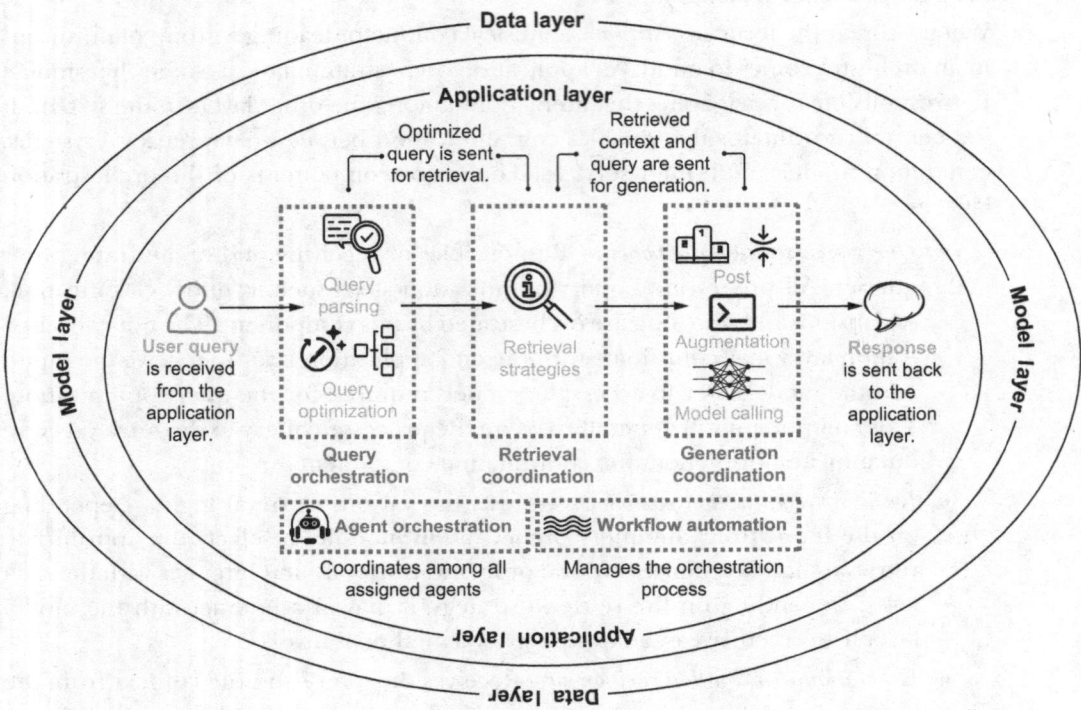

Figure 7.5   The app orchestration layer accepts the user query from the application layer and sends the response back to the application layer.

LangChain and LlamaIndex are the most common orchestration frameworks used to develop RAG systems. They provide abstractions for different components. Microsoft's AutoGen and CrewAI are upcoming frameworks for multi-agent orchestration.

With these four layers (i.e., data, model, model deployment, and application orchestration), the critical RAG system is complete. This core system can interact with the end-software application layer, which acts as the interface between the RAG system and the user. While the application layer is generally custom built, platforms such as Streamlit, Vercel, and Heroku are popular for hosting the application. Figure 7.6 summarizes the critical layers of the RAGOps stack.

Now that you are familiar with the core layers of the stack, let's look next at the essential layers that improve the performance and reliability of the system.

Various service providers offer managed solutions across the layers of the RAGOps stack.

The orchestration layer interacts with all other layers to orchestrate the RAG pipelines.

The orchestration layer receives input from application and returns the response.

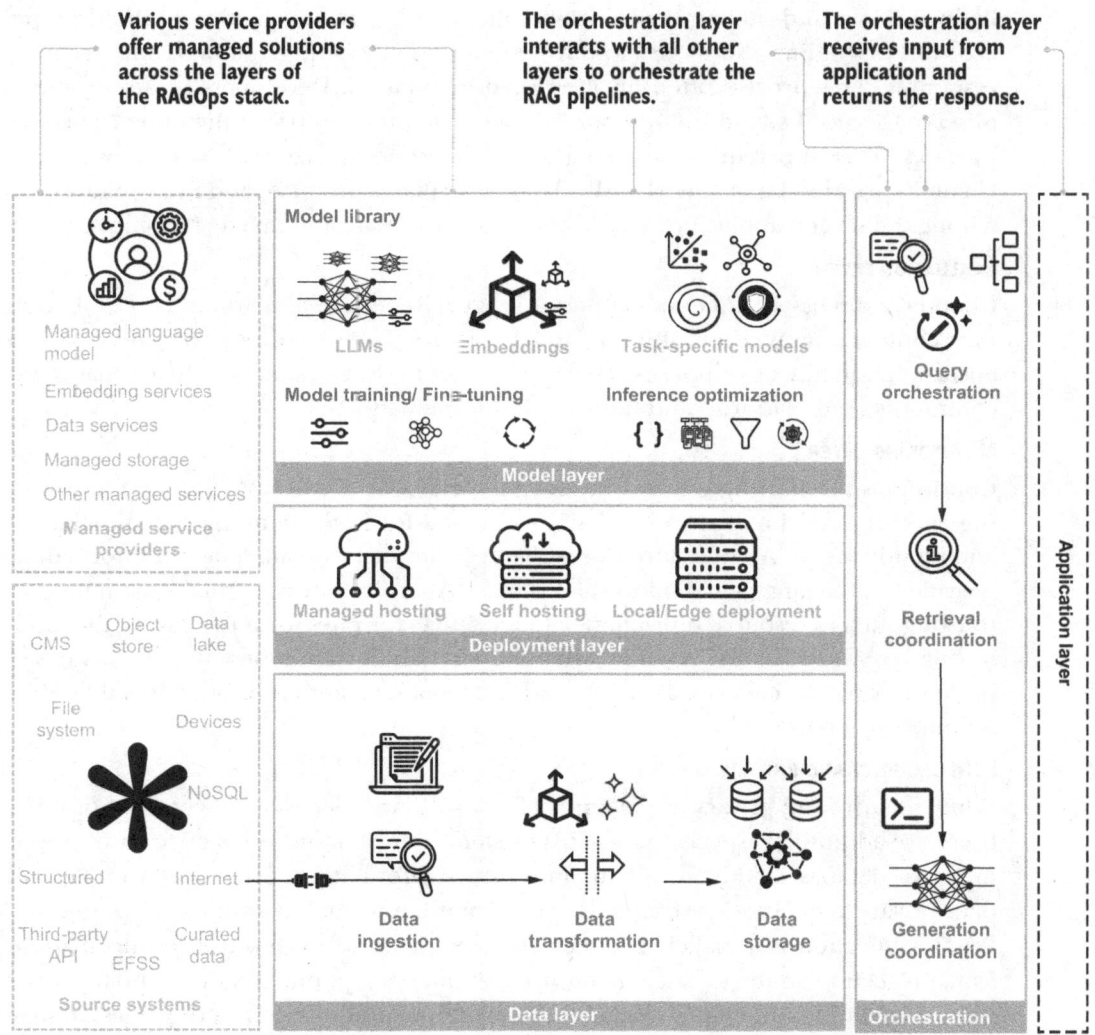

Figure 7.6   Core RAGOps stack where data, model, model deployment, and app orchestration layers interact with source systems and managed service providers, and co-ordinate with the application layer to interface with the user

7.1.2   *Essential layers*

While the critical layers form the core of the stack, they do not evaluate or monitor the system. They do not test the prompting strategies or offer any protection against the vulnerabilities of LLMs. These layers are essential to the system.

PROMPT LAYER

While the generation coordination component of the orchestration layer can simply put together the user query and the retrieved context, poor prompting can lead to hallucinations and subpar results. Proper engineering and evaluation of the prompts are vital to guiding the model toward generating relevant, grounded, and accurate responses. This process often involves experimentation. Developers create prompts, observe the results, and then iterate on the prompts to improve the effectiveness of the app. This also requires tracking and collaboration. Azure Prompt Flow, Lang-Chain Expression Language (LCEL), Weights & Biases prompts, and PromptLayer are among the several applications that can be used to create and manage prompts.

EVALUATION LAYER

Chapter 5 discussed RAG evaluations at length. Regular evaluation of retrieval accuracy, context relevance, faithfulness, and answer relevance of the system is necessary to ensure the quality of responses. TruLens by TruEra, Ragas, and Weights & Biases are commonly used platforms and frameworks for evaluation.

MONITORING LAYER

Continuous monitoring ensures the long-term health of the RAG system. Observing the execution of the processing chain is essential for understanding system behavior and identifying points of failure. Assessing the relevance and adequacy of information provided to the language model is also critical. Apart from this, regular system metrics tracking such as resource utilization, latency, and error rates form the part of the monitoring layer. ARISE, RAGAS, and ARES are evaluation frameworks that are also used in monitoring. TraceLoop, TruLens, and Galileo are examples of providers that offer monitoring services.

LLM SECURITY AND PRIVACY LAYER

While security and privacy are features of any software system, in the context of RAG, there are additional aspects to this. RAG systems rely on large knowledge bases stored in vector databases, which can contain sensitive information. They need to follow all data privacy regulations. AI models are susceptible to manipulation and poisoning. Prompt injection is a malicious attack via prompts to retrieve sensitive information. Data protection strategies such as anonymization, encryption, and differential privacy should be employed. Query validation, sanitization, and output filtering assist in protection against attacks. Implementing guardrails, access controls, monitoring, and auditing are also components of the security and privacy layer.

CACHING LAYER

Caching has become a very important component of any LLM-based application. This is because of the high costs and inherent latency of generative AI models. With the addition of a retrieval layer, the costs and latency increase further in RAG systems. One way to control this increase is to cache responses to frequently asked queries. In principle, caching LLM responses is like caching in any other software application, but for generative AI apps, it becomes more important.

These essential layers stacked together with the critical layers create a robust, accurate, and high-performing RAG system. Figure 7.7 adds the essential layers and their components to the critical RAGOps stack.

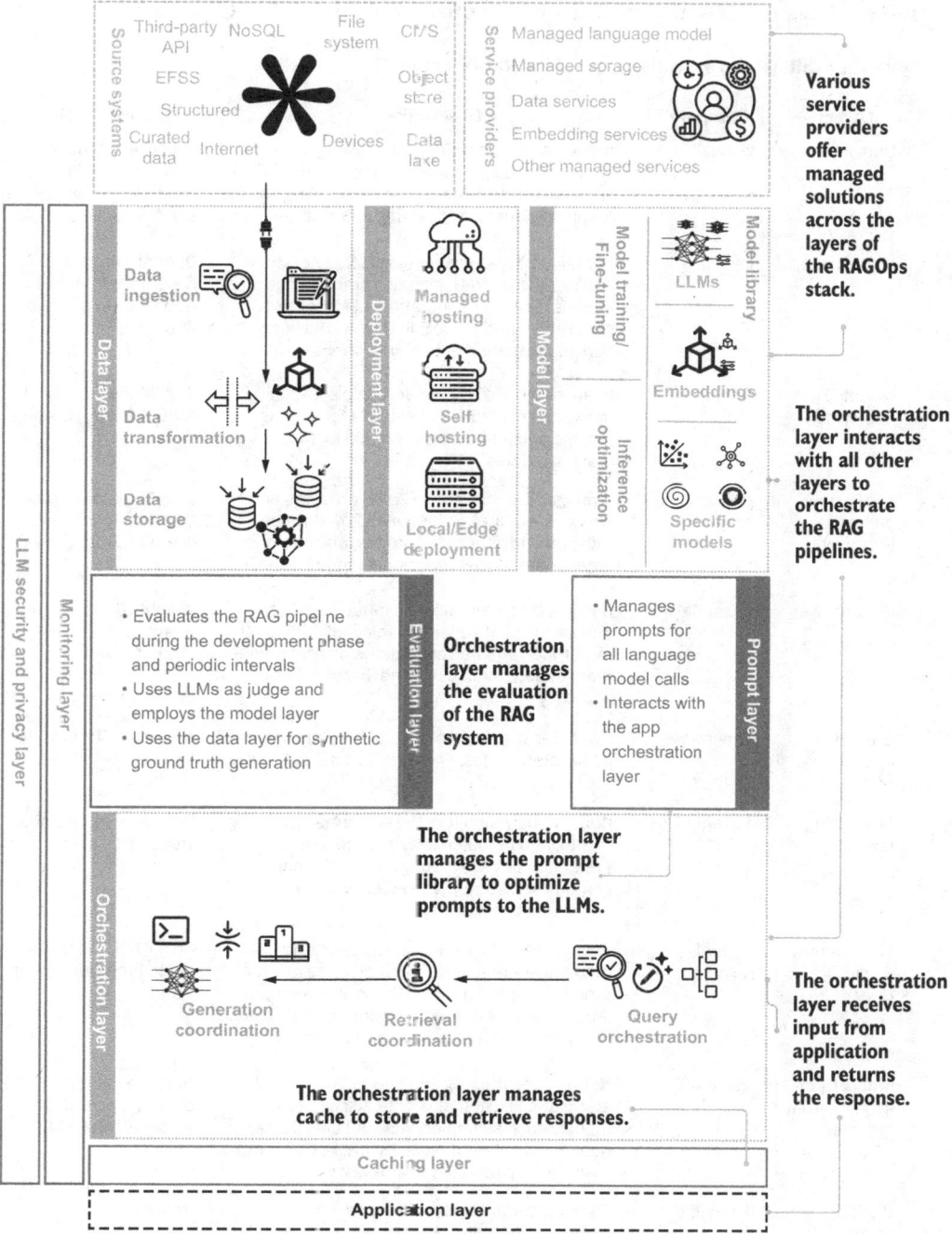

Figure 7.7 Adding essential layers to the critical RAGOps stack lays the path to a robust RAG system for user applications.

Table 7.1 is a recap of the critical and essential layers of the RAGOps stack.

Table 7.1   Critical and essential layers of the RAGOps stack

Layer	Category	Description	Example tools
Data layer	Critical	Responsible for creating and storing the knowledge base via ingestion from various sources, transformation into embeddings or graph structures, and storing for retrieval	AWS Glue, Apache Kafka, FAISS, Pinecone, Neo4j, Weaviate, Milvus
Model layer	Critical	Contains the models required for generation and retrieval in RAG; includes embeddings models for vector generation, LLMs for text generation, and models for query classification, hallucination detection, or re-ranking	OpenAI, Hugging Face Transformers, Google Gemini, Llama, Anthropic
Model deployment	Critical	Ensures the models are accessible, performant, and scalable; responsible for serving models and optimizing inference for fast response times	SageMaker, Vertex AI, NVIDIA Triton, Hugging Face
Application orchestration layer	Critical	Manages the interaction between layers and services, ensures that queries flow through retrieval and generation stages, and coordinates retrieval methods and generation tasks	LangChain, Haystack, Dagster, Apache Airflow, AutoGen, CrewAI
Prompt layer	Essential	Designs and maintains the input queries to ensure the LLM generates relevant, high-quality outputs; ensures continuous prompt refinement to avoid hallucinations and improve accuracy	Weights & Biases Prompts, Azure Prompt Flow
Evaluation layer	Essential	Evaluates the performance of the retrieval and generation stages, ensuring that the outputs are relevant, factual, and accurate.	TruLens by TruEra, Ragas, Weights & Biases
Monitoring layer	Essential	Continuously monitors the performance, health, and resource usage of the RAG system; tracks key metrics such as latency, resource consumption, and error rates to ensure system stability.	Prometheus, Grafana, TruLens, Galileo
LLM security & privacy layer	Essential	Ensures that the RAG system adheres to data privacy regulations and protects against prompt injection or other forms of AI manipulation; implements security strategies such as encryption, access control, and guardrails	AWS KMS, Azure Key Vault, Prompt Injection Guards
Model training/Fine-tuning layer	Essential	Handles the training and fine-tuning of models for specific domains or tasks; fine-tuning models such as embeddings or LLMs using domain-specific datasets ensure better performance for specialized use cases.	Hugging Face, AWS SageMaker, Google Vertex AI, Azure ML
Caching layer	Essential	Caching frequently used queries and responses to reduce the latency and cost associated with repeated retrieval and generation tasks; ensures faster response times for common queries and minimizes resource usage for repeated tasks.	Redis, Varnish, ElasticCache

We will now briefly look at a few enhancement layers, which are not mandatory but may be employed to further improve the RAG systems. Note that there can be several enhancement layers and that they should be tailored to the use case requirements.

7.1.3   Enhancement layers

Enhancement layers are the parts of the RAGOps stack that are optional but can lead to significant gains, depending on the use case environment. They focus on the efficiency, usability, and scalability of the system. Some possible layers are described in the following.

HUMAN-IN-THE-LOOP LAYER

This layer provides critical oversight where human judgment is necessary, especially for use cases requiring higher accuracy or ethical considerations. It helps reduce model hallucinations and bias.

COST OPTIMIZATION LAYER

RAG systems can become very costly, especially with multiple calls to the LLMs for advanced techniques, evaluations, guardrails, and monitoring. This layer helps manage resources efficiently, which is particularly important for large-scale systems. Optimizing infrastructure can save significant costs but is not critical to the system functioning.

EXPLAINABILITY AND INTERPRETABILITY LAYER

This layer helps provide transparency for system decisions, especially important for domains requiring accountability (e.g., legal and healthcare). However, many applications can still function without this in nonregulated environments.

COLLABORATION AND EXPERIMENTATION LAYER

This layer is useful for teams working on development and experimentation but noncritical for system operation. This layer enhances productivity and iterative improvements. Weights & Biases is a popular platform that helps track experiments.

These enhancement layers should be chosen depending on the application requirements. There may be other layers that you may deem fit for your use case.

> ### Managed RAG solutions
>
> Building a RAG system can be complex if you don't have prior knowledge, budget, or time. To address these challenges, service providers offer managed RAG solutions.
>
> OpenAI offers the File Search tool that automatically parses and chunks your documents, creates and stores the embeddings, and uses both vector and keyword search to retrieve relevant content to answer user queries. AWS offers Amazon Bedrock Knowledge Bases, which is fully managed support for end-to-end RAG workflow. Azure AI, such as OpenAI file search, provides indexing and querying. Anthropic offers Claude projects where users can upload documents and provide context to have focused chats.

(continued)

Several other providers offer RAG as a service and can handle video and audio transcription, image content extraction, and document parsing. For quick and easy deployment of a RAG solution, managed service providers can be considered.

We have also discussed several service providers, tools, and technologies that you can use in the development of RAG systems. The choice of these tools and technologies may depend on factors such as

- *Scalability and performance required*—RAG systems need to handle large volumes of data efficiently, while maintaining low latency. As data scales or traffic spikes, the system must remain performant to ensure fast response times. Choose cloud platforms that allow for auto-scaling and variable loads. For high-performance and scalable retrieval, choose the vector databases that can handle millions of embeddings with low-latency search capabilities. Use inference optimization tools to help reduce latency during the generation phase.

- *Integration with existing stack*—Seamless integration with your current technology stack minimizes disruption and reduces complexity. If your system already operates on AWS, GCP, or Azure, using services that integrate well with these platforms can streamline development and maintenance. Choosing tools that natively integrate with your cloud provider, offer strong API support, and ensure that the chosen frameworks support these tools can be highly beneficial.

- *Cost efficiency*—LLMs require much more resources than traditional ML models. Costs, even with pay-as-you-go models, can escalate quickly with scale. Caching and inference optimization can help manage the costs.

- *Domain adaptation*—RAG systems often need to be adapted to specific industries or domains (e.g., healthcare and legal). Pre-trained models might not be fully effective for specific use cases unless fine-tuned with domain-specific data. For domain adaptation, models that can be easily fine-tuned should be chosen. Existing domain-specific models can also be considered.

- *Vendor lock-in constraints*—Since generative AI is an evolving field, using proprietary tools or services from a single vendor may lead to vendor lock-in, making it difficult to migrate to other platforms or adjust your stack as requirements change. Using open source or interoperable technologies where possible helps in maintaining flexibility. Choosing tools that are cloud-agnostic or support multi-cloud deployments to reduce dependency on a single vendor. A modular architecture is advised to swap components without a system redesign.

- *Community support*—Strong community support means access to resources, tutorials, troubleshooting, and regular updates, which can accelerate development and reduce debugging time. This is especially true for rapidly evolving fields such as LLMs and RAG. Tools with active communities such as Hugging Face,

LangChain, and similar are more likely to offer frequent updates, plugins, and third-party integrations.

With the knowledge of the critical, essential, and enhancement layers, you should be ready to put together a technology stack to build your RAG system. Let's now look at some common pitfalls and best practices to consider when building and deploying production-grade RAG system.

7.2 Production best practices

Despite earnest efforts in designing and planning the RAG system, some problems will inevitably creep up during development and deployment. Although RAG is still in its nascent form, some early trends of common mishaps and best practices have emerged. There have been many experiments and learnings derived from them to make RAG systems work. This section discusses five such practices:

- *Latency of the system*—RAG systems can introduce latency due to the need for multiple steps: retrieval, reranking, and generation. High latency can significantly degrade user experience, especially in real-time applications like chatbots or interactive search engines, which happens because each component adds processing time. Effective classification and routing of the queries can help in optimizing latency. A filtering approach is useful in hybrid retrieval, which first filters the embeddings based on keywords or sparse retrieval techniques and then uses similarity search on the filtered results. This reduces the time taken to calculate similarity, especially in large knowledge bases.

- *Continued hallucination*—Despite best efforts, LLMs may continue to generate responses that are factually incorrect or irrelevant to the retrieved content. This may happen if the retrieved data is ambiguous or incomplete. Post-processing validation steps may be required to address these. A common approach is to make RAG systems recommendation oriented rather than action oriented. This means that a human is looped into the system for verification and final action.

- *Insufficient scalability planning*—Early prototypes of RAG systems often work well on small datasets but can struggle as the volume of data or the number of concurrent users grows. Managed vector database services with autoscaling features can be an easier way to plan for growth in demand and computation requirements. Similarly, autoscaling can also be used for the overall application using cloud-native solutions such as AWS Lambda.

- *Domain-adaptation challenges*—The embeddings and language models may not work well in niche or specialized domains. Also, the retrieval model and the language model may not always complement each other well, leading to disjointed or incoherent results. Retrieval models and LLMs are often developed and fine-tuned independently, which can cause a mismatch between the content retrieved and the way the LLM generates responses. It becomes important to fine-tune both the retrieval and generation models together for highly specialized domains.

- *Inadequate handling of data privacy and PII*—Pre-trained models may generate content that includes sensitive information (e.g., personal data and confidential details) due to biases in training data. RAG systems may inadvertently leak sensitive information or personally identifiable information (PII) in their responses, leading to privacy breaches. Data exfiltration, also known as data theft, extrusion, or exportation, is a major threat in the digital world. The solution is to use PII masking and data redaction during both the pre- and post-processing stages. Ensure compliance with privacy regulations such as GDPR or HIPAA and deploy models with privacy filters.

The list of best practices continues to evolve. Latency and scalability are critical for managing user experience and access. The promise of hallucination-free generation and data safety needs to be maintained for the reliability of the system. Table 7.2 summarizes the challenges of and potential solutions to putting RAG systems into production.

Table 7.2   Production challenges and potential solutions

Challenge	Description	Solution
Latency of the system	RAG systems add latency due to retrieval, re-ranking, and generation steps, affecting real-time performance.	Use query classification, hybrid retrieval filtering, and limit similarity searches
Continued hallucination	LLMs may generate incorrect or irrelevant responses due to ambiguous or incomplete data.	Add post-processing validation and make systems recommendation-based with human verification.
Insufficient scalability planning	Early RAG systems struggle with scalability as data and user load grow.	Use autoscaling vector databases and cloud solutions such as AWS Lambda.
Domain-adaptation challenges	Embeddings and LLMs may perform poorly in specialized domains, leading to incoherent results.	Fine-tune both retrieval and generation models for niche use cases.
Inadequate handling of data privacy and PII	Models may expose sensitive data or PII, leading to privacy issues.	Apply PII masking, data redaction, and privacy filters, ensuring compliance with regulations.

In this chapter, we have looked at a holistic RAGOps stack that enables the building of production-grade RAG systems. You also learned about some commonly available tools and technologies, along with a few best practices. This brings us to a close in our discussion of the RAGOps stack. We have now completed part 3 of the book, which means you should be ready to build RAG systems and put them into production. In the last part of this book, we discuss some emerging patterns in RAG-like multimodal capabilities, agentic RAG, and graphRAG, along with closing comments on future directions and continued learning.

Summary

- RAGOps stack is a layered approach to designing a RAG system.
- These layers are categorized into critical, essential, and enhancement layers.
- Critical layers are fundamental for operation; essential layers ensure performance and reliability; and enhancement layers improve efficiency, scalability, and usability.

Critical layers

- *Data layer*—Responsible for collecting, transforming, and storing the knowledge base. Ingestion tools such as AWS Glue, Azure Data Factory, and Apache Kafka enable data collection. Data transformation includes chunking, metadata enrichment, and converting data into vector formats. Tools such as FAISS, Pinecone, and Neo4j are used for storing embeddings and graph data.
- *Model layer*—Includes embeddings models and LLMs for generation. Embeddings models transform the text into vectors, with options from OpenAI, Google, Cohere, and Hugging Face. Foundation models (LLMs) such as GPT, Claude, and Llama generate outputs and evaluate tasks. Task-specific models handle specialized tasks such as query classification and bias detection.
- *Model deployment*—Manages hosting and serving of LLMs and embeddings models. Popular platforms include AWS SageMaker, Google Vertex, and Hugging Face. Inference optimization reduces response time and costs with methods such as quantization and batching.
- *Application orchestration layer*—Coordinates data flow between different components:
  - Query orchestration handles query classification and optimization.
  - Retrieval coordination manages retrieval methods like dense or hybrid search.
  - Generation coordination handles prompt generation and post-retrieval tasks such as re-ranking.

Essential layers

- *Prompt layer*—Ensures prompts are well-engineered to guide LLMs for relevant, accurate responses. Tools such as LangChain and Azure Prompt Flow assist in prompt management.
- *Evaluation layer*—Monitors system performance by evaluating retrieval accuracy, faithfulness, and context relevance. Tools such as TruLens and Ragas provide evaluation frameworks.
- *Monitoring layer*—Tracks system health, resource usage, and latency. Platforms such as TraceLoop and Galileo provide monitoring services.
- *LLM security and privacy layer*—Protects against data breaches and prompt injection attacks. Tools such as encryption, anonymization, and differential privacy should be used to safeguard sensitive data.

- *Caching layer*—Caches frequently generated responses to reduce costs and latency in RAG systems.

Enhancement layers

- *Human-in-the-loop layer*—Adds human oversight to ensure higher accuracy and ethical decision-making.
- *Cost optimization layer*—Reduces infrastructure costs, especially in large-scale RAG systems.
- *Explainability and interpretability layer*—Provides transparency into system decisions, critical for domains such as healthcare and legal.
- *Collaboration and experimentation layer*—Useful for team-based development and continuous improvement.

Production best practices

- *Latency*—RAG systems often introduce latency due to multiple steps. Using techniques such as filtering in hybrid retrieval can help reduce response times.
- *Hallucination*—LLMs may still generate incorrect responses. Post-processing validation and human-in-the-loop systems help mitigate this.
- *Scalability*—Early prototypes may struggle to scale. Managed vector database services with autoscaling can help plan for growth.
- *Domain adaptation*—Embeddings and language models may not perform well in niche domains. Fine-tuning both retrieval and generation models is necessary.
- *Data privacy*—Models may leak sensitive information. PII masking, encryption, and compliance with data regulations are essential for protecting user data.

Part 4

Additional considerations

RAG is an evolving technique, and significant research activity has been ongoing in this field. In this concluding part of the book, you will learn about the popular state-of-the-art variants of RAG and a RAG development framework that will assist you in planning and building RAG systems.

Chapter 8 will teach you about the most important variants of RAG—multimodal RAG, knowledge graph-enhanced RAG, and agentic RAG—along with some other popular ones. Learning about these variants will let you customize your RAG systems to the use case you are building.

Chapter 9 revisits all the concepts discussed in this book, organized within a RAG development framework. This framework will help you strategically plan the development of your RAG system. You'll also get to know a few areas of research that remain open at the time of writing this book.

This concluding part of the book wraps up your introduction to RAG. By the end of this book, you should not only have the foundations to build production-grade RAG systems, but also the knowledge to follow and contribute to ongoing research in this domain.

Graph, multimodal, agentic, and other RAG variants

This chapter covers

- Introducing RAG variants
- Knowledge graph RAG
- Multimodal RAG
- Agentic RAG
- Other RAG variants

The first part of the book introduced retrieval-augmented generation (RAG) and the core idea behind it. The second part dealt with building and evaluating basic RAG systems. Part 3 took RAG beyond the naïve approach and discussed advanced techniques and the technology stack that supports a RAG system. The last part of the book looks at more RAG patterns, and we conclude our discussion with a few best practices and some areas for further exploration.

Chapter 8 looks at some popular RAG variants. These variants adapt different stages of RAG (i.e., indexing, retrieval, augmentation, and generation) to specific use case requirements. The chapter begins by discussing the emergence of these variants and the purpose they serve. We then continue talking about three important variants that have gained prominence in applied RAG. These are knowledge-graph-enhanced, multimodal, and agentic RAG. We also briefly examine other RAG variants that significantly contribute to the evolution of RAG in practical applications. We discuss the purpose and motivation behind each variant. This chapter also breaks down the workflow, features, and technical details of the variants along with their strengths and weaknesses. For simplicity, the code for these variants is not included in this chapter but can be found in the book's code repository.

By the end of this chapter, you should

- Be familiar with the idea and motivation behind RAG variants.
- Have an in-depth understanding of graph, multimodal, and agentic RAG.
- Be aware of several popular RAG variants and the use cases they solve.

There are several limitations of a naïve approach to RAG that affect the overall usability of a standard RAG system. These limitations range from difficulties in understanding relationships across different documents to challenges in handling various data types, as well as concerns regarding system cost and efficiency. Chapter 6 discussed several pre-retrieval, retrieval, and post-retrieval techniques, such as index optimization, query optimization, hybrid and iterative retrieval strategies, compression, and re-ranking, which address different limitations and improve the accuracy of a RAG system. Several RAG patterns that incorporate one or more of these techniques have emerged over time to solve specific use challenges. We refer to them as RAG variants.

8.1 What are RAG variants, and why do we need them?

The universe of applications that rely on RAG is expanding every day. Some of these applications process not just text, but different data modalities such as image, video, and audio as well. Others are being applied in domains such as healthcare and finance, where the effects of inaccurate results are catastrophic. The emerging domain of using LLMs as decision-making agents has also enabled a more adaptive and intelligent RAG system. Apart from factual accuracy, practical RAG applications demand low latency and low costs to enhance user experience and adoption. As the range of applications for RAG has expanded, so need specialized variations of RAG—known as RAG variants—designed to address unique challenges across different tasks and data types.

These RAG variants are adaptations of the standard RAG framework that extend its functionality to meet demands of diverse and complex use cases. By employing advanced pre-retrieval, retrieval and post-retrieval techniques, these variants enhance RAG with capabilities such as handling multimodal data, providing higher accuracy, and better relational understanding. The evolution of these RAG variants makes the system both flexible and domain aware.

While several RAG variants have emerged, the three that we are going to discuss in-depth in the subsequent sections have gained prominence:

- *Multimodal RAG*—Extends capabilities of the standard RAG beyond text data and incorporates other data types such as images, video, and audio. This characteristic enables the system to fetch information from nontextual documents and provide additional context.

- *Knowledge graph RAG*—Integrates knowledge graphs into the retrieval process. This idea was introduced in chapter 6 as part of improving the indexing structure. Knowledge graphs help establish relationships between entities, providing better context, especially in multi-hop queries.
- *Agentic RAG*—Incorporates LLM agents into the RAG framework. These agents enable autonomous decision making across the RAG value chain from indexing to generation. Simultaneously, all components become adaptive to the user query.

In addition to these three, we also touch upon additional variants, such as corrective RAG, self-RAG, and more, but first, we begin by discussing multimodality.

8.2 *Multimodal RAG*

Until now, we have seen that standard RAG systems are effective in managing and retrieving textual data to generate context-aware and grounded responses. However, the scope of enterprise data extends beyond text to image, audio, and video. Standard RAG systems fall short when attempting to interpret nontextual data formats. This is the core motivation behind a multimodal variant of RAG, which extends the capabilities to more data formats.

8.2.1 *Data modality*

Multimodality can be a confusing term for the uninitiated, especially because "modality" varies in meaning across different fields. Grammatical modality relates to the expression of the speaker's attitude, while treatment modality may refer to the medical approach in medicine. In RAG, and AI in general, modality refers to data format. Text is a modality, image is a modality, video and audio are different modalities, and we can also consider tables and code as distinct modalities. Figure 8.1 shows some data modalities, including less common ones such as genomic and 3D data.

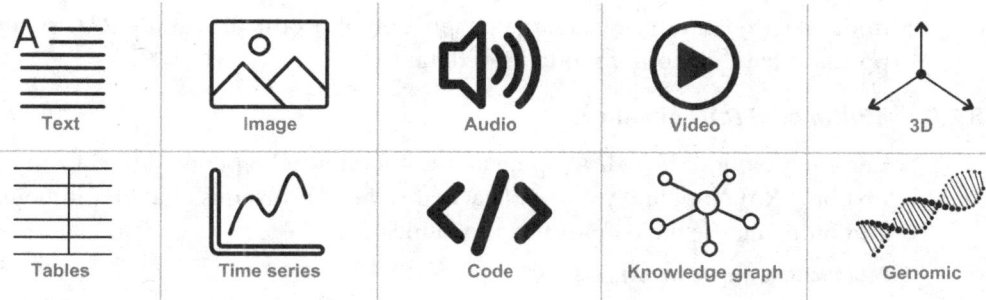

Figure 8.1 Examples of different data modalities

Multimodal RAG is, therefore, the extended variant of standard RAG with the capability to process multiple data modalities. Before diving into the requirements and architectural details of multimodal RAG, let's ponder over the use cases where multimodal RAG is necessary.

8.2.2   Multimodal RAG use cases

There are several industries and functions where a multimodal variant of RAG is required, such as

- *Medical diagnosis*—A diagnostic assistant can work with patient records that may include medical history (in text form), lab results (in tabular form), and diagnostic images (like X-rays, MRIs, etc.), along with studies and research papers that include graphs, charts, or microscopic images. When the patient comes in for a consultation, this assistant can provide a holistic analysis to the doctor.
- *Investment analysis*—Working with financial reports and other filings that have charts showing trends, earnings, and projections along with balance sheets and income statements in tabular form, apart from the usual text commentary, an investment research assistant can provide analysts with crucial information needed to make investment decisions.
- *Buying assistance*—Through an analysis of product images, textual descriptions, product specifications (in tabular form), and customer reviews, a shopping assistant can help the shoppers on an e-commerce website with personalized recommendations.
- *Coding assistance*—Coding assistants retrieve relevant documentation, function usage examples, and code snippets from repositories based on the query context. For example, when a developer asks how to implement a certain API function. The RAG system retrieves precise code snippets and explanations from the documentation, helping the developer avoid time-consuming searches.
- *Equipment maintenance*—Using historical text reports with visual inspection images or video feed, sensor data, and performance tables, a maintenance assistant can provide maintenance recommendations and trends.

These are just a few examples. While standard text-only RAG finds acceptability in the initial stages of a use case, a large proportion of production-grade RAG systems incorporate at least one other modality of data.

8.2.3   Multimodal RAG pipelines

Let's now explore how developing a multimodal RAG pipeline differs from a standard text-only RAG pipeline you have learned so far. An obvious change will be in loading and indexing the data of nontext modalities.

MULTIMODAL INDEXING PIPELINE

Developing the knowledge base for multimodal RAG requires enhancement in each of the four components of the indexing pipelines. Apart from loading and chunking files of different modalities, creating embeddings for multimodal data requires special attention. Let's look at each of the components one by one.

The data-loading step is quite like the standard text-only RAG but now includes connectors and data loaders for nontext modalities. There are several options available. `Pillow`, also known as `PIL`, is a popular Python library for loading images. `Unstructured` is an open source library that includes components for ingesting a variety of data formats. `Pydub` is another Python library that allows the loading of audio files such as WAV and MP3. LangChain provides an integration with the unstructured library. `UnstructuredImageLoader` is a class available in LangChain document loaders for loading images. For audio and video transcription, libraries such as `OpenAIWhisperParser`, `AssemblyAIAudioTranscriptLoader`, and `YoutubeLoader` can be used. Likewise, for tabular data `CSVLoader` and `DataFrameLoader` come in handy. For simplicity, sometimes data of different modalities is transcribed into text.

Chunking for multimodal data largely follows a process similar to text chunking in cases where audio/video data is transcribed and stored as text. However, for raw audio and video data, specific chunking methods can be employed. Voice activity detection (VAD) chunks the data based on silences or background noise in the audio. Scene-detection-based chunking identifies major changes in the scene to segment the video. For tabular data, sometimes row/column-level chunking can be incorporated, and for code, the chunking can be carried out at a function, a class, or a logical unit level. All strategies used for chunking text data such as context enrichment, semantic chunking, and similar are also held here. For images, chunking is generally not done. `semantic_chunkers` is a multimodal chunking library for intelligent chunking of text, video, and audio. It makes AI and data processing more efficient and accurate.

Embeddings is where nuance begins in multimodal RAG. In standard text-only RAG, there are several embeddings models available to vectorize the chunks. But how does one vectorize data of different modalities, such as an image? There are three approaches to deal with this complexity: shared or joint embedding models, modality-specific embeddings, and conversion of all non-text data into text.

Shared or joint embeddings models map diverse data types into a unified embeddings space. By doing this, cross-modal retrieval is enabled, such as finding images based on textual descriptions or generating text from images. Google Vertex AI offers shared embeddings models that generate vectors for all data modalities in the unified embeddings space. Shared embeddings models are also called multimodal embeddings models. While efficient at understanding general image data, multimodal embeddings sometimes fall short when granular understanding is needed, as in charts and tables represented as images and infographics. In figure 8.2, image, text, audio, and video data are plotted in the same 3D vector space.

The modality-specific embeddings approach resemble multimodal embeddings, except that instead of a single embeddings space for all modalities, the embeddings space maps only two modalities. In such a scenario, we need an image–text embeddings model to process text, image, and audio data (e.g., Contrastive Language–Image

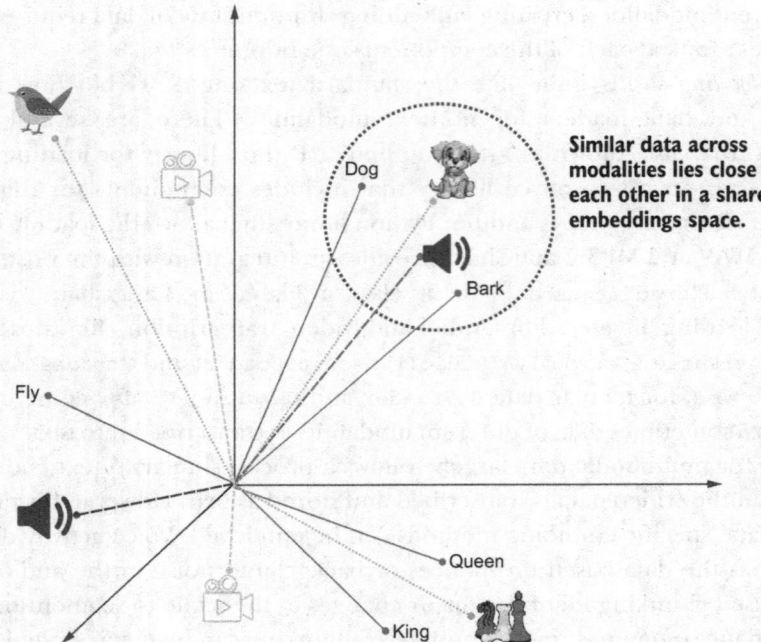

Similar data across modalities lies close to each other in a shared embeddings space.

Figure 8.2 Images, text, video, and audio are plotted on the same embeddings space. Dog, bark, and dog's image are close to each other.

Pretraining, or CLIP) and an audio-text embeddings model (e.g., Contrastive Language–Audio Pretraining, or CLAP). The knowledge base has text, image, and audio embeddings in different embeddings spaces and stored separately. Figure 8.3 is an example of CLIP image–text embeddings where image and text embeddings are projected onto a shared embeddings space.

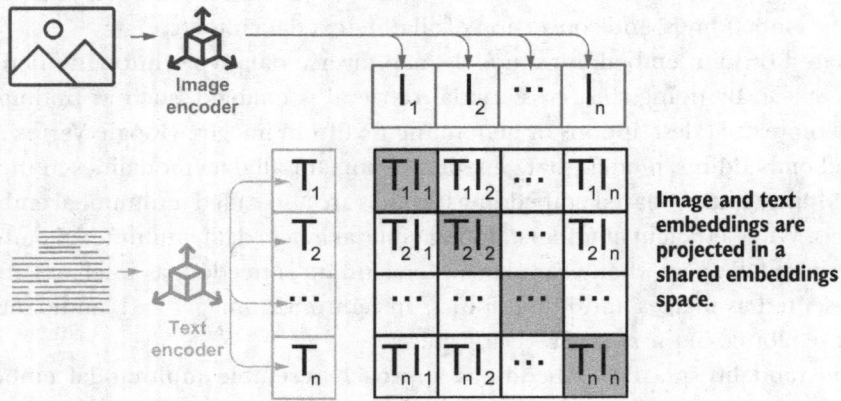

Image and text embeddings are projected in a shared embeddings space.

Figure 8.3   CLIP uses multimodal pre-training to convert classification into a retrieval task, which enables pre-trained models to tackle zero-shot recognition.

Conversion of all non-text data into text is employed to first convert all nontext (image) data into text using a multimodal LLM and then follow the standard text-only RAG approach. (A multimodal LLM is a large language model that processes all modalities of data. You will read more about multimodal LLMs later in this section.) In this strategy, you may notice that we may not be entirely using multimodal data as information loss is bound to occur when converting nontext to text data. In a variation of this strategy, instead of converting all multimodal data into text and using it as text, a two-pronged approach is employed. Here all multimodal data is summarized in text using a multimodal LLM. Embeddings of this text are used to search for during the retrieval process. However, for generation, not only the summary but the actual multimodal file (e.g., a .jpeg) is retrieved and passed to the multimodal LLM for generation. This reduces the loss of information when converting to text.

Embeddings, either multimodal or text, are *stored* in vector databases such as standard text-only RAG. In addition to vector storage, document storage is required to store raw files that can be retrieved and passed to the LLM for generation. Document stores such as Redis can be used to store raw files. When text summaries are used, a key mapping of the summary embeddings to the raw documents must be created. Figure 8.4 shows the indexing pipeline with all three options for embeddings.

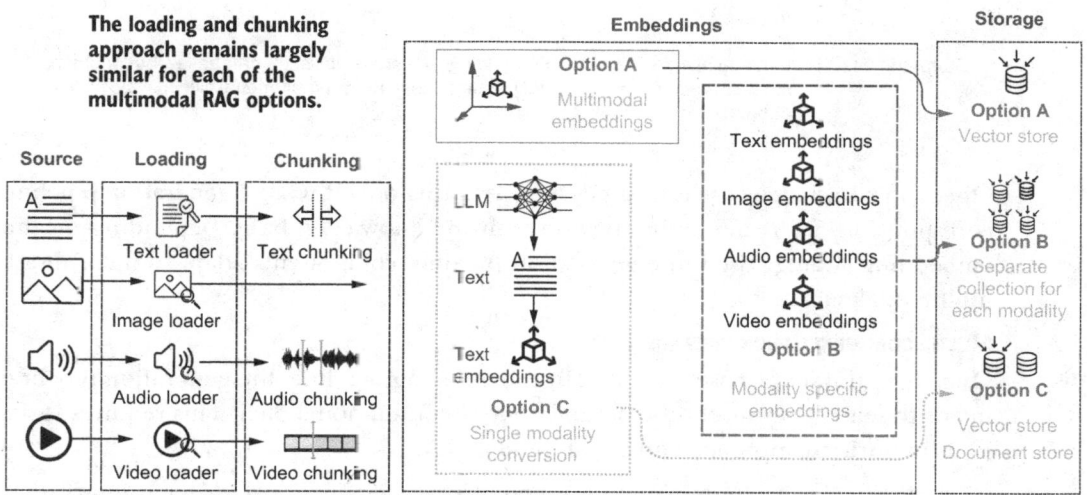

Figure 8.4   Multimodal indexing pipeline presenting three options

While the loading, chunking, and storage components are similar, the embedding component presents several options in multimodal RAG. Table 8.1 compares the indexing pipelines of text-only RAG and multimodal RAG.

Table 8.1   Indexing pipelines of text-only vs. multimodal RAG

Indexing component	Text-only RAG	Multimodal RAG
Loading	Standard text data loaders are used to load documents, such as plain text files, PDFs, and other text-based formats.	Requires connectors for additional data types. For images, libraries such as `Pillow` (`PIL`) and `Unstructured-ImageLoader` in LangChain are used; for audio, we use libraries such as `Pydub` or `OpenAIWhisperParser`, whereas `CSVLoader` and `DataFrameLoader` are used for tabular data. Audio and video transcription tools such as AssemblyAI and YoutubeLoader are also incorporated to preprocess audio/video content.
Chunking	Text data is divided into segments (chunks) based on context or structure (e.g., sentences, paragraphs) and optionally enriched semantically.	Follows text chunking when data is transcribed to text (audio/video). For raw audio, voice activity detection (VAD) can be used to chunk by pauses. For videos, scene detection identifies visual transitions, and tabular data can be chunked row/column-wise. Image chunking is typically skipped.
Embeddings	Text embeddings are created using a single-modality text embeddings model (e.g., OpenAI embeddings or BERT), which vectorizes each chunk for storage and retrieval.	Embeddings can be generated via multimodal embeddings models, which unify all data types in a shared vector space for cross-modal retrieval, modality-specific embeddings such as CLIP and CLAP or converting multimodal data to text first and use text embeddings, although this may cause information loss.
Storage	Embeddings are stored in vector databases.	Embeddings are stored in vector databases, but additional document storage for raw multimodal files may be used.

Once the knowledge base is created, such as in text-only RAG, the generation pipeline is responsible for real-time interaction with the knowledge base. Depending on the embedding strategy used, the generation pipeline components adapt to incorporate multimodal data.

MULTIMODAL GENERATION PIPELINE

Once the knowledge base is created by the indexing pipeline, the generation pipeline needs to search, retrieve, process, and generate multimodal data. This requires variations in retrieval approach and a multimodal LLM:

- *Retrieval*—Depending on the embeddings strategy, the retrieval technique varies:
  - In case a shared multimodal embeddings model is used, the retrieval process follows a similarity search approach, where the user query is converted into a vector form using the same multimodal embeddings, and the documents are retrieved based on their cosine similarity value irrespective of their modality.
  - In the modality-specific embedding approach, because multiple embeddings are present, a multi-vector retrieval approach is employed. For a single query,

documents are retrieved from each modality-specific embeddings space based on similarity. These documents may later be re-ranked before augmentation and generation.

– When nontext data is converted into text, the retrieval process is the same as the standard text-only RAG. In the variation where both text summaries and raw files are used, the retriever first retrieves the relevant summaries from the text embeddings space, and then the files from the document stores mapped to those summaries are also retrieved.

- *Augmentation*—The augmentation step remains the same as text-only RAG, except that the augmented prompt now includes the raw multimodal file accompanying the text prompt.

- *Generation*—Like multimodal embeddings, for processing and generating multimodal data, multimodal LLMs are used. LLMs are limited by their ability to process text data only. Multimodal LLMs are transformers-based models, too, but have been trained on data of all modalities, in addition to text data. There are nuanced differences in the training process of multimodal LLMs, and the readers are encouraged to explore them. However, for building RAG systems, we can use the available foundation multimodal LLMs. OpenAI's GPT 4o and GPT 4o mini and Google's Gemini are popular proprietary multimodal LLMs, while Meta's Llama 3.2 and Mistral AI's Pixtral are open source multimodal LLMs.

While the augmentation step remains similar to text-only RAG, the retrieval step adapts based on the embeddings strategy used, and the generation step swaps the LLMs with multimodal LLMs. The differences in the generation pipelines are highlighted in table 8.2.

Table 8.2 Indexing pipelines of text-only vs. multimodal RAG

Generation component	Text-only RAG	Multimodal RAG
Retrieval	Retrieves similar text embeddings to the query using similarity search	Varies by embedding strategy—in shared embeddings model, a similarity search is employed regardless of modality, converting the query into a multimodal vector. In modality-specific embeddings, multi-vector retrieval is used for modality-specific results, and in text-converted nontext data, a standard text retrieval along with raw files mapped to text summaries is used.
Augmentation	Adds retrieved text to the prompt	Similar to text-only but includes the raw multimodal files alongside the text in the prompt.
Generation	Uses LLMs to generate responses	Uses multimodal LLMs instead of text-only LLMs.

By tweaking the indexing and generation pipelines, a standard text-only RAG system can be upgraded to a multimodal RAG system, as illustrated in figure 8.5.

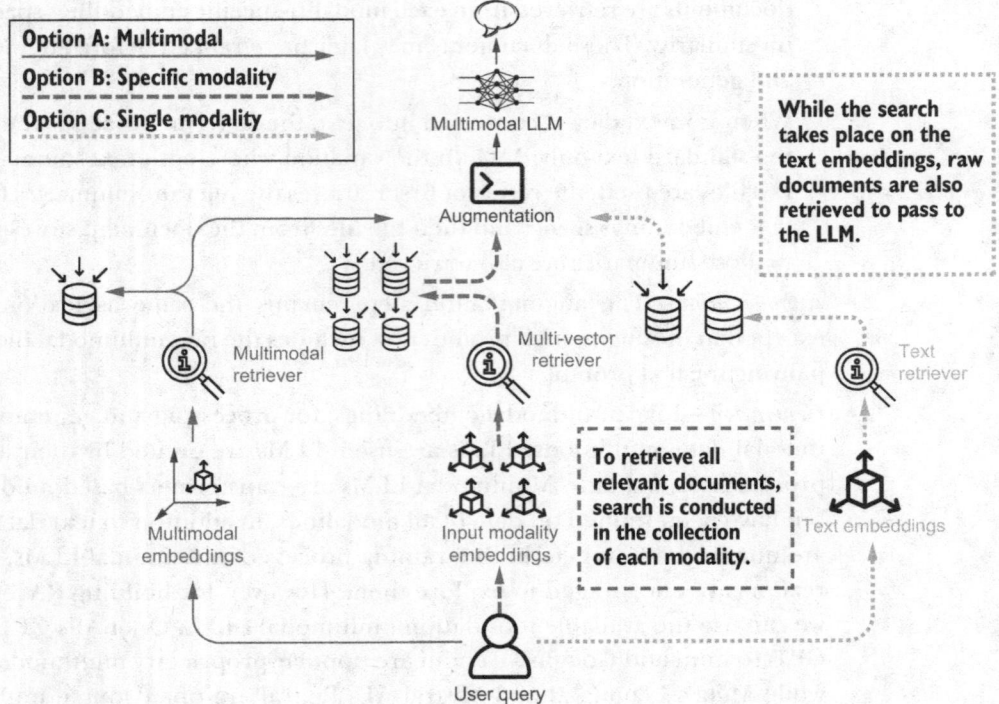

Figure 8.5   For each of the three approaches, the generation pipeline also adapts.

8.2.4   *Challenges and best practices*

Multimodal RAG systems are gaining prominence owing to the diversity present in enterprise data. However, one must note that with multimodality, the complexity of the system increases along with higher latency and more expenditure on multimodal embeddings and generation. Some of the common challenges associated with multimodal RAG are

- Ensuring coherent alignment between different data modalities (e.g., text and images) can be difficult. Utilizing multimodal embeddings projecting different modalities into a common embedding space does create better integration, but these embeddings models can still lead to inaccuracies and must be evaluated.

- Handling multiple data types may increase computational requirements and processing time. Robust preprocessing pipelines to standardize and align data from various modalities are essential. Sometimes, converting multimodal data to text and following a text-only RAG approach may be enough to generate the desired results.

- Not all models are capable of effectively processing and integrating multimodal data of all modalities. Incorporate only those that add significant value to the task to optimize performance and resource utilization.

We have looked at a RAG variant that extends the capability of RAG to different data modalities. However, standard RAG is still deficient when the information is dispersed across different documents. Let s now look at a pattern in which knowledge graphs are used to establish higher-order relationships.

8.3 Knowledge graph RAG

Imagine summarizing a large report or answering complex questions that draw information from diverse sources. For example, a question such as, "What are the main themes in this report?" or "Which products in the catalogue are endorsed by the same celebrities?" are questions that are difficult for standard RAG systems to answer.

In a summarization task such as the "main themes" in a report, there is no chunk of the document that can answer the question completely. Likewise, "endorsed by the same celebrities" is not likely to be present in the data for the retriever to search through.

To answer these kinds of complex questions requiring multi-hop reasoning, identifying contextual relationships, and addressing higher-order queries, a powerful RAG pattern that incorporates knowledge graphs has been widely successful.

This pattern is called *knowledge graph RAG* or simply *graph RAG* (not to be confused with Microsoft's GraphRAG, which is a specific framework of knowledge graph RAG). It must be noted here that graph RAG is not necessarily a replacement for standard vector-based RAG, but a hybrid approach in which both vectors and graphs are used to retrieve context. Before moving forward, The following sections explain what knowledge graphs are and what benefits are inherent to them.

8.3.1 Knowledge graphs

The term *knowledge graph* was popularized by Google somewhere around 2012 by integrating an entity-relationship structure into its search engine to deliver more accurate and context-aware results. The simplest way to understand knowledge graphs is through the node-and-edge structure. Nodes may represent entities such as people, organizations, products, and events, and edges represent relationships between the nodes, such as *is a part of, works at, is related to,* and so on. The nodes and edges can also have attributes such as id, timestamp, and similar. Knowledge graphs, therefore, rely on semantics or meaning to create a shared, human-like, understanding of data. Figure 8.6 illustrates a simple knowledge graph with nodes, edges, and attributes for customer data.

Knowledge graphs offer several advantages over standard structured databases such as SQL by prioritizing relationships and context, which results in deeper data exploration. A standard row–column or a document storage does not allow for context a knowledge graph does.

The storage and data processing in knowledge graphs is unique. Specialized databases such as Neo4j, Amazon Neptune, and TigerGraph are used to store knowledge graph

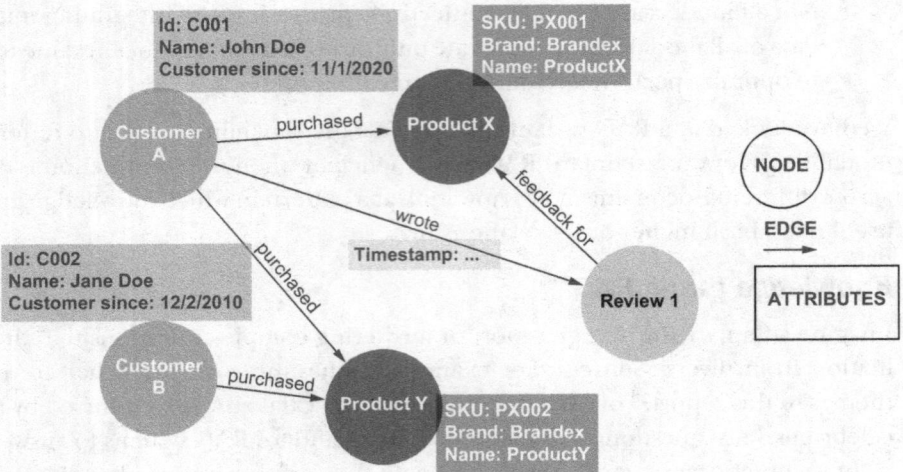

Figure 8.6   Knowledge graph representation of customer activity where nodes (circles) represent entities, edges (arrows) represent relationships, and attributes (rectangles) are the properties.

data, and query languages such as Cypher, Gremlin, and SparkQL are used for graph traversal. Readers are encouraged to learn more about graph databases, but some key concepts to keep in mind are

- *Nodes and edges*—Nodes represent entities, and edges represent relationships to form the graph structure and enable a visual structure to the knowledge.
- *Attributes*—Attributes are properties of entities (nodes) and relationships (edges).
- *Triplets*—Knowledge is represented in triplets such as "customer A purchased product X" (node–edge–node). Here the two entities, "customer A" and "product X," and one relationship, "purchased," form a triplet. These triples are the building blocks of knowledge graphs, capturing facts and relationships in a structured way.
- *Ontology*—An ontology defines the schema or structure of a knowledge graph, specifying the types of entities, relationships, and their properties.
- *Graph embeddings*—Graph embeddings are vector representations of nodes and edges that capture graph structure.
- *Graph query language*—SPARQL, Cypher, and similar languages allow users to retrieve information from the graph, formulating complex queries to find patterns, connections, and insights.
- *Graph traversal*—This is the method of navigating through nodes and edges to discover paths, patterns, and insights, essential for algorithms such as shortest path or recommendation systems.

Because of their inherent focus on relationships and context, knowledge graphs enhance standard RAG for a superior context-aware retrieval.

8.3.2 Knowledge graph RAG use cases

Knowledge graphs can be useful in a variety of use cases where the ability to handle multi-hop relationships, entity disambiguation, and complex networks is required. Standard RAG systems are limited to retrieving isolated information chunks, while knowledge graph RAG can dynamically connect and analyze data points within a network, making it ideal for applications requiring a deep understanding of interrelated data. Here are some examples:

- *Personalized treatment plans*—Knowledge graph RAG can link drugs, treatments, and conditions in a networked format, which allows it to identify potential interactions and customize treatment recommendations based on multiple factors. Standard RAG can retrieve information about a specific drug or treatment but struggles to cross-reference interactions across a network of symptoms, conditions, and treatments.

- *Personalized product recommendations*—Standard RAG can retrieve individual touchpoints or customer reviews but fails to capture the interconnected path a customer follows across their journey. Knowledge graph RAG allows for multi-hop reasoning across transactions, browsing history, and customer feedback, enabling a more holistic analysis of the journey and providing highly relevant recommendations based on relationships between customer behaviors and preferences.

- *Contract analysis*—Standard RAG can retrieve text from individual contracts or clauses but cannot map relationships among contracts, parties, or compliance requirements. Knowledge graph RAG can link contracts, clauses, and parties in a relational network, enabling it to identify conflicts, dependencies, and compliance risks across interconnected legal documents.

While standard RAG can solve simple queries, for processes that require analysis and reasoning on data from multiple sources, knowledge graph can prove to be advantageous.

8.3.3 Graph RAG approaches

Knowledge graph is a powerful data pattern. The approach to using knowledge graphs can be determined by the complexity of the use case and the diversity of data. This section discusses three common approaches that can be followed.

STRUCTURE AWARENESS THROUGH GRAPHS

This is the simplest approach to incorporating knowledge graphs. Recall that in the standard vector-based RAG approach, documents are chunked, and embeddings are created then and stored for retrieval. The problem that may arise is that the information in the adjacent chunks might not be retrieved, and a certain degree of context loss may happen. In section 6.2.1, we discussed a hierarchical indexing structure such as a parent–child structure. The parent document contains overarching themes or summaries, while child documents delve into specific details. During retrieval, the system can first locate the most relevant child documents and then refer to the parent documents for additional context if required. This approach enhances the precision of retrieval, while maintaining the broader context.

An efficient way to store documents in a hierarchical structure is in graphs. Parent and child documents can be stored in the nodes with a relationship "is child of." More levels of hierarchies can be created. In figure 8.7, there are three levels of indexing hierarchy, and while the search happens at the lowest level, parent documents at a higher hierarchy level are retrieved for deeper context.

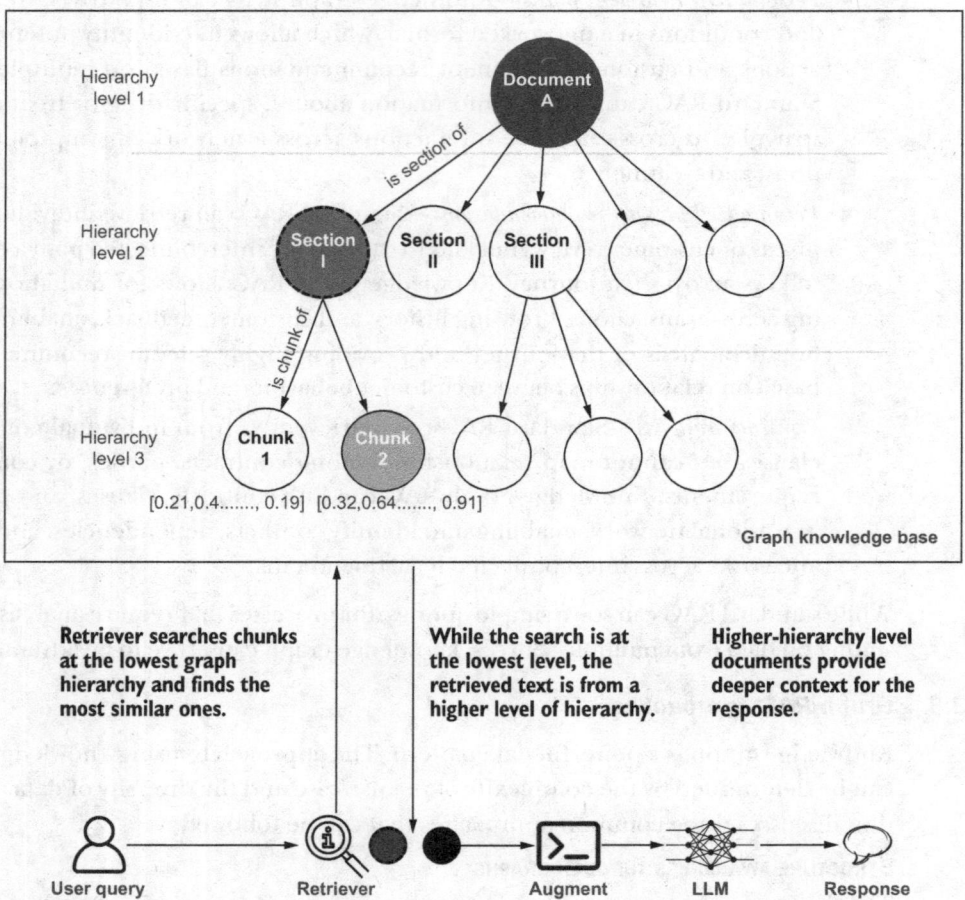

Figure 8.7   While search in a hierarchical index structure happens at the lowest level, retrieved documents are more contextually complete from a higher level of hierarchy.

GRAPH-ENHANCED VECTOR SEARCH

Graphs are not mandatory when implementing hierarchical indexing. The true value of knowledge graphs is realized when connections can be made across chunks. Standard vector-based search on a collection of chunks can be enhanced by traversing a knowledge graph to retrieve related chunks. To do this, a set of entities and relationships are extracted from the chunks using an LLM.

In the retrieval stage, the first step is a usual vector search executed based on the user query. An initial set of chunks is identified that has a high similarity with the user query. In the next step, the knowledge graph is traversed to fetch-related entities around the entities of the chunks identified in the first step. By doing this, the retriever fetches not only the chunks similar to the user query but also related chunks, which leads to deeper context and can be quite effective in solving multi-hop queries. This is often coupled with hierarchical structures and a re-ranking of retrieved documents. Figure 8.8 shows

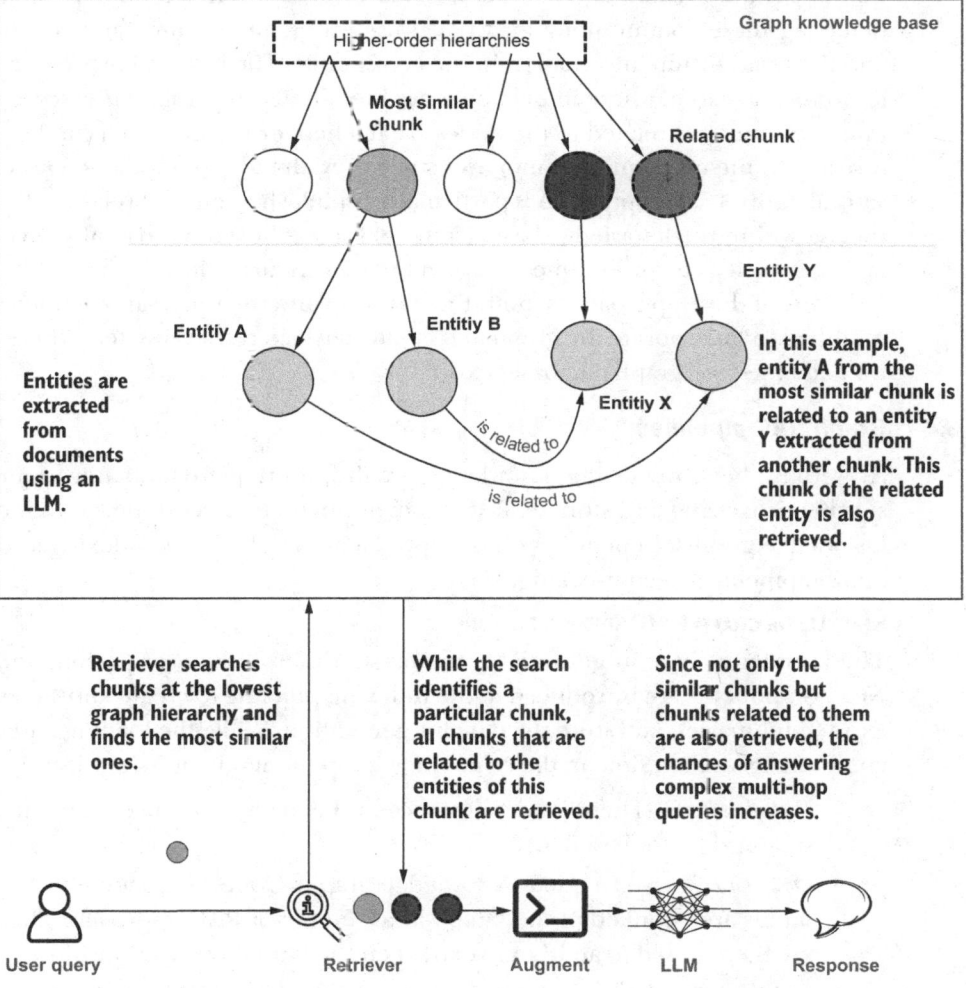

Figure 8.8 Entities and relationships extracted from the chunks play a crucial role. When chunks similar to the user query are retrieved, the chunks that have entities related to the entities of similar chunks are also retrieved.

an enhanced knowledge graph, where chuwnks also have the extracted entities and relationships. During retrieval, in addition to similar chunks, the parent chunks of related entities are also retrieved.

GRAPH COMMUNITIES AND COMMUNITY SUMMARIES

As discussed before, knowledge graphs are about entities and their relationships. Depending on the process, there may be patterns in which certain entities interact more with each other. Graph communities are a subset of entities connected more densely. For example, communities of customers with similar demographics and buying patterns can be identified or clusters of product features that appear together can be discovered. Community detection algorithms such as the Leiden and the Louvain algorithm are employed to detect communities within a knowledge graph. After detecting these communities, an LLM is used to generate summaries of the entities and the relationship information in the community. The retrieval process can be similar to vector search, where initial nodes are identified using a similarity score and community summaries related to the nodes are fetched, or vector search can be employed directly on the community summaries since they already contain a deeper context of several entities. This approach is particularly useful when queries relate to the broader themes within the knowledge base. Figure 8.9 shows how the retrieval at a community level is sufficient to answer questions at a broader thematic level.

In any of these approaches, both the indexing and the retrieval pipeline need to be modified to incorporate the graph and create a hybrid retrieval system where both vector databases and graph databases exist.

8.3.4   Graph RAG pipelines

As we have been discussing, knowledge graph is a unique data pattern that requires specific processing and storage. RAG pipelines need to be customized to incorporate knowledge graphs. Depending on the approach used, both the indexing and the generation pipelines need tweaking.

KNOWLEDGE GRAPH RAG INDEXING PIPELINE

The knowledge base in graph RAG requires a different kind of parsing and storage. New components are introduced in the indexing pipeline to create knowledge graphs, extract summaries, and store the data for generation. While the loading and chunking components remain similar, the remaining components change significantly:

- *Data loading*—There is no difference in the loading of the documents from the standard vector-based RAG.
- *Data chunking*—To create knowledge graphs from the documents, large documents are chunked in the same way as the vector RAG approach. These chunks are then passed to an LLM to extract entities and their relationships.
- *Entity relationship attribute extraction (for graph-enhanced RAG)*—This is a crucial step in graph enhancement because the quality of responses will depend on how well the entities and relationships have been identified. This step can be customized

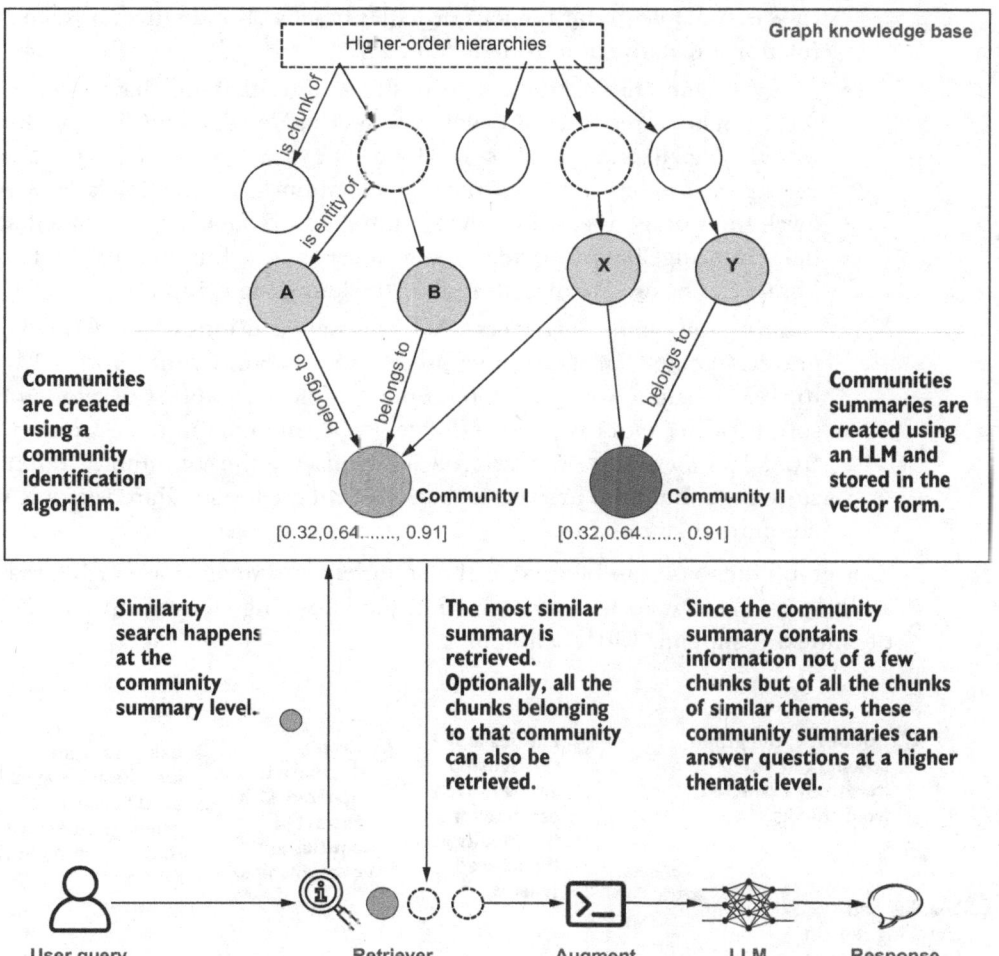

Figure 8.9 Communities club entities under a consistent theme and summarize the information at this group level. Since the summaries are created from a high number of thematically related chunks, these summaries can answer broad queries.

according to the need and complexity of the use case. The simplest approach can be to ask an LLM directly to do the extraction. The exact kind of entities and relationships can also be predetermined, say, allowed entities are "people," "country," and "organization," and allowed relationships are "nationality," "located at," and "works at." There can be another approach in which an LLM is used to identify the schema of the knowledge graph. Attributes can also be added to the entities and relationships. There can be multiple passes of this step to ensure that an exhaustive list has been created. Another step can be employed to remove redundancies and duplication. In LangChain, `LLMGraphTransformer` class is available in the `langchain_experimental` library that abstracts the entity relationship extraction from documents.

- *Storage*—Once the entities, relationships, and attributes have been extracted, these can be stored in a graph database such as Neo4j. LangChain has integration with the Neo4j graph database, and the `Neo4jGraph` library from the `langchain_community` can be used. Since the entity relationship extraction is done at a chunk level, the storage is also iterative, and the graph database is updated after each pass. In LangChain, the `add_graph_documents()` function of the `Neo4jGraph` library can be used to directly update the knowledge graph.

- *Creating community summaries*—As discussed previously, once the knowledge graph is created, an algorithm is used to detect communities, and an LLM is used to create a summary of the community. `Graphrag`, a library developed by Microsoft, provides end-to-end knowledge graph and community summary creation from documents. Another approach is to just use the community summaries and store the summaries in a vector database and use the standard vector RAG on the community summaries.

This graph database can be used as the complete knowledge base or be treated as an addition to the regular vector database in the knowledge base. Figure 8.10 illustrates the indexing pipeline with each step.

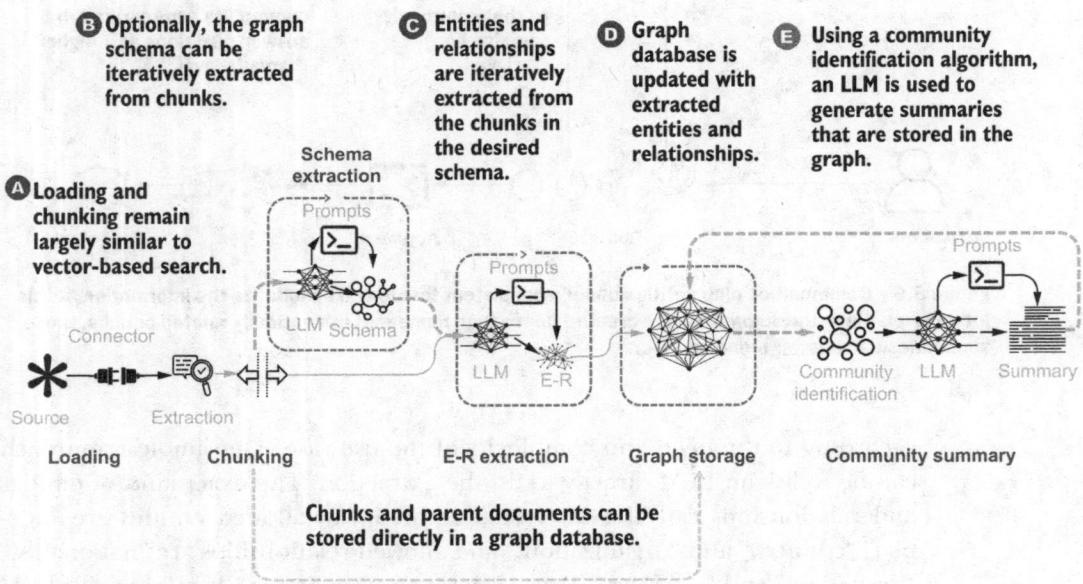

Figure 8.10   Indexing pipeline for graph RAG. Chunks can directly be stored for simple structure-aware indexing, and community summaries can be created and stored with the graph.

GENERATION PIPELINE

Since the nature of the knowledge base in graph RAG is quite unlike standard RAG, it requires significant changes in the generation pipeline. The retrieval process becomes slightly more nuanced than vector retrieval because of an additional step of graph traversal. Graph databases such as Neo4j have introduced vector indexes, via the Neo4j vector search plugin, which represent nodes and attributes as embeddings and enable similarity search. For effective retrieval, the user query (in natural language) is converted into a graph query that can be used to traverse the knowledge graph. Neo4j uses a graph query language called Cypher. For using the Cypher query language, there are a couple of approaches:

- *Template based*—Several pre-defined Cypher templates are created and based on the user query, an LLM selects which template to use. This is an extremely rigid and limiting approach.

- *LLM-generated query*—An LLM generates the Cypher query directly based on the natural language user query. Prompt engineering techniques such as few-shot prompting are employed. This approach is more flexible than a template-based approach, but not 100% reliable.

In LangChain, the `GraphCypherQAChain` class is from the `langchain.chains` library. For better querying, the schema of the knowledge graph is also provided to the LLM:

- *Augmentation*—Depending on the graph query, the response received from the graph database is processed to extract the text that can be augmented to the original user query. Apart from this, the augmentation step is the same as in vector RAG.

- *Generation*—The augmented prompt is sent to the LLM like in the standard vector RAG approach.

While the final generation step and initial data loading and chunking do not require any special adjustment, the rest of the process changes significantly. Table 8.3 summarizes the differences between vector and graph RAG.

Table 8.3 Differences between vector RAG and graph RAG

Step	Vector RAG	Graph RAG
Data loading	Loads documents without specialized preprocessing for relationships	Similar to vector RAG; documents are loaded without special graph handling.
Data chunking	Divides large documents into smaller chunks for embedding and vector storage	Documents are chunked similarly; each chunk is then processed to extract entities and relationships, building a relational structure.
Entity and relationship extraction	Not applicable; focuses on creating embeddings from chunks	Entities, relationships, and attributes are extracted from each chunk using an LLM, potentially in multiple passes to refine and de-duplicate entities and relationships.

Table 8.3   **Differences between vector RAG and graph RAG (*continued*)**

Step	Vector RAG	Graph RAG
Storage	Stores embeddings in a vector database	Entities and relationships are stored in a graph database (e.g., Neo4j), with the option to update the graph iteratively. Tools such as LangChain's Neo4jGraph can automate this process.
Community summaries	Not applicable; primarily relies on similarity search on individual embeddings	Detects communities within the knowledge graph and uses an LLM to create summaries for each community. These summaries can be stored as vectors for a hybrid graph–vector RAG approach.
Retrieval	Performs direct similarity searches on embeddings	Involves graph traversal using Cypher queries, generated either from pre-defined templates or dynamically by an LLM. Neo4j's vector indexes can enhance similarity-based node searches.
Augmentation	Uses retrieved embeddings to augment the user's query	Retrieved nodes, relationships, or summaries augment the user's query. Additional LLM processing might be used to refine responses based on the retrieved graph content.
Generation	Sends the augmented prompt to an LLM for response generation	Like vector RAG but relies on augmented data with graph-derived insights, relationships, and context from the knowledge graph to enrich the response.

8.3.5   *Challenges and best practices*

Despite all the benefits of graph RAG, there are certain challenges that must be considered carefully:

- Merging diverse data sources into a cohesive knowledge graph can be intricate and time-consuming. Start with a focused domain and gradually expand the knowledge graph to manage complexity.

- Due to the iterative LLM processing at different stages, large-scale knowledge graph generation and community summarization from documents are computationally expensive. Therefore, the data for graph RAG must be selected carefully.

- Current similarity measurement techniques may not fully capture the nuanced relationships or structural dependencies in graphs, leading to potential mismatches in retrieved information. Careful use of case-specific evaluation is warranted for acceptable accuracy.

- Each deployment may need custom graph data construction, indexing, and retrieval adaptations, which makes generalization difficult. Keeping the knowledge graph updated with accurate and current information requires continuous effort. Consequently, graph RAG may not be the default RAG strategy.

So far, we have looked at two RAG variants that extend standard RAG capabilities by including multimodal data and graph structures. Next, we discuss one of the most significant concepts in the field of generative AI: agents.

8.4   Agentic RAG

By now, you understand that challenges exist with standard RAG systems. They may struggle with reasoning, answering complex questions, and multistep processes. One of the key aspects of comprehensive RAG systems is the ability to search through multiple sources of data. This can be internal company documents, the open internet, third-party applications, and even structured data sources like an SQL database. So far in this book, we have built systems that can search through a single knowledge base, and for any query, the entire knowledge base is searched through.

Two challenges arise with this approach. First, all information must be indexed and stored in a single vector store, which leads to storage problems at scale. Second, for any query, the entire knowledge base needs to be searched, which is highly inefficient for large knowledge bases. To overcome this challenge, a module that can understand the user's query and route the query to a relevant source is needed. This is one of the limitations addressed by agentic RAG that uses one or more LLM agents for decision-making. Let's first understand what is meant by the term *agent*.

8.4.1   LLM agents

The use of agents in AI predates the popularity of LLMs. The overarching meaning of an AI agent is a software system that can autonomously perceive the environment it is in, make decisions, and perform actions to achieve a goal. Traditionally, AI agents have been developed to execute specific tasks and rely on predefined rules or learned behaviors, like in the fields of autonomous vehicles or robotics. Due to the ability to process and understand language (and now even multimodal data), LLMs are now being seen as a general-purpose technology that can help build autonomous decision-making without explicitly defining rules or environment data. While there is no common definition of an LLM-based AI agent, there are four key components of the system that enable autonomous decision-making and task execution.

The *core LLM brain* is an LLM that assigned a certain role and a task. This component is responsible for understanding the user request and interacting with other components to respond to the user. For example, an AI agent built for travel assistance may have to deal with different types of tasks such as searching for information, creating itineraries, booking tickets, or managing previous bookings.

The *memory* component manages the agent's past experiences. It can be short-term like the chat history of the current conversation or long-term where important pieces of information from previous interactions are stored. For a travel assistant AI agent, short-term memory will hold the current context of the user query, while the ticket booking history or previous travel searches can be fetched from long-term memory.

The *planning* component creates a step-by-step sequence of tasks that will be followed to respond to the user's request. Task decomposition or breaking down complex tasks into smaller, manageable subtasks. ReAct, which stands for reasoning and acting, or reflection, where the agent does a self-assessment of the outcomes, can be part of the planning component.

Tools assist the agent in performing actions on resources external to it. This can be conducting a web search on the internet, querying an external database such as an SQL database, invoking a third-party API such as a weather API, and similar. The core LLM brain is responsible for sending the payload request to the tools in the accepted format. These four components and their interactions are shown in figure 8.11.

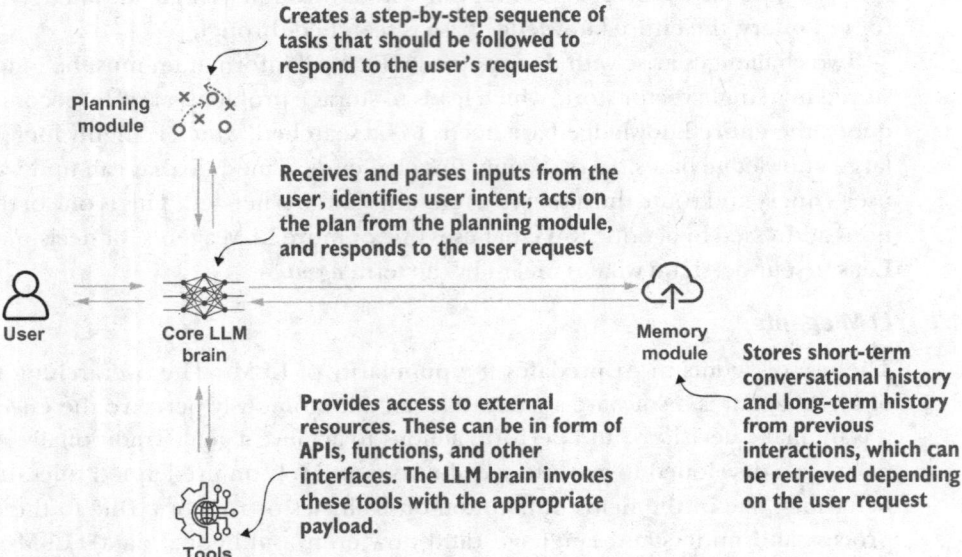

Figure 8.11   An LLM agent's four components break down the user's query, recall the history of interaction with the user, and employ external tools to accomplish tasks and respond to the user.

Since the definition of AI agents continues evolving, these components are not set in stone but are generally agreed upon. To help understand how these components interact, let's take an example of an AI agent built for travel assistance, like the customer service agent of an online travel agency.

Suppose a customer asks a question like, "Is my flight on schedule?" The core LLM brain receives this input and understands that the user intent is to check a specific flight status. At this stage, the core LLM brain can invoke the planning module to decide the course of action required to answer queries of this intent. The planning module may respond with steps such as retrieving booking information from previous interactions (memory), querying the latest flight information from a database, comparing it with previous details from memory, and conveying the result to the user. Here, retrieving the information from the database will require a tool such as an API, which is a prebuilt module that the core LLM brain has access to. The planning module can also bring in conditional steps—for example, if the previous booking information cannot be retrieved from memory, the core LLM brain must prompt the user to provide this information. When the core LLM brain gets the plan from the planning module, it retrieves previous booking information, invokes the tool to retrieve flight information, compares the new information with the old information in memory, and crafts a response based on this analysis. This simple workflow of the agent is illustrated in figure 8.12.

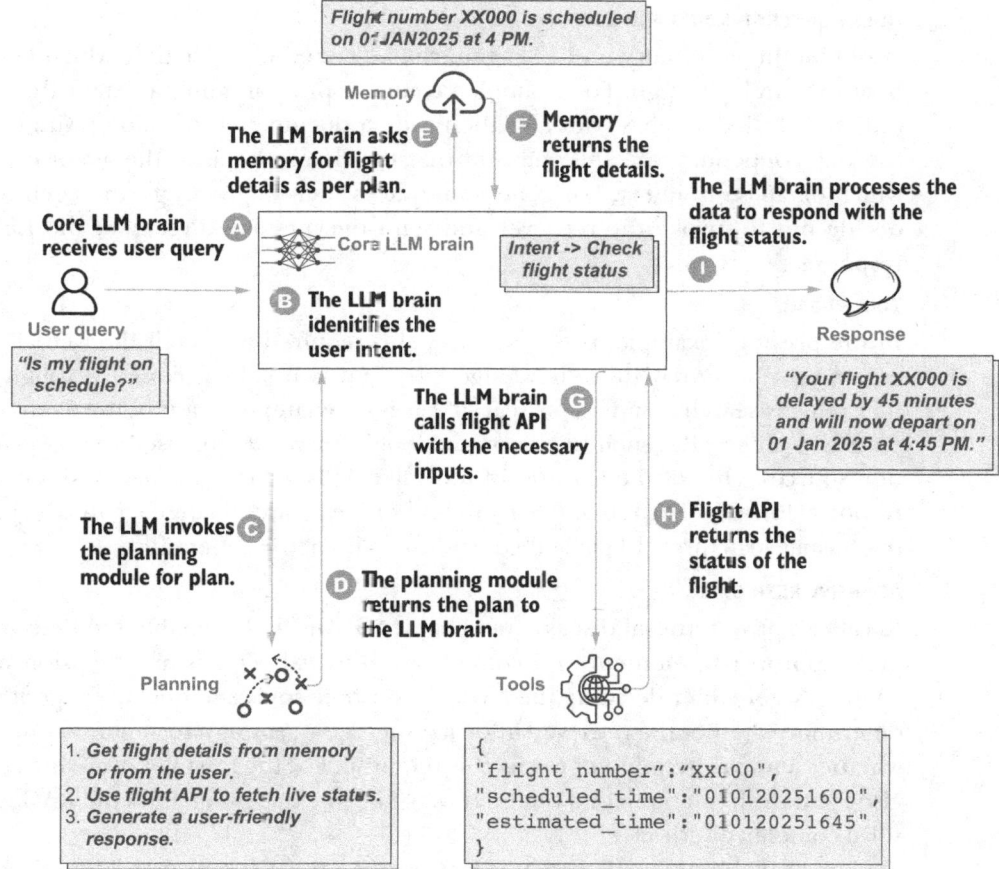

Figure 8.12 A simple task of responding to a user query on flight schedule responded to by an LLM agent by using the planning, memory, and tools modules

This is an example of a simple task. Multiple agents can come together to solve tasks of a higher level of complexity, such as "Plan and book a holiday for me." The field of LLM-based AI agents is quite promising, and readers are encouraged to read more about this evolving domain. For our discussion on agentic RAG in this section, we focus on a few aspects, specifically on tool usage and a little bit of planning. The use cases for agentic RAG span across industries, so it makes more sense to look at the capabilities of agentic RAG.

8.4.2 Agentic RAG capabilities

In our introduction to agentic RAG, we highlighted the challenge in standard RAG using a single knowledge base. Agentic RAG infuses abilities in the RAG system that make the system more efficient and accurate.

QUERY UNDERSTANDING AND ROUTING

Based on the user query, an LLM agent can be tasked with deciding which knowledge base to search through. For example, assume a programming assistant that can not only search the codebase but also the product documentation, along with searching the web. Depending on the question that the developer asks, the agent can decide which database to query. For generic messages such as greetings, the agent can also decide not to invoke the retriever and send the message directly to the LLM for a response.

TOOLS USAGE

In the previous example, the system was also required to search the web. The internet cannot be stored in a knowledge base and is usually accessed through an API that returns search results. This search API is an example of a tool the agent can use. Similarly, other APIs, such as Notion or Google Drive, can be used to access information sources. One of the features of tools like APIs is that they have fixed query and response formats. The job of the agent is to process natural language information into the format structure and parse the response to use it for generation.

ADAPTIVE RETRIEVAL

Recall adaptive retrieval discussed in chapter 6. An LLM is enabled to determine the most appropriate moment and content for retrieval. This is an extension of query routing, where after deciding the most appropriate source to query, an agent can also determine whether the retrieved information is good enough to generate responses or whether another iteration of retrieval is required. For the next iteration, the agent can also form fresh queries based on the retrieved context. This enables the RAG system to solve complex queries.

These capabilities enable agentic RAG systems to be comprehensive and work on a scale. While the indexing and generation pipelines do not change in structure, agents can be invoked throughout the two pipelines.

8.4.3 Agentic RAG pipelines

The capability of LLM-based agents to understand the context and invoke tools can be used to elevate each stage of the RAG pipeline.

INDEXING PIPELINE

The idea of the knowledge base in agentic RAG is no different from standard RAG. Agents can be used across components to enhance the indexing pipeline:

- *Data loading*—Loading data and extracting information is the first and incredibly crucial step of RAG system development. Accurate parsing of information is critical in building an accurate RAG system. Parsing complex documents such as PDF reports can be tough. While there are libraries and tools present for these tasks, LLM agents can be used for high-precision parsing. The importance of metadata in RAG cannot be overstated. It is useful for filtering, more contextual mapping, and source citation. In most scenarios, it is difficult to source rich metadata. LLM agents can be used to build metadata architecture and extract contextual metadata.

- *Chunking*—In agentic chunking, chunks from the text are created based on a goal or a task. Consider an e-commerce platform wanting to analyze customer reviews. The best way for the reviews to be chunked is if the reviews about a particular topic are put in the same chunk. Similarly, the critical and positive reviews may be put in different chunks. To achieve this kind of chunking, we will need to do sentiment analysis, entity extraction, and some kind of clustering. This can be achieved by a multiagent system. Agentic chunking is still an active area of research and improvement.

- *Embeddings*—The role of agents in embeddings can be the selection of the right embeddings model, depending on the context of the chunks. For example, if there is information from multiple domains in the loaded data, there may be a case for using domain-specific embeddings for different chunks. Apart from this, quality control agents can validate embeddings by measuring similarity or alignment with predefined standards or use case requirements. You may also recall from the discussion on graph RAG that agents can also decide to use graph structures for certain chunks.

- *Storage*—There is also a possibility to store chunk embeddings from the same document in different collections owing to the nature of the information. For example, the information related to the installation and troubleshooting of a product can be stored in one collection of a vector database, and product features and advantages can be stored in another. This helps in setting the retrieval up for higher precision. You may notice that the use of agents in chunking, embeddings, and storage are closely related.

Figure 8.13 summarizes how the use of agents can embellish the indexing pipeline. The nature of the knowledge base itself doesn't change, but the process of creation is embellished with agents.

GENERATION PIPELINE

The true advantage of an agentic system lies in how it transforms the entire generation pipeline across all three stages:

- *Retrieval*—Perhaps the most significant use of agents is in the retrieval stage. Query routing to the most appropriate source and the integration of tools to query external sources of information is a crucial feature of agentic RAG.

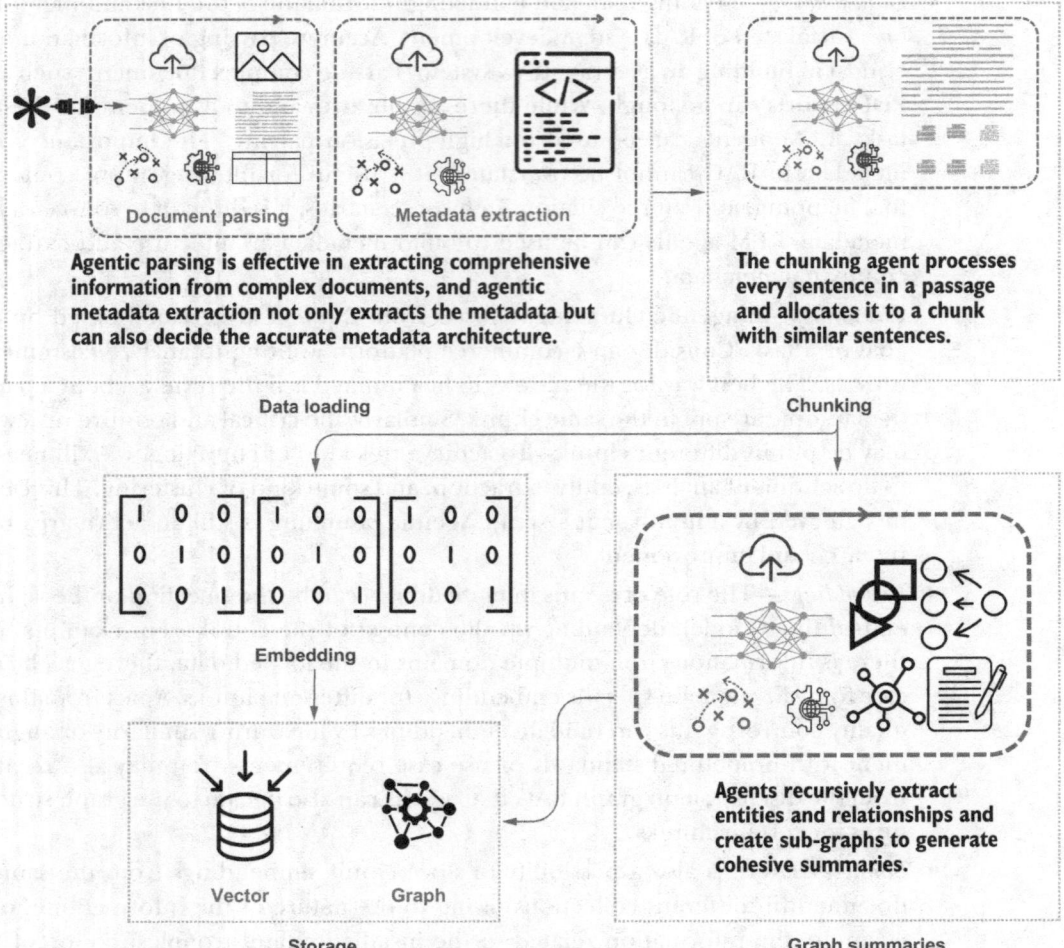

Figure 8.13 Agentic embellishment to the indexing pipeline enhances the quality of the knowledge base.

Adaptive retrieval strategies also bring significant improvement in the retrieval stage.

- *Augmentation*—Agents can choose the correct prompting technique for augmentation, depending on the nature of the query and the retrieved context. Prompts can also be generated dynamically by an agent.
- *Generation*—One of the uses of agentic RAG is also in multistep generation such as IterRetGen or iterative-retrieval generation. In this approach, an agent is used to review the response generated by the LLM in the first pass, and it decides if any further iteration of retrieval and generation is required to completely respond

to the user query. This is particularly useful in multi-hop reasoning and fact verification.

Another way to think about agentic RAG is that wherever dynamic decision-making can improve the RAG system, an agent can be used to autonomously make those decisions. From the previous discussion, you may conclude that agentic RAG is a superior version of standard RAG. Table 8.4 summarizes the advantages of agentic over standard RAG.

Table 8.4 Advantages of agentic RAG

Aspect	Standard RAG	Agentic RAG
Retrieval process	Passive retrieval based on initial query	Adaptive retrieval with intelligent agents routing and reformulating queries as needed
Handling complex queries	Struggles with multistep reasoning and complex queries	Can be used to break down and address complex, multifaceted queries
Tool integration	Limited integration with external tools and APIs	Seamless integration with various external tools and APIs for enhanced information gathering
Scalability	Challenges in scaling due to static processes	Scalable through modular agent-based architecture, allowing for easy expansion
Accuracy and relevance	Dependent on initial query quality; may retrieve less relevant information	Higher accuracy and relevance due to agents' ability to refine queries and validate information

8.4.4 *Challenges and pest practices*

LLM based agents are still evolving and are not foolproof. There are also concerns around the planning and reasoning abilities of LLMs. For implementing agentic abilities into the RAG pipelines, a few aspects should be evaluated carefully:

- The accuracy of tool selection diminishes when a single agent is responsible for invoking a high number of tools. Therefore, the number of decision choices for the agent needs to be controlled.

- No agent can be expected to be accurate all the time. Error rates in multiagent systems can also increase. It is important to establish a failsafe at every stage. The choice of the use case should also be guided by the expected accuracy levels.

- Increased autonomy in decision-making can lead to unintended actions if not properly controlled. In other words, agents can misfire, and establishing explicit boundaries and guidelines for agent behavior is critical.

Multimodal, graph, and agentic RAG patterns have demonstrated significant improvements over the standard RAG pipelines. Multimodal RAG opens the RAG systems to different modalities, graph RAG introduces relational understanding, and agentic RAG infuses RAG systems with intelligence and autonomous decision making. Apart from these three, ongoing research on RAG has resulted in several other frameworks and variations to the standard RAG systems. The next section discusses variants that show significant promise.

8.5   *Other RAG variants*

We have talked about the three major RAG variants in this chapter. Research in the field is bustling, and every week, several papers are released by researchers about their experiments and key findings. Out of these papers, quite a few demonstrate RAG variants that find relevance in practical applications. We close this chapter by briefly discussing four such RAG variants.

8.5.1   *Corrective RAG*

The effectiveness of a RAG system depends on the quality of retrieval. Inaccuracies in retrieval negate all RAG benefits. To address this, the corrective RAG (CRAG) approach evaluates the quality of retrieved documents. It uses a lightweight evaluator and triggers corrective action if the retrieved information is found to be inaccurate. The key CRAG components are

- *Retrieval evaluator*—A model that evaluates the relevance of the retrieved documents and assigns a relevance score to each retrieved document. In the original CRAG paper (https://arxiv.org/abs/2401.15884), the evaluator is a fine-tuned T5 model that assigns a score of being correct, incorrect, or ambiguous.
- *Web search supplementation*—If a retrieved document is classified as incorrect, the system conducts a web search to supplement the knowledge base, ensuring more accurate, up-to-date information.
- *Knowledge refinement*—Retrieved documents classified as correct by the evaluator and the content retrieved from web search are broken down further into smaller knowledge strips, and each strip undergoes evaluation.

Figure 8.14 illustrates the CRAG workflow with the evaluator, knowledge refinement, and web search added to the standard RAG flow.

As for its advantages and limitations, CRAG secures accurate, context-relevant knowledge for generation, particularly in cases where initial retrieval may be flawed. The corrective actions enhance the factual accuracy of the generated content. CRAG is a solution that can be integrated with all RAG pipelines and other RAG variants without causing any disruptions. There are also a couple of factors that need to be considered:

- The additional corrective actions and web search integration may increase response time.
- The performance of the system is closely tied to the accuracy of the evaluator model.

CRAG is an improvement over standard RAG, which uses the retrieved documents as is. The corrective approach makes it effective for accuracy-sensitive applications that demand data verification.

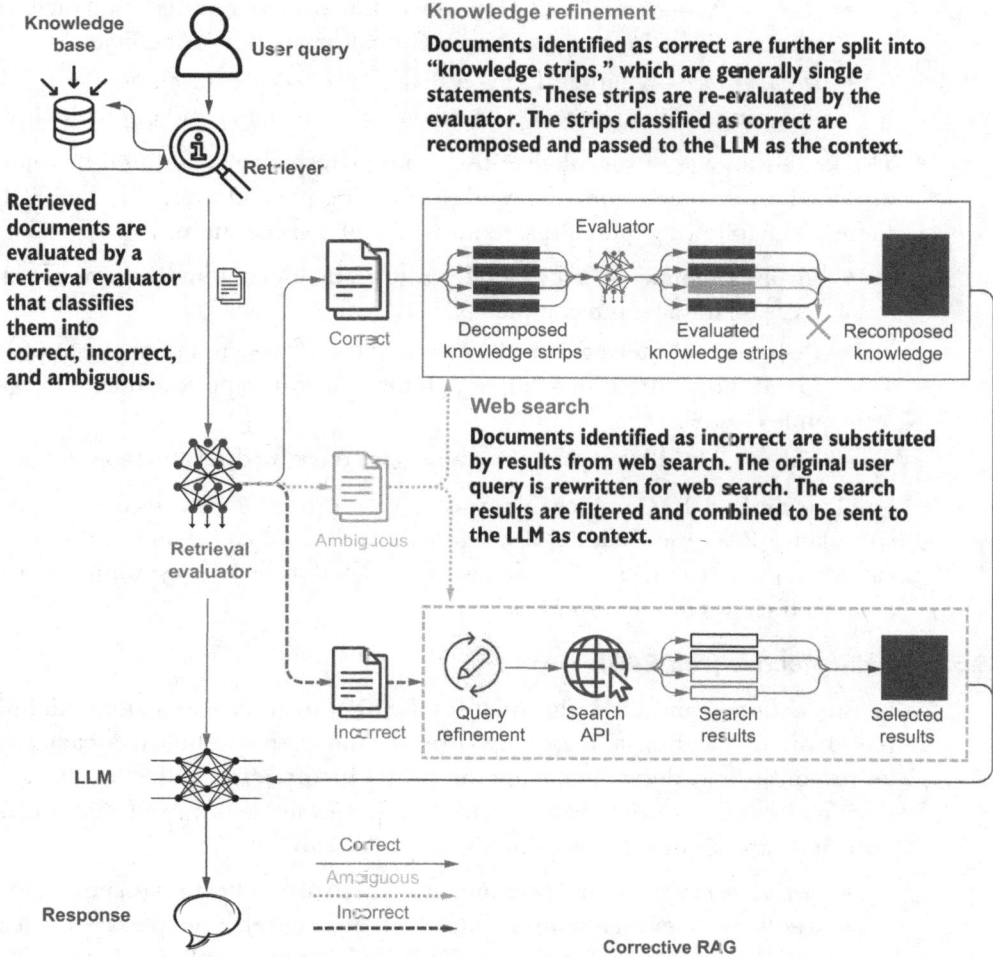

Knowledge refinement

Documents identified as correct are further split into "knowledge strips," which are generally single statements. These strips are re-evaluated by the evaluator. The strips classified as correct are recomposed and passed to the LLM as the context.

Web search

Documents identified as incorrect are substituted by results from web search. The original user query is rewritten for web search. The search results are filtered and combined to be sent to the LLM as context.

Figure 8.14 CRAG corrects the knowledge at the most granular level, hence the name corrective RAG. Source: https://arxiv.org/abs/2401.15884.

8.5.2 Speculative RAG

Latency and redundancy are ubiquitous concerns in RAG systems. Speculative RAG addresses these in a two-step approach. First, small language models parallelly generate multiple answer drafts, each based on diverse subsets of documents. Then, a larger LLM verifies and selects the most accurate draft. The key components of speculative RAG are

- *Document clustering*—Retrieved documents are clustered into topic-related groups, each offering a unique perspective.

- *RAG drafter*—A smaller LLM produces initial answer drafts based on each cluster subset, generating responses and rationales in parallel for efficiency.
- *RAG verifier*—A larger LLM evaluates each draft's accuracy and coherence, assigning confidence scores based on self-consistency and rationale support.

The key advantage of speculative RAG is faster response generation by reducing the workload on the generator LLM and performing parallel draft generation. However, some of the following limitations require careful consideration:

- Involves managing a two-model setup and document clustering, which may increase initial setup complexity.
- Document clustering directly affects draft diversity, and poor clustering can lead to redundant drafts by grouping highly similar or repetitive documents into multiple clusters.
- The smaller LLM may require training for effective draft and rationale generation.

Unlike standard RAG, which incorporates all retrieved data into a single prompt, speculative RAG uses parallel draft generation for efficiency and a dedicated verification step for accuracy, which leads to a reduction in latency, while improving the factual efficiency of the responses.

8.5.3   *Self-reflective (self RAG)*

Self-reflection in an LLM is the ability of the LLM to analyze its actions, identify potential errors or flaws in its reasoning process, and then use that feedback to improve its responses and decision-making. Self RAG incorporates reflection to dynamically decide whether to retrieve relevant information, evaluate retrieved content, and to critique its output. The key components of self RAG are

- *Reflection tokens*—Self RAG trains an LLM to use "reflection tokens," which help it assess the relevance, support, and usefulness of retrieved passages. These tokens are designed to guide the model in judging the quality of both the retrieved content and its generated response, adding layers of control and adaptability. A *retrieve token* indicates whether retrieval is needed. Similarly, the *relevance token* determines whether a passage is relevant, the *support token* verifies whether the generated response is fully supported by retrieved content, and the *utility token* scores the usefulness of the response.
- *Dynamic retrieval decision*—The model uses reflection tokens to determine if retrieval is necessary based on each segment of the response and skips retrieval if it is unnecessary at any step.
- *Self-critique*—The model critiques its output at each generation step, applying reflection tokens to guide retrieval and refine the response in real time.

Adaptive retrieval in self RAG reduces unnecessary retrievals, and self-reflection results in better accuracy, factual consistency, and relevance. However, some limitations need to be considered:

- Processing multiple passages in parallel and self-reflection may increase computational demands.
- The additional training and use of reflection tokens require fine-tuning of thresholds.

Self RAG is one of the most cited techniques in research on RAG. Its dynamic adjustment of retrieval based on task needs evaluates output quality, achieving superior accuracy.

8.5.4 RAPTOR

Recursive abstractive processing for tree-organized retrieval, or RAPTOR, is a RAG variant designed to handle hierarchical relationships in data. It creates a multilevel, tree-based structure of recursive summaries, capturing both granular details and overarching themes in long documents. Like graph RAG, RAPTOR uses a tree structure to achieve similar objectives. Here are the key RAPTOR components:

- *Chunk clustering and summarization*—Chunk embeddings are clustered based on similarity, and an LLM is used to summarize the clusters. Soft clustering with Gaussian mixture models allows text segments to belong to multiple clusters.
- *Recursive tree construction*—RAPTOR builds a multilayered tree by using chunks, clusters, and summaries in a bottom-up process.
- *Dual querying mechanisms*—A top-down approach starts traversing down to select the most relevant nodes at each level based on cosine similarity to the query. Another single-layer search retrieves context across all tree nodes irrespective of the levels.

Like graph RAG, RAPTOR enables better multi-hop reasoning and thematic question answering by incorporating both granular and high-level summaries. However, tree structures are complex to manage and RAPTOR comes with its set of challenges:

- The recursive clustering and summarization steps can be computationally intensive, especially for very large documents.
- Effective retrieval hinges on the quality of the clustering; errors in initial clustering can propagate up the tree.

Unlike standard RAG, which may struggle with multilayered content, RAPTOR's hierarchical model allows targeted retrieval, optimizing for both specificity and contextual relevance.

This chapter explored RAG variants that use advanced techniques to improve RAG systems for specific use cases. Multimodal pipelines give RAG systems access to previously unusable data, graph RAG provides the ability of relational analysis, and agentic RAG introduces autonomous decision-making for complex tasks. Each RAG variant addresses a certain aspect of improvement in standard RAG systems. Corrective RAG focuses on factual relevance, RAPTOR builds relational intelligence for hierarchical data, speculative RAG is built for efficiency, and self RAG makes the system adaptive.

With this chapter, we are almost at the end of our discussion on RAG. The last chapter discusses some of the independent considerations and best practices across different stages of RAG system lifecycle.

Summary

Introducing RAG variants

- RAG variants are adaptations of the naïve RAG framework that extend its functionality to specific use cases.
- These variants address challenges, such as processing nontextual data, improving relational understanding, enhancing accuracy, and enabling autonomous decision-making.
- Three major RAG variants were discussed in depth: multimodal, graph, and agentic RAG.
- Other promising RAG variants are corrective RAG, speculative RAG, self RAG, and RAPTOR.

Multimodal rag

- It extends RAG capabilities to handle multiple data modalities such as text, images, audio, and video. It can be used for
  - *Medical diagnosis*—Analyzing text, images (X-rays), and tabular data (lab results)
  - *Investment analysis*—Processing financial documents, charts, and balance sheets
  - *Equipment maintenance*—Combining text reports, visual inspections, and sensor data
- As for the pipeline enhancements, multimodal RAG introduces multimodal embeddings (shared or modality specific), transcription tools, and specialized chunking methods to indexing pipeline. In the generation pipeline, it employs multimodal LLMs (e.g., GPT-4o, Google Gemini).
- Multimodal RAG has high computational requirements and increased latency. Information loss is possible during text conversion of nontext modalities.

Knowledge graph RAG

- It enhances retrieval and reasoning through relationships represented in a graph structure. It can be used for
  - *Personalized treatment plans*—Linking drugs, conditions, and symptoms for customized recommendations
  - *Contract analysis*—Identifying dependencies and compliance risks across interconnected legal documents

- As for the pipeline enhancements, the knowledge graph RAG extracts entities, relationships, and attributes from chunks to create a graph in the indexing pipeline. As for the generation pipeline, it incorporates graph traversal using graph query languages such as Cypher.
- Building and maintaining knowledge graphs is complex and computationally expensive. It also requires custom adaptations for each deployment.

Agentic RAG

- It introduces LLM-based agents for autonomous decision-making and dynamic query routing. Agentic RAG can be used for
  - Query understanding and routing to relevant data sources
  - Adaptive retrieval and multistep generation
  - Integration with tools such as web search APIs and external databases
- With regard to pipeline enhancements, agentic RAG enhances chunking, metadata extraction, and embeddings selection with agentic decision-making in the indexing pipeline. In the generation pipeline, it dynamically augments prompts and employs iterative retrieval-generation workflows.
- Agentic RAG requires robust controls to prevent unintended actions by agents. High computational overhead and multiplied error rates in multiagent systems.

Other RAG variants

- Corrective RAG (CRAG) Focuses on factual accuracy by evaluating retrieved content. It also adds corrective steps such as web search supplementation and knowledge refinement.
  - *Advantages*—Enhances accuracy and can integrate seamlessly with other RAG pipelines
  - *Challenges*—Increased response time and dependency on the evaluator model
- Speculative RAG reduces latency by generating multiple drafts in parallel using smaller LLMs. A larger LLM verifies and selects the most accurate draft.
  - *Advantages*—Faster response generation
  - *Challenges*—Requires careful document clustering and draft diversity
- Self RAG incorporates reflection tokens for adaptive retrieval and self-assessment of generated content.
  - *Advantages*—Superior accuracy and factual consistency
  - *Challenges*—Computationally demanding and requires fine-tuned thresholds
- RAPTOR builds hierarchical relationships through tree-structured summaries.
  - *Advantages*—Optimized for multi-hop reasoning and thematic queries
  - *Challenges*—Computationally intensive and relies on effective clustering

RAG development framework and further exploration

This chapter covers

- A recap of the concepts covered in this book using a six-stage RAG development framework
- Areas for further exploration

The previous eight chapters covered a wide breadth of retrieval-augmented generation (RAG), including a conceptual foundation, critical components, evaluation methods, advanced techniques, the operations stack, and essential variants of RAG. By now, you should be equipped with the necessary information required to develop RAG systems.

This concluding chapter summarizes the discussion and recaps all the previously discussed concepts. To accomplish this, we put all the different aspects of developing RAG systems together and came up with a RAG development framework. Across the six stages of this RAG development framework, we recap the concepts covered in this book along with some best practices. This framework not only covers the technical aspects but also looks at the development process holistically.

RAG is a rapidly evolving technique. At the end of this chapter, we also discuss some of the ideas that you can explore further. Some of these approaches to incorporating context may compete with the RAG technique, while others may be complementary.

By the end of this chapter, you should

- Have reviewed and consolidated your understanding of key RAG concepts.
- Get a solid understanding of the RAG development framework.
- Be ready to build and deploy RAG systems.

Often, the problem statements that the developer of a RAG system is presented with will be open ended. For example, an e-commerce platform wants to develop a buying assistant, or the marketing function wants a research agent to track and summarize competitive information. So, how does one navigate from an open-ended problem statement to a fully developed RAG system? It becomes very important that this journey is guided by a thought process. For this purpose, let's define and discuss a framework for developing RAG systems.

9.1 RAG development framework

The process of developing RAG systems is not very different from developing an application that uses a machine learning model. We have seen that a RAG system can be complex and include several components. It goes beyond the elements such as models, data, and retrievers. It requires a service infrastructure to make the system available to users. Evaluation, monitoring, and maintaining the systems becomes as important as developing and deploying them. It all begins with an understanding of requirements and a conceptual design. To address all these aspects, a RAG development framework that will assist us in building RAG systems is proposed here. This framework involves the following six stages:

1 *Initiation*—This stage involves understanding the problem statement, aligning the stakeholders, gathering system requirements, and analyzing these requirements to draft a high-level system architecture.

2 *Design*—At this stage, design choices for RAG pipelines are made, and the suite of tools to develop the system is developed. In addition, different layers of the RAG operations stack are conceptualized.

3 *Development*—This stage involves developing a working prototype of the desired RAG system. All required models are trained, and the required APIs are developed. This stage leads to the creation of the knowledge base and the development of the application orchestration layer.

4 *Evaluation*—During this stage, the retrieval and generation components are evaluated, along with testing the end-to-end system performance. At the end of this stage, the system is ready for deployment.

5 *Deployment*—During this stage, the system is made available to end users. The deployment strategy is also decided at this stage.

6 *Maintenance*—This final stage is an ongoing one that involves system monitoring, incorporating user feedback, and keeping abreast of technological enhancements.

Bear in mind that the RAG development framework is not a linear process, but flexible, iterative, and cyclic. Figure 9.1 illustrates the cyclic nature of the six stages of the RAG development framework, showing the key artifacts of each stage.

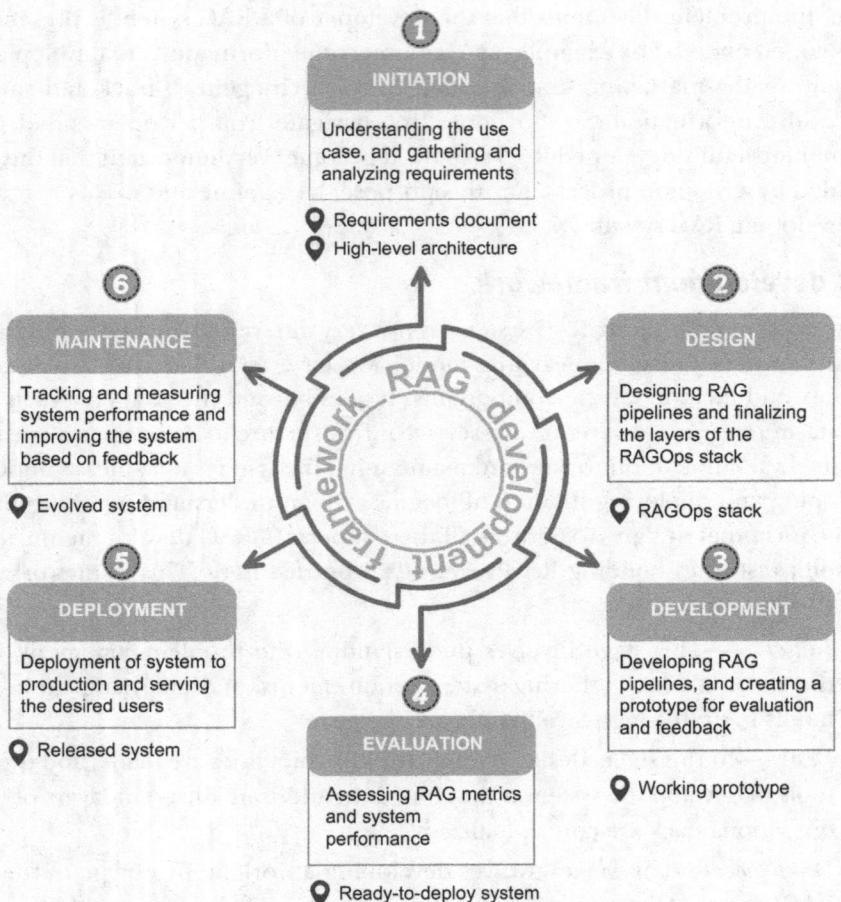

Figure 9.1   The six stages of the RAG development framework are iterative and cyclic. At each stage, specific artifacts can be created.

Each of the stages involves certain activities. We look at these activities one by one and discuss the best practices associated with them. We begin with the initiation stage.

9.1.1 Initiation stage: Defining and scoping the RAG system

The journey toward a successful RAG system begins with the initial interactions with the stakeholders. This is an opportunity to gain an in-depth understanding of the problem statement and the user requirements. It is an exploratory stage and sets the direction of the project.

USE CASE IDENTIFICATION

A lot of the choices a developer will make in the development process of a RAG system depend heavily on the use case being addressed. Even a basic understanding of the industry domain/function and a simple definition of the use case is enough to answer crucial starting questions about the system. The requirement of a RAG system needs to be assessed here. Recall from chapter 1 the challenges that RAG solves: RAG overcomes training data limitations, knowledge cut-off date, and LLM hallucinations to bring factual accuracy, reliability, and trust to the system. It is important to assess whether these RAG benefits are pivotal to the use case. There can be LLM applications that may not even require RAG. Here are some questions you may need to ask at this stage:

- Does the system require data that may not be present in the training set of an available LLM?
- Does the system require data that is current or updates frequently?
- Does the system need to quote or generate facts? How crucial is the accuracy of the generated facts?
- Will the users benefit if the sources are cited?

A use case evaluation card as the one shown in figure 9.2 can help in assessing whether a RAG system is required to solve the use case. Use cases such as creative writing, language translation, sentiment analysis, grammar correction, and so forth do not generally require a RAG system unless some nuance of the use case warrants it.

Apart from this, the industry domain and function can also give an early indication of the system requirements. For example, use cases from the healthcare and finance domain may require more security and compliance measures, while a use case from sports may require processing of quickly updating information.

This initial assessment of the use case may provide early insights, but a detailed understanding and analysis of the requirements is necessary before proceeding further.

GATHERING OF REQUIREMENTS

Developing the right RAG system means meeting the stakeholders' needs and wants. Understanding these needs and wants is a crucial step. Gaining this understanding is an interactive and investigative process. Most stakeholders and end users may have limited knowledge about technology and how a RAG system is built. It is therefore important to know what a successful application would mean to them. These requirements can range from the features needed in the system to the expected scale and the

Use case	Use case evaluation questions				Is a RAG system required?
	System requires data that may not be present in training set?	System requires data that is current or updates frequently?	System generates facts?	Are users looking for sources?	
Creative writing assistance	No: LLMs do not need any additional data for creative writing.	No: LLMs do not need any current information for creative writing.	Maybe: Creative writing may not necessarily need generated facts.	No: User expectations from creative writing do not need any source citation.	✗ No
Customer support bot	Yes: Product/Company specific information may not be present in LLM training data.	Yes: Product information, inventory levels, and order information changes frequently.	Yes: All generated information is factual.	Maybe: Sources may enhance customer experience.	✓ Yes
Language translation	No: LLMs do not need any additional data for language translation.	No: LLMs do not need any current information for language translation.	No: Facts, if any, will be the same as provided in the prompt.	No: The source of information will always be the prompt.	✗ No
Spelling and grammar correction	No: LLMs do not need any additional data for checks.	No: LLMs do not need any current information for checks.	No: No additional facts need to be generated.	No: The source of information will always be the prompt.	✗ No

Figure 9.2   A use case evaluation card with the evaluating questions can help in assessing whether a RAG system is required to address the use case.

desired performance of the system. A good way to gather requirements may be to look at them through different lenses, such as

- *Business objectives*—These requirements relate to the main business reasons for building these systems, such as increasing click-through rates, saving process costs, improving customer satisfaction, and so forth. Technical developers may not directly be responsible for business metrics, but these business metrics can act as the leading light in the development process of the system.
- *User needs*—These are the core requirements of the users for whom the system is being developed. Expressing these needs helps in determining the inputs and outputs of the system along with other functionalities such as multilingual support and source citation. These needs are also key in determining the types of user queries that the RAG system can expect.

- *Functional requirements*—These are the core functionalities of the system, such as the supported data types, number of documents to be retrieved and length/tone/style of generation, and similar. Functional requirements are influenced by user needs and business objectives. They are also the main influencers of the development process.
- *Non-functional requirements*—These are requirements about the performance, scalability, reliability, security, and privacy of the system. There may be additional requirements such as legal and compliance, especially for regulated industries.
- *Constraints*—One should also focus on any constraints that the system should be cognizant of, such as access to the internet, availability of data, cost, and integration with existing systems.

A customer service system, for example, may be envisioned to reduce customer query resolution time, requiring quick response time and a constraint of integrating with existing customer support platforms. An illustrative requirement document for the above can look like the one shown in figure 9.3, detailing out different types of requirements.

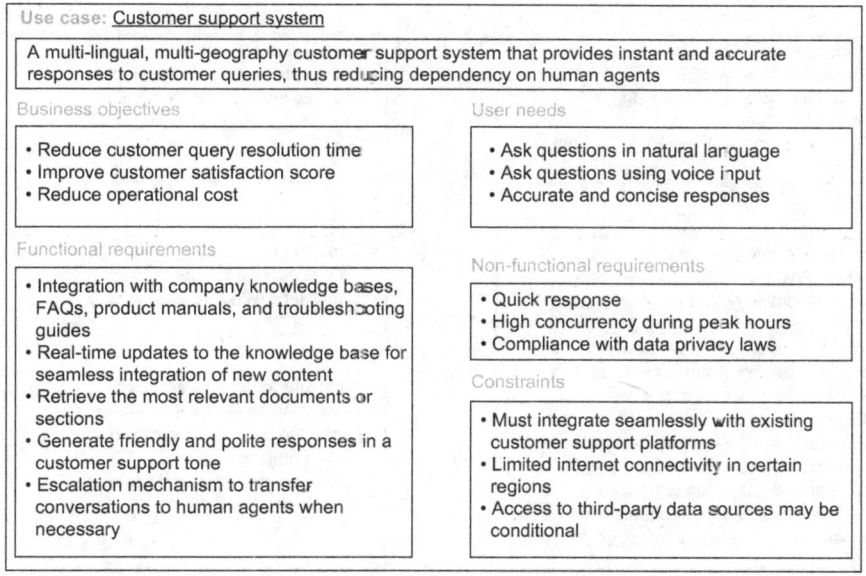

Figure 9.3 An illustrative requirements document for a customer support system requiring RAG

REQUIREMENTS ANALYSIS

Eliciting requirements from the stakeholders is a major activity in the initiation stage. These raw requirements then need to be analyzed. The requirements should be clear, precise, and quantifiable so that they can lead to specific development steps. For example, a non-functional need for a quick response may be too vague. Instead, a better requirement is that 90% of queries should be responded to within 2 seconds. Similarly, a constraint of limited internet connectivity can lead the developer to believe that a completely offline system is required. Such vagueness in the requirements needs to be addressed in further interactions with the stakeholders.

At this stage, it is also important to define the success criteria on which the system will be evaluated. A few success metrics need to be defined and agreed on. For developers, these success metrics should be different from the business objectives since business outcomes may depend on factors beyond their control. Latency, throughput, percentage of queries resolved, and similar, are good criteria for success metrics. Figure 9.4 presents an illustrative requirements document after an analysis of the success metrics. It is an improvement on the previous requirement document shown in figure 9.3.

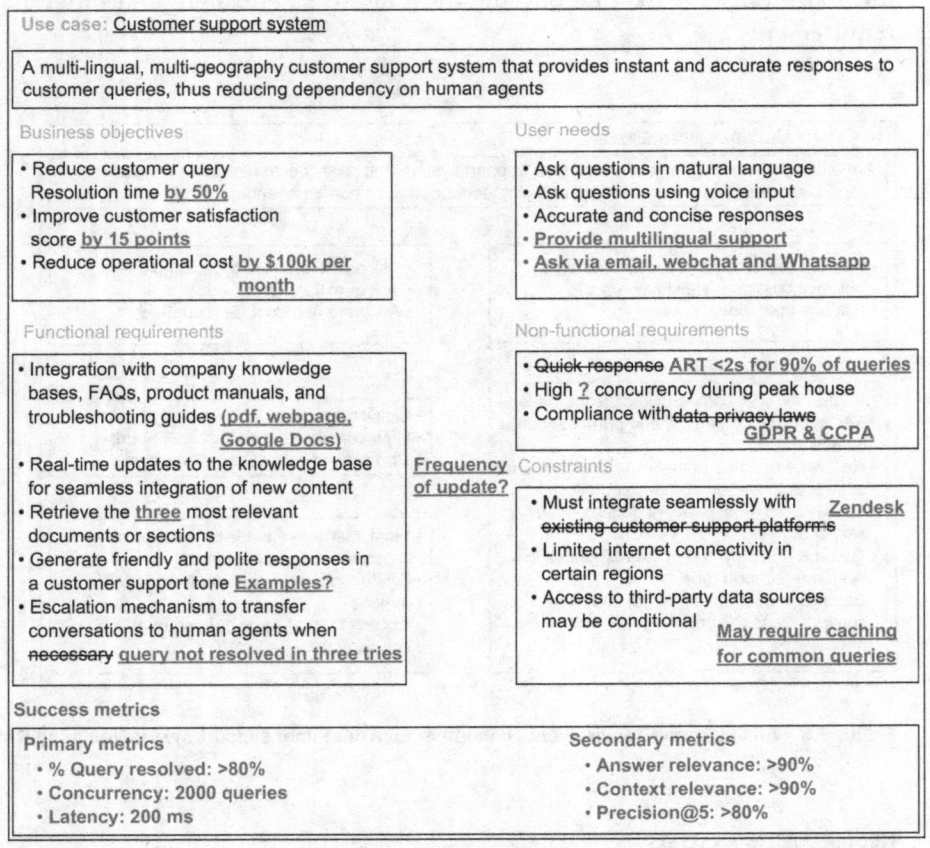

Figure 9.4   Illustrative requirements document with success metrics defined and requirements analyzed for clarity and precision

HIGH-LEVEL ARCHITECTURE

Once the requirements are understood well, the initiation stage can be deemed complete. It is good practice to close the initiation stage with a high-level architecture diagram that can be used as a starting point for the design stage. This architecture can be used to bring alignment among stakeholders and discuss the requirements further. The focus of this high-level architecture is to illustrate the system inputs and outputs. Since data plays such a crucial role in a RAG system, this high-level architecture should also include the data component. As illustrated in figure 9.5, for a multichannel customer support system, the system must allow inputs and outputs from and to different channels.

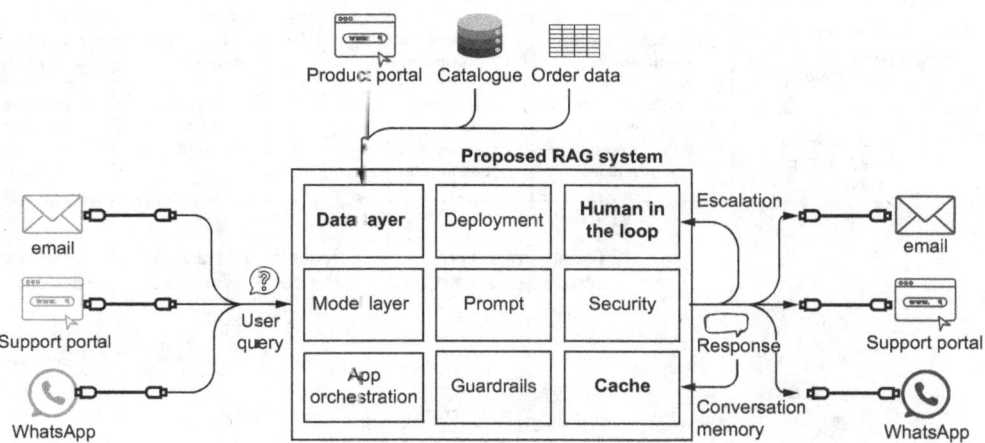

Figure 9.5 High-level architecture of a proposed customer support bot highlighting inputs and outputs, along with the data, human-in-the-loop, and cache layers

A first go/no-go decision or the going forward strategic call can be taken on the completion of the initiation stage. Once the stakeholders are aligned, all the RAG operations layers for the system can be designed in the next stage.

9.2 Design stage: Layering the RAGOps stack

With a clear understanding of the use case and the requirements, developers can start planning for the development. In the design stage, the high-level architecture is refined to map out RAGOps stack, and the choices around tools and technology are made. At this stage, we design the indexing and generation pipelines along with other components such as caching, guardrails, and the like.

9.2.1 Indexing pipeline design

In the requirement-gathering step, we identify the data sources. During the design stage, we double-click on these data sources to identify the nature of the source systems, file types, and nature of the data itself to determine the development steps for the knowledge base. Recall from chapter 3 that the knowledge base is created for a RAG system via the indexing pipeline. Components such as data loading, chunking, embeddings, and storage form the indexing pipeline. In chapter 7, we also discussed that the data layer of the RAGOps stack enables this by extracting, transforming, and loading the data. Figure 9.6 summarizes the indexing pipeline components and the data layer.

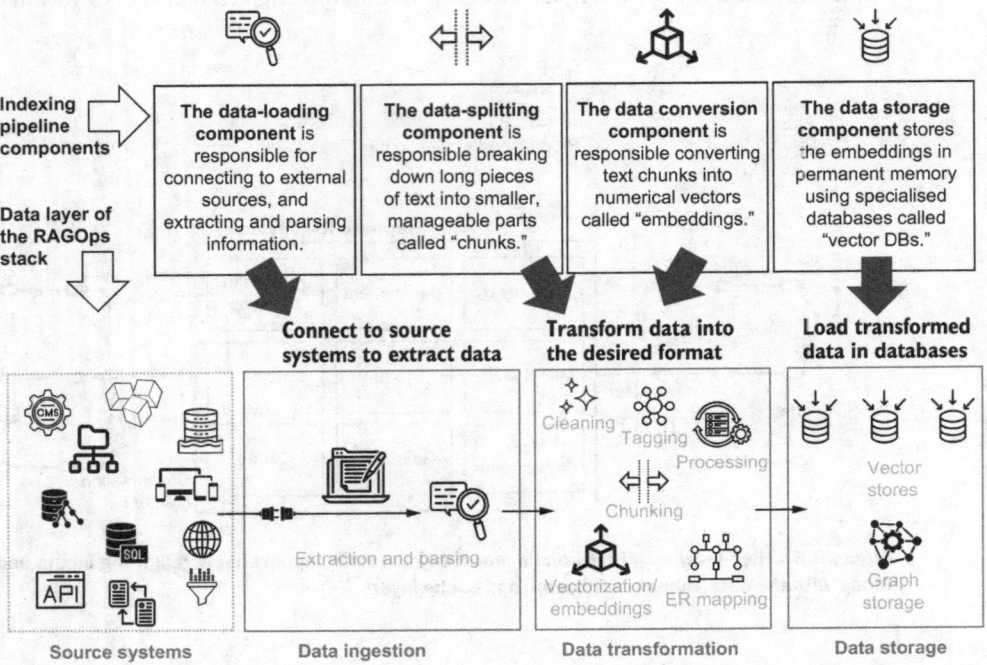

Figure 9.6   The indexing pipeline of the RAG system is executed using the data layer in the RAGOps stack.

Now let's look at some important points of consideration that will help us when making the choices for the indexing pipeline design.

DATA INGESTION

When you're working with less data, like a few PDF files or a couple of websites, *data ingestion* is a relatively simple step. However, in production-grade systems, the complexity increases with the scale of the data. Special attention needs to be given to the source systems and the file formats. Here are a few questions about connecting to source systems that will help in designing the data ingestion component:

- Which source systems will the data layer need to connect to?

- Are the connectors readily available? If yes, which tools or services are required to establish these connections?
- Which connectors will need to be developed? Which technology will these connectors be developed on?
- Is access to open internet required? How will the system connect to the internet?

The following group of questions is about parsing files:

- Which file formats will be ingested?
- How will the web pages be scraped, if required?
- Do we have the necessary parsers for the different file types?
- Is some special parsing technique required to be developed?
- Can there be more than one modality of data in a single file?

The answers to these questions will determine the tools you will need to use for ingesting data and the parts that will need to be developed.

DATA TRANSFORMATION

Once the data is ingested, the *transformation step* converts the data into a suitable format for the knowledge base. In the data transformation step, the data will first be cleaned and pre-processed. A good practice is also to extract metadata information. Sometimes, other preprocessing steps such as PII data redaction or resolving conflicting information are required.

After pre-processing, the data will be chunked using a suitable chunking technique. Chunk size, overlap size, and the chunking strategy should be decided at this stage. Chunking can be fixed size, structure driven, semantic chunking, or agentic chunking.

Once the chunks are created, they need to be transformed for retrieval. We have discussed approaches such as embeddings and knowledge graphs. For use cases that require relational understanding between chunks, knowledge graphs should be explored. The creation of vector embeddings is almost mandatory in all RAG systems. To create vector embeddings, pre-trained embeddings models can be used. However, sometimes, due to the peculiarity of the domain, embedding models may need to be fine-tuned.

Let's now look at some of the questions that should be considered at this stage. The first group of questions is about pre-processing:

- How noisy is the data? What algorithms and techniques can be used to clean up the data?
- Is structured data like tables or JSON present?
- Is metadata readily available, or should it be extracted?
- What algorithms or models should be used for metadata extraction? (Note: All models sit in the model library of the model layer of the RAGOps stack.)
- Does the data contain sensitive information that needs to be masked or redacted? What techniques will be used to execute this?
- Are there any other data protocols or guidelines that need to be followed?

When it comes to chunking, consider asking the following questions:

- Is the chunk size pre-determined? If not, what chunk sizes should be experimented with?
- Is the data in a format that will warrant structured chunking?
- What techniques and models will be employed for semantic chunking, if required?
- Is a chunking agent readily available, or will it need to be built? Which models, algorithms, and tools will be used by the chunking agent?

The following group of questions covers graphRAG:

- Is a hierarchical indexing structure required?
- Do we need to extract entities and relationships for relational context? Do we have the necessary budget?
- What approaches are we going to take for entity-relationship extraction?
- Are we using any frameworks for graph extraction?
- Which models are going to be used?

As for embeddings, ask the following:

- Which embeddings model will we use? Are there any domain-specific embeddings models available that will be more useful?
- Are multimodal embeddings required?
- Do we need to fine-tune embeddings for our use case? Do we have the training data for fine-tuning? How will the training data be sourced?

Data transformation steps require significant thought and effort. This is also where significant costs can be incurred, especially in using agents and employing graphRAG.

DATA STORAGE

The final component of the data layer is the storage. Depending on the choices made during the data transformation, the storage will comprise vector stores, graph databases, and document stores (if necessary). At this stage, we should also keep in mind that a cache store may be required in the application that can be a part of the data layer. We will discuss caching separately. Some of the questions pertinent to data storage are

- Can all data be stored in a single collection, or are multiple collections required?
- Can we manage the vector database or do we require a managed service?
- What is the current scale of data and how is it likely to grow?
- Which vector database will we use?
- Do we need a graph database? Which graph database will we use?
- Do we need to store raw documents or images? Which document store will we use for this purpose?

With the storage in place, the creation of the knowledge base can be executed. It is important to note that the choices at this stage should be flexible. You should also keep options available for tools, services and libraries that can be experimented with during development. You'll also have to estimate the costs associated with different steps of this stage and ensure that the stakeholders are aligned with these costs.

With the data layer of the RAGOps stack, the design of the indexing pipeline is complete. You may also note that the indexing pipeline also interacts with the model layer where embeddings models and LLMs along with other task specific algorithms sit.

9.2.2 Generation pipeline design

We have discussed that the real-time interaction of the user with the knowledge base is facilitated by the generation pipeline. In chapter 4, we developed the three main components of the generation pipeline—the retrievers, augmentation via prompts, and generation using LLMs. Apart from these three components, query optimization in the pre-retrieval stage and context optimization in the post-retrieval stage are advanced components of the generation pipeline. Sometimes, even post-generation, response optimization is conducted to better align the responses. The generation pipeline is powered by the model layer of the RAGOps stage, which has the LLMs, the retrievers, embeddings models, and other task-specific models. The generation pipeline is brought alive by the app orchestration layer of the RAGOps stack. Let's discuss the design of the generation pipeline in the following six steps: query optimization (pre-retrieval), retrieval, context optimization (post-retrieval), augmentation, generation, and response optimization (post-generation).

QUERY OPTIMIZATION

Query optimization techniques are employed to help retrieval better align with the query. Several techniques are employed for transforming and rewriting queries. For agentic RAG, query routing is an important aspect of this step. Some of the questions to help finalize the nature of query optimization are

- How many types of queries can the user ask? Do each of these query types require different downstream processes?
- Are there multiple collections in the knowledge base that need to be selected before the search?
- Are user queries expected to be short or generic?
- Are users looking for precise responses?
- How much processing time can be afforded to query optimization?
- Which models and techniques will be used for query optimization?

Query optimization is optional but may be unavoidable when the data in the knowledge base is voluminous. It must also be noted that query optimization can add to the latency of the system.

RETRIEVAL

Retrieval is a pivotal component of RAG systems. There are many retrieval techniques and strategies discussed in this book. The quality of the RAG system hinges on the accuracy of the retrieval component. You may use a dense embeddings similarity match for simple RAG systems. In more complex systems, you will need to use hybrid, iterative, or adaptive retrieval strategies. The questions to ask at this stage are

- Does our retrieval component need high precision, high recall, or both?
- Can the queries be resolved with a simple similarity match?
- Do we need graph retrieval?
- Will searching through the entire data be prohibitively long? Do we need filtering?
- Will a single pass retrieve all necessary documents?
- Will the information from the retrieved documents lead to more questions?
- Which models and techniques will we use for adaptive, recursive, or iterative retrieval?
- Which retrieval algorithms should we try?
- Are there any providers or libraries that we will leverage?
- How will we estimate the cost of retrieval?
- How many documents should be retrieved for acceptable levels of coverage?
- Does ranking in retrieved results matter?

Retrieval, especially in large knowledge bases, can lead to significant latency and should be optimized for speed and accuracy.

CONTEXT OPTIMIZATION

Once the results are retrieved from the knowledge base, they need to be sent to the LLM for generation along with the original user query. However, once the results are retrieved to sharpen the context, certain optimization techniques such as re-ranking and compression can be applied. These techniques filter, compress, and optimize the retrieved information to reduce noise and increase the precision of the context. To validate the need for context optimization, a few questions can be asked:

- Will the amount of information retrieved overwhelm the LLM?
- Will the retrieved information fit the context window of the LLM?
- Is there a possibility of the retrieved information being noisy?
- Have a lot of documents been retrieved? Do we need to discard a few?
- Which techniques can be used to sharpen the retrieve context to the query?
- Are there any services or libraries that we can use?
- Can we afford the time taken for this optimization?

Optimizations like this are very helpful in making the context precise and improving the overall quality of the RAG system, but they do add to the processing time and cost.

AUGMENTATION

Augmentation is the process of adding the retrieved context to the original query in a prompt that can be sent to the LLM for generation. While it may seem a simple step, there can be many nuances to it. All the use case context along with the retrieved context also needs to be passed. Sometimes, you may need to pass examples of desired responses or the thought process. In cases where you need to use the LLMs internal parametric knowledge, this can also be specified in the prompt. Key questions to ask at this stage are

- What is the system prompt or the overall persona that we need the LLM to take?
- Does the response require nuanced analysis? Can that be passed as a chain of thought?
- Do we want to restrict the responses to the context only?
- What kind of examples should be given?
- Will different query types need different prompting techniques?

Augmentation is done through prompts, and prompts can be managed by the prompt layer of the RAGOps stack. Prompting affects the cost and latency since the LLM-s processing depends on the number of tokens passed in the prompt.

GENERATION

Generation is a core component of all generative AI apps and contains an LLM that takes a prompt as input and generates a response. The nature of the LLM determines the efficacy and efficiency of the RAG system to a large extent. There are several choices that you will need to make:

- Should an open source model be used? Do we have the skills and resources to use them?
- Should a proprietary managed LLM be used?
- Will we need to fine-tune an LLM for our use case?
- How large a model do we need? What capabilities do we need to address?
- How can we estimate the cost of the generation component?
- Are there any deployment constraints to be considered?
- Will the models need optimization for deployment?
- Are there any security implications to be considered?
- Are there any ethical or legal implications to be considered?

The selected LLMs will sit in the model library. All training fine-tuning activities and optimization are carried out in the model layer of the RAGOps stack. LLMs can be costly to train and use. Using the right LLM is key to the success of the RAG system.

RESPONSE OPTIMIZATION

Sometimes, the response from the generation component may be further processed before presenting the results to the user. This can range from evaluating the response for relevance to checking the format and appending the responses with the retrieved sources. Some questions that can help with the assessment at this stage are

- Does the response from the LLM be presented to the user as is?
- Is there any kind of verification that the responses need to go through?
- What is the impact of a sub-optimal result?
- Are there any workflows that need to be triggered based on the responses?

Response optimizations are highly subjective and closely coupled to the use case, but it is a consideration that should not be overlooked.

With these seven steps, the generation pipeline design is complete. The model library and the training/fine-tuning components of the RAGOps stack can be covered with the necessary tools, platforms, and algorithms. The orchestration of the generation pipeline can also be finalized depending on the choices made during this stage. The prompt layer can also be addressed after finalizing the augmentation techniques. Figure 9.7 shows the generation pipeline design with the overarching question of each step.

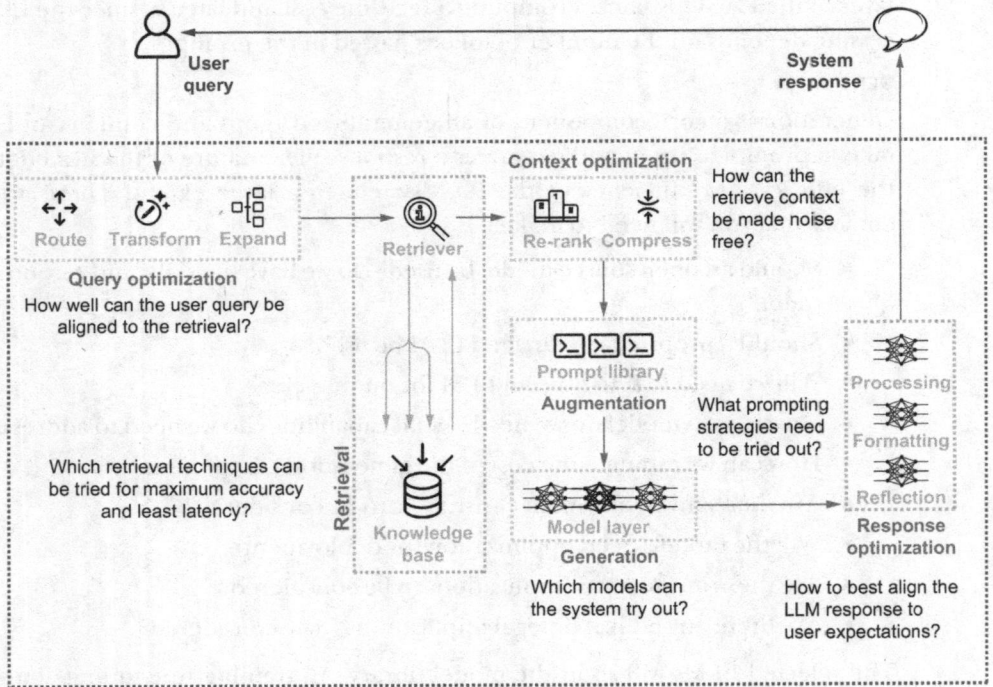

Figure 9.7   Key questions need to be answered to make the choices for the generation pipeline.

This completes the design choices of the core RAG pipelines. The model, prompt, and the orchestration layers are largely complete by this stage. But there are more design considerations regarding security, guardrails, caching, and other use case requirements.

9.2.3 Other design considerations

While well-designed core RAG pipelines complete the critical layers of the RAG system, other system considerations and business requirements also need to be addressed:

- What kind of guardrails are required in the system? Should the user queries be restricted? Is there any kind of information that should not be output?
- Is it possible and useful to cache certain kinds of responses?
- Do we need human supervision or action at any stage in the system?
- How will the models be protected from adverse attacks?
- Is there any approval workflow required in the system?
- Are users looking for explainability?

These questions will help address the essential and enhancement layers of the RAGOps stack. You should be able to have a complete view of the necessary components, tools, platforms, and libraries for the development of the RAG system. The last choice to be made is on deployment options.

You can choose between a managed deployment on the cloud, a self-hosted deployment on a private cloud, a bare metal server, or local/edge machines. The choice will largely be driven by the business constraints but can have an effect on the design choices of the pipelines. Fully managed deployment favors managed services for storage and compute to reduce development complexity and ensure scalability, self-hosted solutions need a special focus on a design with modularity and optimization techniques to handle limited infrastructure, and in edge deployment, you should emphasize lightweight components and efficient retrieval strategies due to resource constraints.

With all these design elements finalized, experimentation can begin for the development of the RAG system.

9.2.4 Development stage: Building modular RAG pipelines

The development stage of the RAG development framework focuses on implementing the design choices into a functional RAG system. The ideal way would be to build the RAG pipelines in a modular fashion, which involves decomposing the system into distinct, interchangeable components, each responsible for a specific function. This approach enhances flexibility, scalability, and maintainability, allowing for tailored configurations to meet diverse application requirements. A few activities in the development stage involve training and fine-tuning models; creating APIs or microservices for different components; and creating an orchestration layer using different tools, services, and libraries.

MODEL TRAINING AND FINE-TUNING LLMS

For most systems, a pre-trained foundation LLM and embeddings models will meet the requirement. There may be instances where you may need to fine-tune models for domain adaptation. In rare cases, you may choose to train language models from scratch. In such cases, the development of RAG systems may take a back seat, and training the models will be the core of the development effort. You can follow a progressive approach when deciding whether to fine-tune embeddings models and LLMs.

When creating embeddings using a pre-trained model, you will need to assess if a similarity search yields relevant results. To do this, you can also create ground truth data. The ground truth data can be a set of manually curated search queries and their matching documents. If the embeddings model can retrieve the documents accurately, you may use the pre-trained model. If not, you can either look for another embeddings model more suited for the use case domain or fine-tune the pre-trained embeddings model for the use case domain.

Similarly, if a pre-trained LLM generates desired results by prompting alone, you can use the model as is. In cases where you desire a specific style, vocabulary, or tonality, you can choose to fine-tune a model.

If the system warrants other models such as query classification, harmful content detection, usefulness, and similar, they will also need to be trained.

MODULE DEVELOPMENT

Different RAG pipeline components should be developed as independent modules in the form of packages, APIs, or other modular frameworks. Some of the modules can be

- *Data loading and parsing*—Responsible for connecting to the source system and parsing file formations
- *Metadata extraction*—Responsible for extracting and tagging metadata
- *Chunking*—Responsible for creating chunks from documents
- *Embeddings*—Responsible for converting chunks into vector embeddings
- *Storage*—Responsible for storing embeddings into vector databases
- *Query optimization*—Responsible for aligning user query with retrievers
- *Retrieval*—Responsible for efficient retrieval of documents
- *Augmentation*—Responsible for maintaining and invoking the prompt library
- *Generation*—Responsible for using the LLMs to generate responses
- *Memory*—Responsible for storing conversations, user preferences, and similar

These are only a few examples. Modularity will be dependent on the complexity of the components. For example, if you are convinced that fixed-size chunking is sufficient for your use case, you may not develop an independent chunking module. Conversely, if you assume that LLMs may need to be changed as the system evolves with the technology, you can create the generation module that allows for quick and easy replacement of models. Figure 9.8 recalls the modular RAG design discussed in chapter 6.

ORCHESTRATION

Finally, you will develop the orchestration layer that will manage the interaction among the different modules that you have developed. This enables the workflow of your RAG

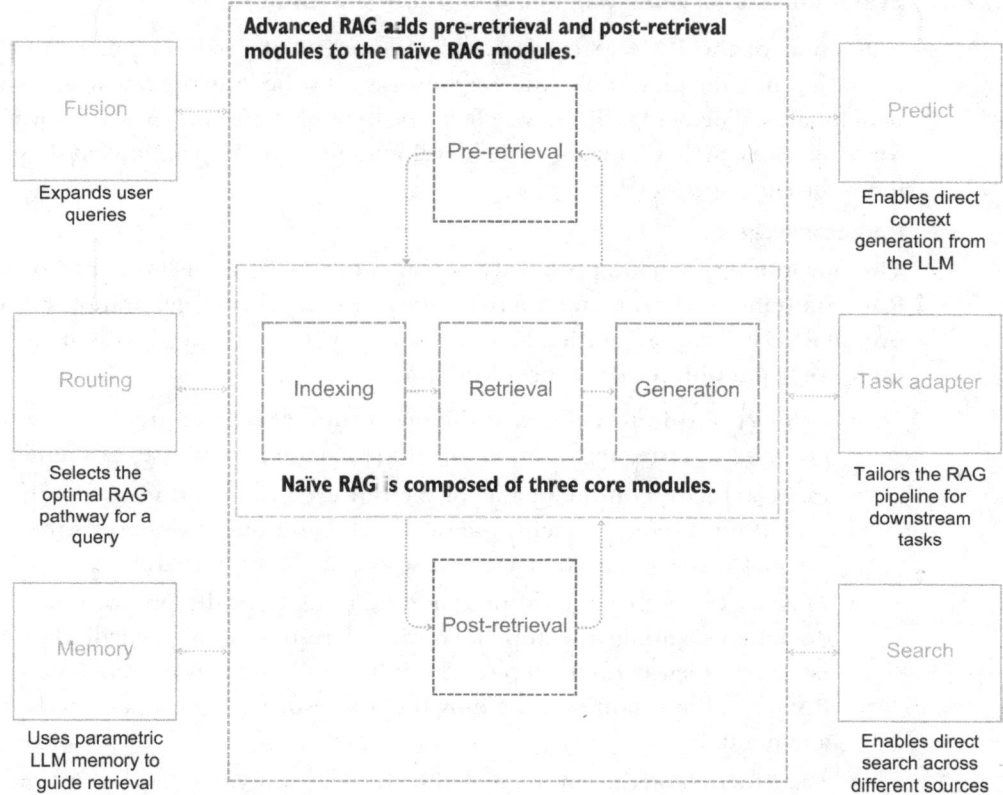

Fusion

Expands user queries

Routing

Selects the optimal RAG pathway for a query

Memory

Uses parametric LLM memory to guide retrieval

Advanced RAG adds pre-retrieval and post-retrieval modules to the naïve RAG modules.

Pre-retrieval

Indexing → Retrieval → Generation

Naïve RAG is composed of three core modules.

Post-retrieval

Predict

Enables direct context generation from the LLM

Task adapter

Tailors the RAG pipeline for downstream tasks

Search

Enables direct search across different sources

New modules interact with the advanced/naïve RAG framework, as well as with each other.

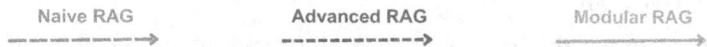

Naive RAG   Advanced RAG   Modular RAG

Figure 9.8   Modular structure allows for flexibility and scalability of individual components.

system. This workflow should be flexible enough to adapt with feedback for different query types.

You will also have access to various managed services, frameworks, libraries, and tools that you can integrate with any of the modules. For example, LangChain is a framework that provides libraries for most components of a RAG framework. You can use these libraries for quick and easy development. However, for components that you desire more control over, you may need to build the functionality from scratch.

Development is an experimentation-driven iterative process. To finalize the different components of the RAG system, you will need to evaluate them and benchmark them against the goals you had set in the initiation stage.

9.2.5   *Evaluation stage: Validating and optimizing the RAG system*

Evaluation of the RAG system is a key component of its development process. All the different strategies, tools, and frameworks must be evaluated against some set of benchmarks. The actual business effect can only be measured post-deployment, but some metrics can be evaluated at the development stage. We can look at these metrics in two broad categories.

RAG COMPONENTS

The purpose of evaluating the RAG system is to assess the performance of different RAG components. To this end, there can be retriever-specific, generation-specific, and overall RAG evaluation metrics. Here is a summary of these metrics discussed in chapter 5. We begin with retriever-specific metrics:

- *Accuracy* is typically defined as the proportion of correct predictions (both true positives and true negatives) among the total number of cases examined.

- *Precision* focuses on the quality of the retrieved results. It measures the proportion of retrieved documents relevant to the user query. It answers the question, "Of all the documents that were retrieved, how many were relevant?"

- *Precision@k* is a variation of precision that measures the proportion of relevant documents among the top 'k' retrieved results. It is particularly important because it focuses on the top results rather than all the retrieved documents. For RAG, it is important because only the top results are most likely to be used for augmentation.

- *Recall* focuses on the coverage that the retriever provides. It measures the proportion of the relevant documents retrieved from all the relevant documents in the corpus. It answers the question, "Of all the relevant documents, how many were retrieved?"

- *F1-score* is the harmonic mean of precision and recall. It provides a single metric that balances both the quality and coverage of the retriever.

- *Mean reciprocal rank, or MRR,* is particularly useful in evaluating the rank of the relevant document. It measures the reciprocal of the ranks of the first relevant document in the list of results. MRR is calculated over a set of queries.

- *Mean average precision, or MAP,* is a metric that combines precision and recall at different cut-off levels of 'k' (i.e. the cut-off number for the top results). It calculates a measure called average precision and then averages it across all queries.

- *nDCG* evaluates the ranking quality by considering the position of relevant documents in the result list and assigning higher scores to relevant documents appearing earlier.

Here is the summary of generation specific metrics:

- *Coherence* assesses the logical flow and clarity of the response, ensuring that the information is presented in an understandable and organized manner.

- *Conciseness* evaluates whether the response is succinct and to the point, avoiding unnecessary verbosity, while still conveying complete information.

We conclude with a summary of overall RAG metrics:

- *Context relevance* assesses the proportion of retrieved information relevant to the user query.
- *Faithfulness* or *groundedness* assesses the proportion of the claims in the response that are backed by the retrieved context.
- *Hallucination rate* calculates the proportion of generated claims in the response that are not present in the retrieved context.
- *Coverage* measures the number of relevant claims in the context and calculates the proportion of relevant claims present in the generated response.
- *Answer relevance* assesses the overall effectiveness of the system by calculating the relevance of the final response to the original question.

Recall the triad of RAG evaluation from chapter 5. Figure 9.9 shows the pairwise interaction between the user query, retrieved context, and the generated response, which calculates the RAG specific metrics.

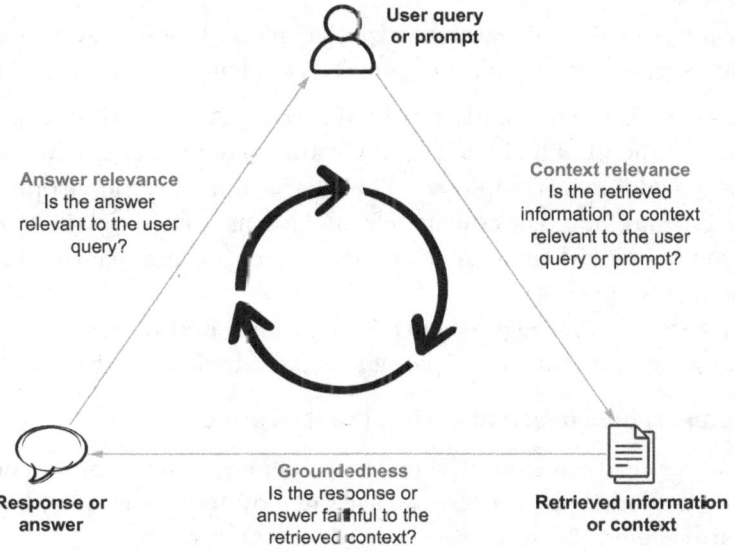

Figure 9.9   The triad of RAG evaluation proposed by TruEra

To calculate some of these metrics, a ground truth dataset is required. Ground truth is information known to be real or true. In RAG, and the generative AI domain in general, ground truth is a prepared set of prompt–context–response or question–context–response examples, akin to labeled data in supervised machine learning parlance. Ground truth data created for your knowledge base can be used for the evaluation of your RAG system.

You can measure these metrics for different components. For example, you can check if context relevance increases by replacing a hybrid retrieval strategy with an adaptive one. You can also check the effectiveness of query and context optimization. You can also compare two service providers for a particular component.

SYSTEM PERFORMANCE

System performance metrics relate to the non-functional requirements of the system, which affect the usability of the system more than the accuracy of the system. Some of these metrics are

- *Latency*—Measures the time taken from receiving a query to delivering a response. Low latency is crucial for user satisfaction, especially in real-time applications.
- *Throughput*—Indicates the number of queries the system can handle within a specific time frame. Higher throughput reflects the system's ability to manage large volumes of requests efficiently.
- *Resource utilization*—Assesses the efficiency of CPU and GPU usage during operations. Optimal utilization ensures cost-effectiveness and prevents resource bottlenecks.
- *Cost per query* calculates the average expense incurred for processing each query, encompassing infrastructure, energy, and maintenance costs.

Latency and cost get special attention in LLM-based systems. This is because of the inherent nature of the LLM architecture. RAG adds to both latency and cost. Therefore, the impact of additional components like filtering during retrieval, optimizations, and retrieval strategies should be evaluated from this lens. Sometimes the stakeholders may also ask you to evaluate some use case-specific metrics, and that should also be a part of this evaluation stage.

When your system is thoroughly evaluated and improved to meet all the benchmarks, it is ready to go. You can now deploy it to make it available to the intended users.

9.2.6 *Deployment stage: Launching and scaling the RAG system*

Once the system is ready to ship, it needs to be deployed into a production server accessible by the intended users. There are a few deployment techniques that are popular for software systems, which can also be used for RAG systems.

BLUE–GREEN DEPLOYMENT

Blue–green deployment maintains two separate environments named blue and green. The existing system is in the blue environment, and the new RAG system is put in the green. Once the green environment is tested and verified, all traffic is directed to the green environment, and the blue environment is deactivated. The advantage of this blue–green deployment is that it is possible to test the production environment without affecting the live traffic. Consequently, there is zero downtime and an easy option for a rollback if any problem is encountered. However, it is a costly option since the entire production environment is duplicated. Indexing pipelines can be updated in the green environment without affecting the live system. Changes to retrieval strategies or embeddings models can be safely validated before production use.

CANARY DEPLOYMENT

Canary deployment gradually releases the new RAG system to a small number of users. If it performs well with these users, it is expanded to all users. Canary deployment allows for real-time user feedback that enables early detection of problems. However, it adds feedback and monitoring complexity and multiple versions to manage. It can test changes in retrieval algorithms, embeddings, or generation models on limited queries or specific regions.

ROLLING DEPLOYMENT

Rolling deployment is used when there are multiple production servers. The new RAG system is deployed to one server incrementally at a time before moving to the next. So, there is no complete downtime and only a part of the system is offline at one time. It may become complex if problems arise mid-deployment. The rollback can become tedious when some servers are updated, while others are not.

SHADOW DEPLOYMENT

Shadow deployment mirrors live traffic to a new version of the system running alongside the old one, without exposing the new RAG system's responses to users. By doing this, the system can be tested without affecting the users. However, it requires duplication of the infrastructure much like the blue–green deployment.

A/B TESTING

A/B testing involves deploying two versions of the RAG system (A and B) to separate subsets of users and comparing their performance to determine the better option. This can also be done for new systems. It enables direct comparison and provides clear insights into performance. However, it requires robust mechanisms to split traffic and collect performance metrics. It allows for experimenting with different LLMs or retrieval strategies and variations in prompting and augmentation techniques.

INTERLEAVING EXPERIMENTS

Interleaving experiments compare two RAG systems by blending their outputs into a single result set shown to users. Results from both systems are interleaved, and user interactions are attributed to the originating system to determine which performs better. This approach provides fast feedback and reduces bias by comparing systems under identical conditions. However, the attribution of user engagement to the correct system can be complex.

The choices for the deployment strategy can depend on factors like such as tolerance, and using strategies such as shadow, canary, and blue–green can mitigate risks in mission-critical systems. It also depends on the scale, and rolling deployments make sense for large-scale systems. Small new RAG systems can be also deployed all at once.

Now that the system is available to the users, you will start getting real-time feedback, and the success and failure of the system will also depend on how you react to the feedback. To measure and improve the system, continuous monitoring is required.

9.2.7   *Maintenance stage: Ensuring reliability and adaptability*

Deploying a RAG system into production is only the first milestone in the journey toward an evolved contextual AI system. Explicit user feedback, evolving technology, and changing user behavior present previously unexplored challenges that the system may encounter. It is therefore essential to be continually vigilant and monitor the system performance. There are several reasons why a RAG system may fail in production. There are operational reasons such as compute resource constraints, sudden spikes in load, and malicious attacks. The reason can also be a shift in the type of data in the knowledge base or a change in user queries. It is therefore essential to measure a few metrics:

- RAG component metrics that were evaluated before deployment need to be continuously monitored for degradation.
- Changes in user behavior can be tracked by analyzing the nature of user queries.
- System performance metrics such as latency, throughput, and similar should also be continuously monitored.
- Additional metrics such as error rates, system downtime, malicious attacks, and similar should also be tracked.
- User engagement metrics such as customer satisfaction scores or repeat engagement can indicate the usability of the system.
- Business metrics such as revenue effects and cost savings should also be tracked.

This development framework completed its cycle with maintenance. However, it is not a linear process. New requirements and business objectives will emerge. This will re-initiate the development cycle for an improved RAG system. This development framework will prove to be a good reference resource while building RAG systems.

We conclude this book and end the discussion on RAG in the next section with some additional considerations to keep in mind as the generative AI domain evolves.

9.3   *Ideas for further exploration*

Like any technology, even with RAG, there are some complementary and some competing ideas that coexist. You may hear about these techniques and sometimes be challenged to defend the use of RAG. There are also common points of failure for RAG systems that need attention.

9.3.1   *Fine-tuning within RAG*

Supervised fine-tuning (SFT) of LLMs has become a popular method to customize and adapt foundation models for specific objectives. There has been a growing debate in the applied AI community around the application of fine-tuning or RAG to accomplish tasks. While RAG enhances the non-parametric memory of a foundation model without changing the parameters, SFT changes the parameters of a foundation model and therefore influences the parametric memory. RAG and SFT should be considered as complementary, rather than competing, techniques because both address different parts of a generative AI system. You may prefer fine-tuning over RAG if there is a change required in the writing style, tonality, and vocabulary of the LLM responses. In their paper "Retrieval-Augmented Generation for Large Language Models: A Survey" (https://arxiv.org/abs/2312.10997), Gao and colleagues plot the evolution of prompt engineering to RAG and fine-tuning. This is illustrated in figure 9.10, demonstrating the need for fine-tuning with the increase in the need for model adaptation.

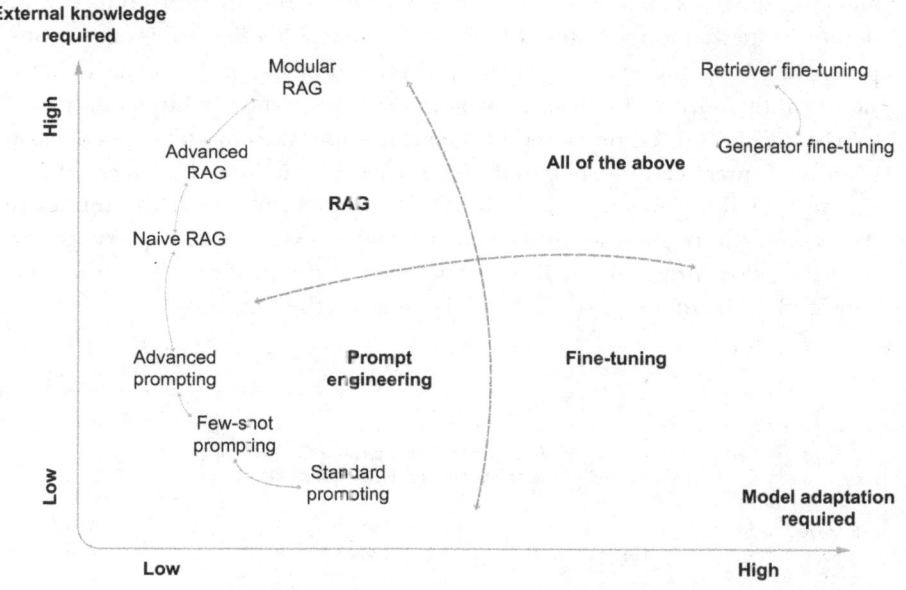

Figure 9.10 **Prompt engineering requires low modifications to the model and external knowledge, focusing on harnessing the capabilities of LLMs themselves. Fine-tuning, however, involves further training the model. Source: https://arxiv.org/abs/2312.10997.**

Fine-tuning methods for both retrievers and generators hold immense potential for significantly improving RAG performance. Retriever fine-tuning enhances the ability of retrieval models to accurately capture semantic nuances relevant to specific domains, using methods such as contrastive learning, supervised embedding fine-tuning, LM-supervised retrieval, or reward-based fine-tuning. Generator fine-tuning complements this by adapting language models through methods such as fusion-in-decoder (FiD), prompt tuning, latent fusion techniques, and parameter-efficient fine-tuning (PEFT). Combining these approaches within a hybrid fine-tuning framework can align the retrieval and generation components more effectively, leading to higher accuracy, reduced hallucinations, and improved adaptability to domain-specific tasks.

9.3.2   *Long-context windows in LLMs*

Context windows in LLMs keep growing significantly with iteration. As of this writing, Claude 3.5 sonnet supports a window of up to 200,000 tokens, while GPT-4o, O1, and variants can process 128,000 tokens. Google Gemini 1.5 leads with a massive 1-million-token context window. It is possible that when you read this book, there may be models with even longer context windows. So, in a lot of cases, we can just pass the entire context such as a long document to the model as part of the prompt. This would eliminate the need for chunking, indexing, and retrieval in cases where the knowledge base is not too large. In their paper, "Retrieval Augmented Generation or Long-Context LLMs? A Comprehensive Study and Hybrid Approach" (https://arxiv.org/abs/2407.16833), Li and colleagues systematically compare RAG and LLMs with long-context windows. They demonstrate that long-context LLMs outperform RAG with a few exceptions. However, processing long contexts directly with LLMs can be computationally expensive. RAG is significantly more cost-efficient owing to processing shorter inputs. A hybrid approach such as SELF-ROUTE proposed in the same paper uses model self-reflection to decide whether a query can be answered with retrieved chunks or if it needs the full context. Figure 9.11 illustrates the SELF-ROUTE approach, in which the model receives the query with the retrieved chunks and determines whether the query can be answered based on this information. If yes, it generates the answer. If no, the full context is provided to the model, and the model generates the final answer.

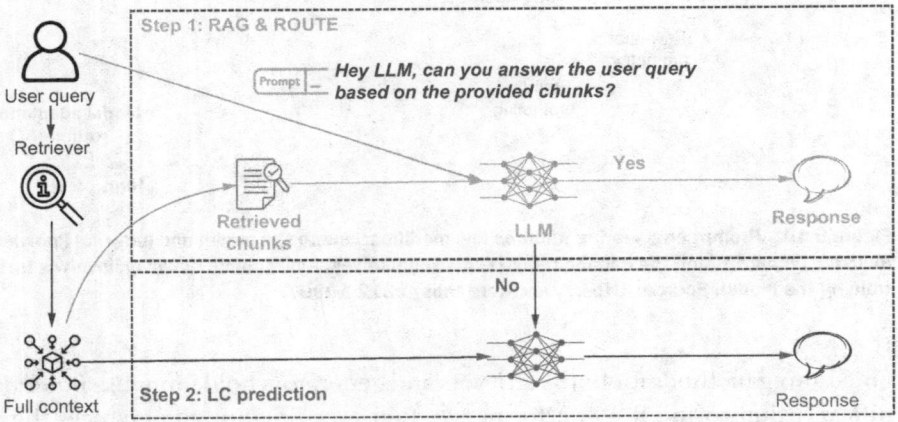

Figure 9.11   A hybrid approach utilizing RAG and long context in LLMs can lead to better performance without adversely increasing the costs.

9.3.3   *Managed solutions*

With the growing popularity of RAG and its significance in generative AI applications, many service providers offer managed RAG pipelines in which several RAG components can be configured without the need for custom development. For example, knowledge bases are an Amazon Bedrock capability that facilitates implementation of the entire RAG workflow. Azure AI Search provides indexing and query capabilities, with the infrastructure of the Azure cloud, and Vertex AI RAG Engine is a component of Google's Vertex AI platform that facilitates RAG. There are also independent service providers such as CustomGPT, Needle AI, Ragie, and so forth that provide managed RAG pipelines. As with managed solutions across technologies, the factors to consider are cost, applicability to the use case, flexibility, and control over components.

9.3.4 Difficult queries

Some key reasons for failures in RAG systems are related to the types of queries. As RAG developers, it is important to keep focusing on these query types so that the technique can be improved. Some of these are

- *Multi-step reasoning*—RAG struggles with queries needing multi-hop retrieval (e.g., "What nationality is the performer of song XXX?").
- *General queries*—Vague or broad questions are hard to retrieve relevant chunks for (e.g., "What does the group think about XXX?")
- *Complex or long queries*—Complex queries challenge the retriever's understanding.
- *Implicit queries*—Questions requiring comprehensive context understanding can't be addressed by RAG alone.

We have come a long way in our discussion on RAG. This chapter provided an exhaustive summary of the contents of this book, from the benefit of RAG to the best practices in building RAG systems. At the risk of repetition, RAG is an important and evolving technique in the field of generative AI. I hope you had a good time reading this book. I'll leave you with the following closing thoughts:

- Remember to remain familiar with the principles of contextual AI powered by RAG.
- Have faith in your ability to build complex RAG systems.
- Always bear in mind the development challenges and strategies to overcome them.
- Understand the ethical and legal concerns around generative AI.
- Be on top of the rapidly changing trends.

Summary

RAG development framework

- The RAG development framework provides a structured approach to building, deploying, and maintaining retrieval-augmented generation systems.
- It addresses the complexity of RAG systems by incorporating six iterative and cyclic stages: initiation, design, development, evaluation, deployment, and maintenance.

- The framework emphasizes both the technical and operational aspects of RAG system development.

RAG development framework stages

- **Initiation stage**
  - Focuses on understanding the problem statement, aligning stakeholders, and gathering requirements.
  - Emphasizes use case identification and assessing the need for RAG, using tools like use case evaluation cards.
  - Involves requirements gathering across business, functional, and non-functional needs.
  - Concludes with drafting a high-level architecture diagram for alignment and strategic decision-making.

- **Design stage**
  - Transforms high-level architecture into detailed pipeline designs for indexing and generation.
  - Incorporates choices around chunking, embeddings, and retrieval strategies.
  - Addresses additional considerations such as guardrails, caching, security, and deployment strategies.

- **Development stage**
  - Implements modular RAG pipelines, enabling flexibility, scalability, and maintainability.
  - Activities include training/fine-tuning models, creating independent modules (e.g., chunking, retrieval, generation), and building orchestration layers.

- **Evaluation stage**
  - Validates RAG system components and overall performance using metrics such as context relevance, faithfulness, precision, recall, latency, and cost per query.
  - Employs ground truth datasets for benchmarking and optimization.

- **Deployment stage**
  - Includes deployment strategies like blue-green, canary, rolling, and A/B testing to ensure smooth transitions and minimal disruption.
  - Emphasizes real-time user feedback and system scalability.

- **Maintenance stage**
  - Ensures system reliability through continuous monitoring of component metrics, user behavior, and performance metrics.
  - Adapts to evolving use cases, technological advancements, and user feedback.

Best practices in RAG development

- Modular design improves adaptability and ease of updates.
- Ground truth datasets are essential for accurate evaluation and fine-tuning.
- Deployment strategies should align with system criticality, scale, and risk tolerance.
- Regularly monitor for changes in user behavior, data, and performance to maintain reliability.

Ideas for further exploration

- **RAG vs. fine-tuning**
  - RAG complements fine-tuning by enhancing non-parametric memory, while fine-tuning adapts parametric memory for style, tonality, and vocabulary.
  - Use cases may benefit from hybrid approaches, depending on specific needs.
- **Long-context windows in LLMs**
  - Advances in LLMs (e.g. 200k+ token contexts) can reduce reliance on chunking and retrieval for smaller knowledge bases.
  - Hybrid models such as SELF-ROUTE combine RAG with long-context processing to optimize cost and accuracy.
- **Managed solutions**
  - Services such as Amazon Bedrock, Azure AI Search, and Google Vertex AI RAG Engine offer prebuilt RAG pipelines, simplifying deployment and reducing development effort.
- **Handling difficult queries**
  - Multi-step reasoning, general queries, and implicit questions remain challenges for RAG systems.

index